MAVERICKS OF *Style*

Sunset from the room of 31 Union Square West, New York City, circa 1980. Polaroid sx-70. Courtesy of the Estate of Antonio Lopez and Juan Ramos.

URI MCMILLAN

MAVERICKS OF
Style

THE SEVENTIES IN COLOR

DUKE UNIVERSITY PRESS
Durham and London 2025

© 2025 Duke University Press
All rights reserved
Printed in the United States of America on acid-free paper ∞
Project Editor: Lisa Lawley
Designed by Dave Rainey
Typeset in Adobe Jenson Pro by Westchester Publishing Services

Library of Congress Cataloging-in-Publication Data
Names: McMillan, Uri, author.
Title: Mavericks of style : the seventies in color / Uri McMillan.
Description: Durham : Duke University Press, 2025. | Includes bibliographical references and index.
Identifiers: LCCN 2024060615 (print)
LCCN 2024060616 (ebook)
ISBN 9781478032519 (paperback)
ISBN 9781478029168 (hardcover)
ISBN 9781478061373 (ebook)
Subjects: LCSH: Jones, Grace. | Burrows, Stephen, 1943- | Lopez, Antonio, 1943–1987. | Fashion—New York (State)—New York—History—20th century. | Arts—New York (State)—New York—History—20th century. | African American artists—New York (State)—New York—History—20th century. | African American fashion designers—New York (State)—New York—History—20th century. | Hispanic American artists—New York (State)—New York—History—20th century. | Fashion and art. | Nineteen seventies. | New York (N.Y.)—Social life and customs—History—20th century.
Classification: LCC GT617.N4 M455 2025 (print) | LCC GT617.N4 (ebook) | DDC 746.9/209227471—dc23/eng/20250528
LC record available at https://lccn.loc.gov/2024060615
LC ebook record available at https://lccn.loc.gov/2024060616

Cover art: Pat Cleveland and Stephen Burrows at the home of fashion photographer Sante Forlano, ca. 1971. Courtesy of Charles Tracy Archive.

Duke University Press gratefully acknowledges the generous support of the University of California, Los Angeles, Division of the Humanities and the Division of Social Sciences, which provided funds toward the publication of this book.

This project was supported by the Andy Warhol Foundation Arts Writers Grant.

To those who dare to dream, create, and live outward

contents

ix		Cast of Characters
1		Introduction. Insurgent Aesthetics
23	1	Mundane Made Spectacular: ANTONIO LOPEZ
75	2	Neophyte to Muse: GRACE JONES
121	3	Color That Moves: STEPHEN BURROWS
165		Afterword. Style Is a Feeling
179		Acknowledgments
183		Notes
209		Bibliography
225		Index

Cast of Characters

PRIMARY CHARACTERS

Stephen Burrows	Black American fashion designer, master of color and the "disco dress," mambo dancer, O Boutique cofounder, connoisseur of jersey and chiffon, friend of Pat Cleveland and Bethann Hardison
Pat Cleveland	Biracial, Harlem-raised model, Ebony Fashion Fair alum, bubbly runway walker, *Soul Train* dancer, Halstonette, one of "Antonio's Girls," Stephen Burrows's fitting model and muse
Grace Jones	Jamaica-born model and recording artist, an African mask and Cubist sculpture, bon vivant and "art groupie," Jean-Paul Goude's onetime paramour, Richard Bernstein's "art mother," one of "Antonio's Girls"
Antonio Lopez	Puerto Rico–born fashion illustrator, Kodak Instamatic artist, lover of the street, flashy dresser and

	dancer, lifelong collaborator with Juan Ramos, credited with "discovering" Grace Jones and Jerry Hall
Juan Ramos	Puerto Rico–born art director, former window dresser, elegance personified, lifelong collaborator with Antonio Lopez, partner of Paul Caranicas

SECONDARY CHARACTERS

Joey Arias	Performance artist, Club 57 habitué, salesperson and window dancer at Fiorucci, friend of Antonio Lopez and Klaus Nomi
Anthony Barboza	Erudite Black commercial and fashion photographer, member of Kamoinge Workshop, early collaborator with Grace Jones
Richard Bernstein	Bronx-born Jewish commercial illustrator, quaalude lover, friend of and collaborator with Grace Jones, Andy Warhol's favorite local artist
Bobby Breslau	Deft leathermaker, member of Stephen Burrows's commune, Halston's handbag designer, friend of Andy Warhol and Keith Haring
Paul Caranicas	Greece-born painter, student at École des Beaux-Arts and DJ at Le Bureau, friend of Antonio Lopez, partner of Juan Ramos
Angelo Colon	Model for Antonio Lopez, body double for Grace Jones
Betty Davis	Lusty funk siren, self-professed "Nasty Gal," wife of Miles Davis, frequent collaborator with Antonio Lopez
Potassa de la Fayette	Leggy Dominican partygoer with Grace Jones and Pat Cleveland, informal model of Antonio Lopez

Victor Fernandez	Piscean Latin-about-Manhattan, frequent model for Antonio Lopez, assistant designer to Stephen Burrows
Jean-Paul Goude	French graphic designer, Antonio Lopez's friend and Union Square neighbor, collaborator with and one-time paramour of Grace Jones
Jerry Hall	Texan model, Grace Jones's Paris roommate, muse of and briefly engaged to Antonio Lopez, model for Stephen Burrows
Halston	Iowa-born fashion designer, lover of Ultrasuede, friend of Stephen Burrows, Studio 54 enthusiast, friend of Pat Cleveland
Bethann Hardison	Black American model, fierce runway walker, Stephen Burrows's first showroom model, friend of Pat Cleveland, Halstonette
Elsa Peretti	Italian jewelry designer, model, friend of Halston, member of Stephen Burrows's commune
Rock Steady Crew	Legendary Bronx-based b-boy crew, collaborators of Antonio Lopez
Roz Rubenstein	Cofounder of O Boutique, member of Stephen Burrows's commune
Ming Smith	Black American model, fine-art photographer, sole female member of Kamoinge Workshop, friend of and collaborator with Grace Jones
Willi Smith	Lead designer for WilliWear, geeky brother of model Toukie Smith, friend of Stephen Burrows, friend of Bethann Hardison

André Leon Talley	Andy Warhol's receptionist at *Interview* magazine, chic social diarist, interviewer of Grace Jones, champion of Stephen Burrows
Charles Tracy	Puerto Rico–born fashion photographer, member of Stephen Burrows's commune, collaborator with Antonio Lopez
Andy Warhol	Pittsburgh-born Pop artist, Antonio Lopez's friend and Union Square neighbor, friend of Pat Cleveland, collaborator with Grace Jones
Stephen Burrows's models	Alva Chinn, Naomi Sims, Billie Blair, Norma Jean Darden, Renauld White, Deanna Lambert, Iman
Antonio Lopez's models	Jane Thorvaldson, John Stavros, Jessica Lange, Donna Jordan, Virginia Shaddick MacGregor, Jean Eudes Canival, Tina Chow, Paloma Picasso, Amina Warsuma, Nina Gaidarova, Annabel D'Huart, Jay Jenkins, Arrow, Carol LaBrie, Toukie Smith, Divine
Settings	Paris, Palace of Versailles, Fire Island, the gritty streets of New York City, Enchanted Gardens (The Enchanted Garden, Douglaston Golf Course [now Douglaston Manor], 6320 Commonwealth Boulevard, Douglaston, NY), Studio 54 (254 West Fifty-Fourth Street), Max's Kansas City (213 Park Avenue South), Paradise Garage (84 King Street), Fiorucci (125 East Fifty-Ninth Street), Cinandre (11 East Fifty-Seventh Street), O Boutique (236 Park Avenue South), Stephen Burrows World boutique at Henri Bendel (10 West Fifty-Seventh Street), Antonio Lopez and Juan Ramos's studios (876 Broadway and 31 Union Square West), Anthony Barboza's studio (10 West Eighteenth Street), department store windows, bathtubs and showers, broom closets

I thought this was how artists moved to New York, alone, that the city was a mecca of individual points, longings, all merging into one great light-pulsing mesh, and you simply found your pulse, your place.

Rachel Kushner, *The Flamethrowers*

Introduction

Insurgent Aesthetics

Amid the enormous economic precarity and persistent political upheaval that roiled the United States in the 1970s, New York City was an urban metropolis on the verge. But what, exactly, it was on the brink of depended entirely on whom you asked.

Across the country, the decade seemed like a parade of bad news: an oil embargo and stubbornly high gas prices, Richard Nixon's resignation following the Watergate scandal, the persistent stagflation, and looming fears of a recession. But this gnawing cynicism was particularly pernicious in New York City. Despite completing the World Trade Center in Lower Manhattan in 1973, a phenomenal architectural and financial achievement, the city barely escaped bankruptcy two years later. And that fiscal crisis was often blamed on populations of color, particularly impoverished Black and Puerto Rican residents, who were perceived as draining social services while not paying enough taxes.[1] The summer of 1976 was the beginning of serial killer David Berkowitz's yearlong spree of violence. And, amid this terror, the city suffered a crippling twenty-five-hour blackout in July 1977, resulting in widespread looting. Times Square, bursting with peep shows, adult bookstores, and xxx porn theaters by decade's end, was a sleazy vortex of prostitution and crime. Graffiti was widely perceived as an uncontrollable and inescapable public nuisance. And the South Bronx, already devastated by the construction of the Cross Bronx Expressway, was a charred landscape, a national symbol of dysfunction, as landlords burned their buildings to pocket the insurance money.

However, as those with the means fled the city for more serene surroundings, more and more artists found a home. After all, "The Big Apple," specifically downtown Manhattan, was the place to go if you wanted to make a name for yourself. Cheap rents attracted the ambitious. And consequently, among all the awfulness—*because* of all the awfulness—a thriving and sprawling network of creative, eager people bloomed: hairstylists, aspiring filmmakers, performers, musicians, photographers, visual artists. From SoHo to the East Village to Tribeca, casual conversations over drinks or on the dance floor—whether at the East Village's Club 57 or Tribeca's Mudd Club—often led to artistic collaborations. And that spirit of openness and experimentation permeated the work subsequently created; friendship and art-making went hand in hand. Hand-drawn, xeroxed flyers, which would later become collector items, epitomized the DIY ethos of the time. Poetry readings, performance art, "trash" film screenings, and whimsical theme parties proliferated. Nightclubs hosted art exhibitions. Painters designed clothes. Fashion boutiques morphed into impromptu parties. Together and independently, these hopeful artists shared a dogged pursuit: creativity inseparable from hedonism. As the city seemed on the verge of falling apart, downtown seemed to bubble with artistic scenes—ever-mutating, irreverent, overlapping.

This flowering of aesthetic energy downtown also manifested in heady sonic innovation as disco culture became a distinctive paradigm. Starting in the early 1970s, racially mixed crowds (often predominantly gay men) gathered at word-of-mouth parties and underground clubs. Dancing became a form of communal pleasure and spiritual rebirth.[2] At 647 Broadway, David Mancuso hosted the Loft, an early predecessor; he used LSD and music to deprogram people's minds and bring them together. And DJs, in tandem, became legendary inspirations who smoothly blended disparate genres and, later in the decade, debuted 12-inch singles. For instance, Paradise Garage's resident spinner Larry Levan became as talked about as the club's spectacular sound system. Writer Hilton Als likened Levan's skill to a narcotic high: "Levan's music was like the sound of cocaine: one intense burst of thinking and feeling joined to another by a bass line."[3] People began looking for vinyl records of songs they had heard the night before. In this expansive milieu, DJs were celebrated as an integral part of a growing tapestry of artists, recognized for their ability to mold sound into color and emotion.

Meanwhile, in contrast to the effervescent energy bubbling south of Fourteenth Street, uptown was the locus of culture with a capital C. Though a mere subway ride away, it was a universe apart. On the Upper East Side, "Museum Mile" was a twenty-three-block stretch of Fifth Avenue anchored by some of the most exclusive arts institutions in the world, including the Met and the Guggenheim. And as bastions of respectability, they catered to established artists—not quirky neophytes. The offices of *Vogue* were also nearby, across the street from Central Park, projecting and disseminating ideals of American fashion to the masses. Uptown was also home to the city's luxury department stores, like Henri Bendel on Fifty-Seventh Street and Fifth Avenue, known for its white-and-chocolate-brown striped hat boxes and its moneyed (and adamantly slim) clientele. Pop artist Andy Warhol and fashion designer Halston, who each became wealthy household names in the 1970s, lived on the Upper East Side. Uptown's upper-crust respectability and elite social networks coexisted with downtown's edgier, laid-back environs and artistic efflorescence. And those two worlds started to mingle more, eroding seemingly clear-cut geographical borders and cultural limits.

Much has been written about this heavily mythologized moment. The grit of 1970s New York seems magical. And there is ongoing "nostalgia for the sequined glory days of 1970s bohemia."[4] But our myths, like all myths, are partial. Incomplete. Our exuberant and constant retelling of this legendary time has also been influenced by our blind spots, washing out crucial dimensions of this moment in the city. In doing so, once-prominent historical subjects and their assemblages of friends-turned-collaborators have been overlooked in our storytelling.

Artists of color—critical contributors to the riveting downtown cultural scene, yet whose prodigious and outsize talents were also, somewhat surprisingly, recognized uptown—exist only on the margins of our understandings of this now-romanticized time. And that is primarily because of their race. Too often, they are characterized as marginal figures—people who circulated in the same spaces as more important artists or perhaps even briefly dated a member of a collective, but are not themselves worthy of serious and sustained consideration. Repeatedly, they are assigned stock parts with a few lines in the cultural histories of the period. They typically serve as the local color, hovering in the shadows while the spotlight remains on the era's major, and nearly always white, characters. In short, they are stubbornly situated as mere footnotes to a larger story.

And yet the inverse is more accurate: Much of the innovation of this period came from these artists. These artists of color were the ones most able to see that culture was more expansive than what was exhibited in the hushed (and Eurocentric) spaces of museums. Instead, they noticed that culture was on bold display everywhere: in the blossoming locales downtown, the bustling streets of Harlem and the South Bronx, and the spray paint–drenched subways that traversed them all. And that culture multiplied in the subterraneous nightclubs where disparate groups—Black and Puerto Rican breakdancers, gay men and their fashionable female friends, even choreographer Alvin Ailey alongside his students and instructors in their Capezio shoes—commingled. The result was an ongoing exchange of energy, which was not left on the musty dance floor but was absorbed into everyday life. By combining these putatively low sensibilities with allusions to high art, artists of color continually created experimental and cutting-edge forms, eventually appropriated or belatedly recognized by gatekeeper institutions and arbiters of culture. In other words, the New York City of our myths would not have fully emerged without this ill-defined but essential gathering of Black and Brown artists.

This book is an intimate journey through the lives and work of three artists of color: Antonio Lopez, Grace Jones, and Stephen Burrows. It offers a kaleidoscopic view of these figures and their eclectic orbits of friends during the creative explosion that was 1970s New York City. Each primarily expressed themselves through a specific form: fashion illustration (Lopez), modeling (Jones), and fashion design (Burrows), but also confidently crossed over into other mediums. Lopez, for instance, swapped markers and pens for a Kodak Instamatic camera during this period. And Jones made a notable pivot later in the decade, reincarnating herself as a dazzling disco diva. Each partook in the joys of working together—a practice that, I believe, was a defining feature of this era. They built networks with like-minded individuals who prized imagination—people who keenly understood that where you came from and who you were was much less important than who you *imagined* yourself to be. They each envisioned New York City as fertile stomping grounds for their artistic practice, where inspiration could be easily gleaned from the colorful din of the street or the crisp pages of a fashion magazine. Together, these polymaths offered a textured and profoundly original way of seeing—each providing, in other words, a slightly different version of the 1970s as they staged art, performance, and fashion that pushed the cultural needle radically forward.

These characters each charted idiosyncratic paths while merging downtown attitude with uptown glam. Lopez, by all accounts playful, sexy, and charismatic, was already well-known by the late 1960s for modernizing fashion illustration with fresh forms and psychedelic color. In the 1970s, he and his lifelong collaborator Juan Ramos devised album covers, designed clothes, and participated in a renaissance of diasporic Puerto Rican creatives. Jones, striking and supple with an angular face often likened to an African mask, was a struggling model at the decade's dawn. By the end of the 1970s, after a brief stint in Europe, she became a successful model, a wild performer, and an object of fascination for artists like Andy Warhol and Keith Haring. Burrows, a boyish wunderkind who favored muscle tees and mirrored sunglasses, had gained notice by the end of the 1960s for his handmade leather garments. In the ensuing decade, he became synonymous with tropical-hued jersey and chiffon dresses that resembled paintings on the body.

At first glance, Grace Jones, Antonio Lopez, and Stephen Burrows may seem like improbable protagonists in this story. They did not have the imprimatur of elite art schools, nor did they necessarily aspire to become serious artists. Lopez and Jones, for instance, were both college dropouts. Lopez briefly studied at Fashion Institute of Technology (FIT) but left to work at *Women's Wear Daily*, the industry trade journal. He quickly ascended the ranks and landed his first cover within a few months. Likewise, Jones was enrolled at Onondaga Community College in Syracuse at one point, with the modest goal of becoming a Spanish teacher. She left to join a traveling theater troupe, briefly became a nudist, and first experimented with LSD while living in a hippie commune in rural Pennsylvania. Burrows's original aim was to become an art teacher, given his propensity for drawing and "strong color."

He spent two years at the Philadelphia Museum College of Art before transferring to FIT and moving to New York City.

Furthermore, given their backgrounds, their rise to stardom in the 1970s seemed unlikely. Lopez and Burrows were the second- and third-generation progeny of garment trade workers—sample hands, sewists, and mannequin dressers. Their families were indeed part of the American fashion industry, but only as the invisible Black and Brown labor that ultimately sustained it. Lopez and Jones, moreover, came to the United States as children from the Caribbean. The former, born in Puerto Rico, was raised in East Harlem, while the latter, born in Jamaica, eventually migrated with her family to upstate New York. Not just by the sheer size of their talent but by their insistence on breaking the rules did they overcome steep social hierarchies designed to keep them in their place. All three bypassed the gallery system, the usual track to recognition in the polite art world, as they figured out what it meant to be bona fide artists. Instead of the typical pecking order, the collectives they each nurtured and were nurtured by operated with relentless variety: as a type of school, an incubator of big ideas, and a perpetual party.

Antonio Lopez, Stephen Burrows, and Grace Jones belonged to prismatic and interlocking social worlds that, while erroneously remembered as secondary to the glittery silver of Andy Warhol's Factory or the art-punk sensibilities of Club 57, were deeply impactful. Despite their humble and (in the cases of Lopez and Jones) immigrant backgrounds, they each became cosmopolitan and forward-thinking iconoclasts whose gifts reverberated outward—past the graffitied subway cars and the newly completed Twin Towers.

Yet, while these three artists created through community, their most compelling canvas was their personal style. In other words, these creators constantly reinvented themselves, evolving with each phase of their work. Their punchy aesthetic and performance-based disruptions found analogues in their oft-discussed and ardently original self-presentations. They lacked the hallmarks of more traditional routes to artistic eminence, be it financial capital or the patronage of an accomplished elder. However, what they each possessed in abundance was a confident and influential sense of self. As they staged themselves, over and over, they became pathbreaking mavericks who happily disobeyed boundaries between commercial and fine art. In short, they inhabited style and made art.

Pat Cleveland, Billie Blair, Alva Chinn, Bethann Hardison, and Sean Bryne at a fashion show, New York City, circa 1975. Kodak Instamatics. Courtesy of the Estate of Antonio Lopez and Juan Ramos.

As we have seen, these creatives were not simply *of* the 1970s; they actively shaped it. They did so by manipulating their individualistic style, that inherently amorphous apparatus of cultural cachet, and even challenging what that term meant. Again, while Lopez, Jones, and Burrows were extremely fashionable people and repeatedly interpellated as such by their peers and the press, they each recognized that style was much more expansive than a mere vehicle of personal expression; instead, it was an artistic medium and an intentional form of communication—a nonverbal conduit for meaning. And by learning how to harness it, whether through the drape of jersey fabric, the tilt of a head, or the arrangement of mannequins in a department store window, they could each translate their audacious worldview to a broader public.

Style surfaces in these pages as both a noun and a verb. It can refer to the set of unique characteristics inherent in a work of art, such as line, shape, or color. These characteristics are often so distinct that they can be recognized in other works manufactured by the same person or group. (Burrows's lettuce hem is one of many examples.) Style is thus an artistic signature that audiences can "read" for clues about the artist's intentions or the climate a collective lived and worked in.[5] (Think of Lopez's repeated use of a three-by-three grid for his series of Kodak Instamatic works.) Style, however, is also closer to a practice or a *doing*. (Here, we need look no further than Jones's staging of herself as an aesthetic subject.) It is also a manner of living (as in Burrows's fashion "commune"). And style is a powerful vehicle when subordinate groups, those who ostensibly lack power, wield it. Subcultures manipulate style to reveal their group identities to each other (see: gay men's clever and coded use of handkerchiefs in this period) and as a type of defiant messaging directed at the public (see: the boisterous visual language of graffiti).[6] As we examine this decade more closely, we find again and again that the most meaningful connoisseurs of style are the overlooked individuals on the margins of society who utilize whatever is readily available to speak about their most urgent concerns.[7]

The tenacity of these artists meant that, sooner or later, the so-called tastemakers began to herald the singular work they constructed or actively participated in, but such emerging fame did not occlude experiences of racial bias or homophobia.[8] Some critics spent more time trying to situate these creators into prefabricated narratives centered on their racial backgrounds than recognizing their aesthetic finesse. In such efforts, tortured and biased, we see a recurrence of the burden of representation that is repeatedly foisted onto queer artists and artists of color, where their identities are privileged more than their art. And sometimes, these artists' work was misunderstood or blatantly censored, particularly when it openly flaunted queer desire or exhibited pleasure in self-objectification.

The specific hardships these artists faced also reveal the vast complexities frequently ignored in static portrayals of race in this fraught moment. The stories of these three artists showcase, for instance, the linkages between psychedelic drugs and creativity among these Black and Brown cognoscenti. They force us to confront the manifold realities of artistic subjects who resist recuperation in the revolutionary ethos of Black Power or doctrines of racial uplift. And once again, they reveal the presence of figures who are often elided in the prototypical narratives of this historical moment, be it hippie communes, the "peacock revolution," or the rise of boutique culture in New York City.

Likewise, if their boldness was apparent in how they chose to stage themselves as racial and sexual minorities, it was also evident in their unabashed use of bright, sumptuous colors. The artists and performers I gather here repeatedly gravitate to a chromatically intense spectrum. Lopez's use of a fluorescent pink, or the blood-red favored by Burrows, transported viewers to a Shangri-la-like aesthetic dimension and temporarily estranged them from pressing economic and political realities. And that reality—New York City in the 1970s—was often bleak: diminished social services, widespread vandalism, persistent robberies, and the scorched tenement buildings of the Lower East Side.

Still, amid these entrenched structural problems, a seemingly endless array of innovations emerged. Gay men repurposed the long-abandoned Pier 48 in Greenwich Village for street cruising and casual sex; artists began living and working in expansive, sunlit SoHo lofts once used for manufacturing; and figures like Burrows, Lopez, and Jones were purveyors of an aesthetic revolution, albeit in a minor key.[9] Living on the social edges of society, so often the wellspring of avant-garde art, they channeled their desires—for pleasure, for the new, for an intangible *more*—into raucous color and indefatigable fun. Hence, when Roland Barthes grumpily decried the artifice-laden "openly chemical" colors of Pop Art—colors that were "never shades, since nuance is banished from them"—he could have been discussing Lopez's Kodak Instamatic photo series or the airbrushed album covers Richard Bernstein made for Grace Jones.[10]

If the seventies were the decade of color, the ensemble of peers discussed in these pages were virtuosos of insurgent chromatics. This rebellion was waged not through political organizing, as it was in the sixties, but through the turf war of the aesthetic. In other words, while seemingly superficial, the heated debates about aesthetic practices—such as the artistic merits of color photography, or lack thereof, as some critics argued—were often a cover for more significant concerns. The aesthetic was not as openly democratic as it might appear; debates often arose over who had the privilege to shape it and for whose advantage. Moreover, the artistic use of color was not wholly cleaved from racial identity as color. For instance, Americans typically understood "loud" colors to belong *elsewhere*: confined to urban landscapes like barrios or exported to the blistering sun of Latin America and the Caribbean. When used at all, racy colors were to be tamed within the relative safety of interior design.[11] But these luscious shades and highlighter hues were precisely the types of color that these artists repeatedly deployed and adorned themselves with. Colors that evoked the dreamy hallucinogenic effects of an acid trip. Colors that, in an Afro-diasporic sense, possessed palpable energy—like Burrows's fiery red. Colors that "popped," especially when paired with brown skin. "Hot equator colors," as one fashion journalist aptly described Burrows's plush dresses. Lush, saturated colors that exceeded the optical and seemed to spill over into the other senses—like the gold lamé unitard Jones wore when she performed at Studio 54. Colors that had movement. And colors that seemed to symbolize futurity. Collectively, they offered a shared sense that color was not simply decorative but a potent repository of knowledge, feelings, and memories.

Mavericks of Style, therefore, seeks to complicate, undo, and expand past the rote frameworks and casual assumptions that too often underlie our discussions of artistic practice. Fashion design, long regarded as a secondary art form, is given equal billing with visual art. Pop Art is recast as a genre generative for artists of color in the United States, not just white men. Along the way, the artist and the model are revealed as mutually transformative. And the fetish of sole authorship is scrapped for a more pluralistic perception of bodies at play in the act of creation. The care the assorted players in this book exhibited toward each other was not simply the precondition for what they made together. Their friendships were, in themselves, art forms too.

Thus, if the development of an artist's style is a product of their social environment, then *Mavericks of Style* continually illuminates the cohort's

FASHION IDEAS SHAPE

Naomi and Deanna greet sunrise (left) on the beach in "worm" dresses of rayon jersey ($130)—to wear over bikinis or nothing at all. Renauld shows O's classic tunic ($70) and flared pants ($40) both in wool jersey. At right, Naomi comes through the beach plume in an "Egyptian" suit—burned-leather wrap skirt, appliquéd jersey jacket and "worm" pullover ($315, complete). The girls' jersey suits (below right) look like sports sweaters over dresses (Naomi's, $200; Deanna's, $130). Skullcaps are $5. What inspires Stephen's designs? People on the streets, sports gear, rock music and sex—the anatomy clothes "are sex," he points out.
As hair stylist, brother Franklyn Welsh updates coiffures of the '30's like Deanna's, and fluffs the family Afros.

Look magazine, 1970. *Left to right*: Naomi Sims, Renauld White, Deanna Lambert. Courtesy of Charles Tracy Archive.

influence on creation. What these Black and Brown creatives constructed was inseparable from the communities they formed; these peers understood collaboration as a given, as they lived and worked together or in close proximity. Each of the principal characters in the book was enmeshed in the artistic ecosystems of others whose so-called solo projects were, in fact, spiderweb-like structures that often intersected with one another. They made work not just alongside each other but *because* of each other.[12] Lopez worked with Jones and drew Burrows; Jones wore clothes by Lopez and Burrows; Burrows and Lopez both had connections to *Vogue* and shared model Pat Cleveland; Cleveland made films with Lopez, went on *Soul Train* with Burrows, and partied at Enchanted Gardens with Lopez and Jones. Jones dated, worked, and lived with Jean-Paul Goude, whose studio was near Lopez's; Cleveland met Halston through Burrows; Lopez, like Burrows, frequented Max's Kansas City; Andy Warhol's Factory was close to both Lopez's and Goude's studios, and he watched horror movies with Cleveland.[13] If we peel back the palimpsest-like layers of these people and their art, friendship and love frequently surface as the critical supports enabling their work to flourish—or even to exist in the first place.

Grace Jones herself acknowledges this: "Back then, it seemed that everything and everyone was connected. There was some kind of nuclear magnet that brought all of us together. I always say it was as if an octopus linked me to Andy (Warhol), Jean-Paul (Goude), Antonio (Lopez), and Richard (Bernstein). Nowadays, artists don't really work together anymore, but we all inspired and respected each other and collaborated together. We had the best, best times doing what we wanted to do and having fun with it."[14]

As Jones suggests, these trailblazers lived life as an ongoing art project, filled with color and fashion, music and travel, heartbreak and laughter. They journeyed together to far-flung places like Brazil and Puerto Rico or more local haunts like Fire Island, staging impromptu photo shoots in pools or on the beach. They elevated partying to an art form in their collective pursuit of the get-down. They actively sought forms of beauty while widening the watercolor-like palette they used to conjure it into being. At the same time, Antonio Lopez, Grace Jones, and Stephen Burrows did not wait for others to identify them as "artists." They forcibly, if belatedly, claimed that title for themselves. They were masters at creating spellbinding worlds that lasted the duration of a darkly alluring performance or came alive when a swath of canary-yellow chiffon undulated on its wearer. And the rhythm of their lives attests to how they traversed the streets of New York City and beyond. These pages are a tribute to their steely determination in art and life and their shared attempt to project a new vision of the 1970s in sultry, bombastic color.

Throughout *Mavericks of Style*, these New York City–based artists move between varying fields of expertise in a dual effort: they seek to explore new aesthetic forms and to melt the edges between seemingly disparate disciplines. In this cultural history, I trace a loose assembly of the artistically inclined, from models to leather-makers to graphic designers, all living and working in 1970s New York City. Rejecting the hierarchical order implicit in traditional categories, they collectively develop increasingly sophisticated artistic practices that span multiple genres. Inspired by these creatives' wildly imaginative, cross-disciplinary approach, I employ, in Kandice Chuh's words, a "deliberately promiscuous" reading practice that utilizes insights from multiple schools of thought without being beholden to their apparent limits.[15]

How can these provocateurs' noted aversion to boundaries—between high and low cultures, fashion and art, or commercialism and creativity[16]—encourage a breakdown in the rigid and often-policed divisions between bodies of knowledge?[17] Put differently, an open-ended interpretative method can more fully attune to the porous flows between differing sensibilities, influences, and cultures discussed here. For instance, recognizing Antonio Lopez's immense artistry requires us to understand his "context-switching," as he freely pivoted to whatever medium best suited his purposes at each moment.[18] In doing so, the imprint of his point of view moves across various material objects—make-up-inspired vinyl record covers, tulle skirts, or steamy photography.

As such, *Mavericks of Style* draws on concepts from disciplinary and interdisciplinary fields, including cultural studies, visual culture, queer and feminist theory, art history, and ethnic studies. It is aligned with the onus of performance studies to privilege artists as "not only culture makers but also theory producers," as José Esteban Muñoz has argued, while also contributing to the field's attention to "critical experiments in sound, visuality, space, and text," as Alexandra Vazquez elegantly puts it.[19]

Moreover, I understand the aesthetic as the broad range of stimuli the human sensorium discerns. *Mavericks of Style* dovetails with scholarship tracking the "ways in which aesthetic practices could alter the world and our experience of it," such as the image and object world of mass culture, while also critiquing aesthetics as a regime often wielded against minoritarian subjects.[20] Thus, I follow the lead of scholars like Muñoz, Anne Cheng, Amber Musser, and Jillian Hernandez, among others, turning toward the ornamental, campy, synthetic, surface-oriented, and excessive as foundational (albeit feminized and racialized) aesthetic properties.[21] Furthermore, this text's attention to "distinct forms of image-making" and "performative approaches to being seen and represented" corresponds with work tracing the intermingling of gesture, desire, and affect that occurs inside and outside the representational frame; these scholars also highlight photography's "other histories," or its complicity in sustaining visual taxonomies of racial difference and Western superiority.[22]

Similarly, art history has been criticized for its "focus on Western perspectives, dominant narratives, and canonic images" while treating racial difference as "an unwanted or uninvited guest, an intrusive presence that cheapens and distracts attention from the concerns of materiality and form."[23] These appraisals indicate the need for fresh methodological perspectives in the field, widening our purview to include performance and aesthetic works that stage provocative encounters for the spectator and offer counterintuitive examples of how (and where) meaning is produced. It also means redirecting our gaze to marginalized historical figures and unorthodox archives that remain underexamined. In the following discussion, I construct an alternative model, continually revealing sites and scenes of "uncommon beauty"—Paradise Garage, Fiorucci, O Boutique, breakdancing, sportswear, voguing, Blackness, and latinidad.[24] They take their cues (and audiences) from queer nightlife, hip-hop, or a shared sense of diasporic cultural pride, for instance, rather than the museum or gallery. *Gesture*, a keyword in performance studies, also serves as a valuable rubric for analyzing the artistic works below. "After all, the gesture is small, oftentimes barely perceptible, and as performance studies scholars, this is what we are trained to catch, in an artwork, in an everyday interaction, in the way a dancer moves a muscle, etc.," as Iván A. Ramos reiterates.[25]

In addition, this book emerges from topics that transcend any field of study per se—modeling, department store window performance, and hippie communes, to name a few. In what follows, I reveal the influence of overlooked but vital historical figures and defamiliarize well-known ones. I suggest a more extensive understanding of artistic practice, which supersedes the usual lines of demarcation—hastily drawn but rigidly imposed—between visual art, performance, and fashion design.

Mavericks of Style is also, avowedly, a queer history. I foreground figures whose orientation to the world was queer, and I value elusive forms of evidence that more traditional histories may obscure. While *queer* is often used exclusively to denote nonnormative forms of sexuality and identity, I conceive of queerness differently. What if queerness is more indicative of a directional compass that suggests how a person perceives everyday life and how they move through it? In this way, queerness refers less to one's sexual proclivities and more to one's approach to navigating the world.[26] Lopez, Jones, and Burrows cut a dashing figure not just in terms of how they looked (or dressed or danced) but also in how they traversed New York City and contributed to various artistic enterprises and commercial industries. Again and again, they choreographed ingenious possibilities for personal and aesthetic expression and thus daringly mapped new terrains.[27] Their objective, as Jonathan Flatley and Anthony Grudin write about Warhol, was "making room for alternative, queer ways of feeling and being with others in the world" via artistic expression.[28]

Queerness also indicates the "differential aesthetic valuing" of Black and Brown cultural producers, in Jillian Hernandez's words, as well as what they valued as objects of beauty, such as the poetry of the street, the sensory bliss of the disco, and the zest of the Black model.[29] This echoes Ann Cvetkovich's suggestion, in an essay on queer collecting practices, that "to love the wrong kind of objects is to be queer."[30] My attention to both ephemera and chatty, secondhand narration in this book echoes our growing scholarly insistence on these as different forms of evidence that subvert, or queer, more prototypical notions of the "fact" or proof. This methodological approach attaches value to performances, for instance, that only existed in the time of their duration but live on through documentation and the memories of those who were there.[31] Despite their negative valences, it recognizes gossip and rumor as generative sources of knowledge and (art) history.[32]

Amid all this, I recognize that *Mavericks of Style* is also an act of curation. My selective arrangement of visual media and textual description conjures this story into being. My sequencing of drawings, photographs, and print advertising runs on a parallel track to the written word, as this book is not just a cultural study but a visual history of style, as practiced by this artistic ensemble and their compatriots. (After all, one could argue that Lopez, Jones, and Burrows were curators in their own right.) Furthermore, this book is also a queer curatorial project, one that understands curation as not just the juxtaposition of aesthetic objects but also as an intimate care for the past and a duty to translate its importance to others.[33] That care is particularly important for objects, persons, conversations, and onetime events typically deemed unimportant, as well as for those whose names, when not elided entirely, are badly mangled: I was initially disappointed that neither Stephen Burrows's name nor his O Boutique appeared in a cultural history of Max's Kansas City until I realized that his full name and boutique were misspelled as "Steven Barrow's Au Boutique."[34] I "care about" and "care for" these aesthetic practices, as Gayatri Gopinath puts it, by writing about them and indulging in the generative frictions produced by considering them alongside one another.[35] That sense of fidelity and affection also manifests in my studious documentation of the places these figures touched and the specific friendships and extensive "*life*-world[s]" they built.[36]

As a result, in each chapter, I reconstruct a spatial cartography of select sites in New York City of the late 1960s and 1970s, places instrumental in the artistic and personal development of Lopez, Jones, and Burrows. I describe venues, both noteworthy and obscure, where they partied, pranced, and performed, where others helped refine their image, and where they imparted their aesthetic signature, their style. We crisscross the city and sometimes temporarily escape it, as I transport us to little-known hair salons, nondescript artist studios, buzzy boutiques, posh department stores, funky discos, and formal runway presentations. I also apply that subway map vision to their sundry working relationships and kinship networks, often a confluence of both. I describe like-minded affiliations (Grace Jones and Ming Smith's mutual identity as Black models), track mentor and mentee dyads (Antonio

Lopez and Joey Arias at Fiorucci), and pinpoint more asymmetrical dynamics based on aesthetic inspiration (Stephen Burrows and his muse Pat Cleveland). In doing so, I aim to showcase the glossy and glamorous but also gritty and soulful projects they created together, where style and substance coexisted in equal measure. And, in this vivid rendering of the recent past, I hope to draw a new map of where artistic experimentation and camaraderie roamed in 1970s New York City, manifested in its singular—if until now ignored—progenitors.

Mavericks of Style contributes to a small but growing body of literature, especially in recent years, on key artistic collectives on the East (and West) Coast that overlap with the historical period distilled here. In Southern California, for instance, these include the East LA–based Chicanx group Asco, who pointedly rejected the "collective" label. It also indexes the loosely organized Studio Z, an assemblage of Black artists who worked out of a former dancehall in South LA. Both groups thrived, despite lacking the institutional support of museums, because of their willingness to share resources and present their works in nonart contexts, such as the Route 110 underpass and the median strip of Whittier Boulevard.[37] Meanwhile, the Kamoinge Workshop—a Harlem-based network of Black fine art photographers—nurtured their members' desires to sharpen their technical aptitudes and proudly foreground Black diasporic subjects as archetypes of beauty. (One of these was Grace Jones.) First formed in the early 1960s, this working group exhibited and published together most fiercely in the early 1970s. Two other groups that originated in New York during this period— "Where We At" Black Women Artists Inc. in 1971 and the Nuyorican Poets Café in 1973—were both the result of informal gatherings of like-minded peers: the former's initial meeting in Dindga McCannon's Brooklyn home and, in the latter's case, Miguel Algarín's living room on East Sixth Street.[38] For each ad hoc group, the sixties' various political and social upheavals were critical underpinnings of a shared aesthetic philosophy and institutional critique.[39]

This study is also in dialogue with scholarship focused less on overt identifiable sets of artists and more on the nocturnal spaces they congregated in. For instance, the oddball energy circulating in Club 57 and the Mudd Club led to unique forms of artistic exchange. And both are firmly centered in any recounting of Lower Manhattan's vibrant party scene in the late 1970s, spilling over into the early 1980s. However, neither appears to be a home for the primary characters of this book. One reason may be that while identity play, especially gender nonconformity, was a defining theme of Club 57, racial diversity was not.[40] Consequently, the few Black artists who frequented the venue did not make it their preferred base. The Mudd Club, which opened in Tribeca in 1978, featured punk and disco in the same space as avant-garde performances and art exhibitions.[41] While not a regular presence, Pat Cleveland mentions singing at the Mudd Club in her memoirs.[42] At least one artist recalls witnessing the runway legend's "long-forgotten performance."[43] But a similar ethnic homogeneity haunts the historical record. The noted exceptions—graffiti artist Fred Braithwaite (later known as Fab 5 Freddy), visual artist Jean-Paul Basquiat, and Michael Holman (who formed the experimental band Gray with Basquiat in 1979)—were habitués of both spaces. And yet, Basquiat and Braithwaite struggled to get into either club before becoming more recognizable, which is a testament to the painfully slow inclusion of people of color into the city's burgeoning art-punk club scene at the tail end of the decade.[44] Meanwhile, the prominence of midtown's Studio 54 and its Queens-based predecessor, Enchanted Gardens, in the following pages may seem antithetical to the genealogies of New York City's downtown party networks.[45] This is primarily because neither was located downtown. However, that dissonance, too, is instructive. In short, we need a more expansive account of the feedback loop between club culture and artistic freedom in the 1970s, especially for the chic polymaths of color I highlight here.[46]

Moreover, my focus on identifying specific networks of affiliation and shared artistic impulses suggests a *generational* aesthetic dissent. Typically, generations are thought to be united by their mutual experience of the era's defining events. For instance, Woodstock, the March on Washington, the Stonewall Riots, and the Vietnam War symbolize the political agitation and daring of the sixties generation, an era of seismic sociopolitical "shocks." In contrast, the seventies have been identified as the "Me" decade, a term coined by writer Tom Wolfe in 1976; the decade traded sixties communalism for individualistic role-play, "compulsive artifice," and "soul style."[47] In short, "the 1970s as a 'me' decade is remembered as relentlessly superficial and self-obsessed."[48] The common point of view I track in these pages—toward deeply saturated colors, for instance—indicates a different metric for understanding how their collective predispositions were initially shaped: the similarity of their "impressions." In other words, a generation consists of people who share identical impressions, drawn from their experiences during youth, their country of birth, age, or university education. "The early impression is the key to understanding how a shift in attitude or a new aesthetic has come about," art historian James Meyer argues.[49]

For instance, model Pat Cleveland recalls money being scarce growing up in Spanish Harlem with her painter mother, Lady Bird, and aunt Helen, both nurses' aides at Bellevue Hospital. However, that poverty was augmented by the "will to adorn," in Zora Neale Hurston's words, which they freely indulged in when designing clothes for the costume balls they hoped to attend.[50] In Cleveland's words, "As far as I'm concerned, my true education centered on the creative mess that existed in our living room. And what a glorious mess it was: There were sequins, strings of pearls, peacock feathers, large exotic fans, beads, and bent wire hangers loaded down with fabrics."[51] She describes how, soon after *Sputnik* entered space, her mother and aunt constructed a four-foot-high replica of planet Earth that Lady Bird wore to New York City's Beaux Arts Ball in 1958. Cleveland's anecdote, set during her formative years, illustrates how she, like others in this book, absorbed a tutelage in style as a means for extravagant self-expression that often required creative resourcefulness. It demonstrates how histories are defined just as much by our individual lives—not to mention the stories we tell about ourselves and our friends—as they are by epochal events. Thus, I meditate on the careers and kinship networks of our primary and secondary characters to understand the recent past, a time that is both near (memory) and far (history).

In my elastic understanding of the seventies, I suggest that this milieu's propulsive energies extend beyond the decade itself, bookended by the late 1960s and the early 1980s. In this manner, I concur with other historians in suggesting that clear-cut delineations of decades are artificial; such temporal divisions ignore how history and memory both linger and persist. Moreover, in this project, a taut focus on the ten years beginning in 1970 is unrealistic, given that, for instance, Burrows and Lopez had both gained notoriety by the end of the sixties. As a result, their aesthetic interventions in the following decade are better understood when contextualized within the longer trajectory of their artistic development as they sharpened their skills and ventured into different arenas. The same is true for Jones, a fierce performer whose iconic image is so synonymous with the late seventies that it has become visual shorthand for it, especially the excesses of Studio 54. A broader inquiry into her fledging attempts at modeling from the late 1960s into the early 1970s provides a more nuanced understanding of how she created her distinct persona with crucial coconspirators, becoming a canvas for others and a muse for herself. This looser frame around the seventies reveals, on the one hand, how the recent past animated what these artists designed and, on the other hand, the fascinating afterlives of acts that persisted long after their creation.

Finally, *Mavericks of Style* is a multisensorial project. It aims to hear the "groove" of Juan Ramos and Antonio Lopez's artistic practice. It seeks to recreate the intoxicating atmosphere in which Grace Jones's cosmopolitan glamour flourished. And it attempts to capture the kinetic motion of Stephen Burrows's ethereal, rainbow-bright dresses. I repeatedly showcase assorted innovations in form as they individually and collectively fashioned the era. I also privilege photography as source material, attending to its illusory mysteries and mythological qualities.[52] Such a mandate necessitates, in Tina Campt's words, "looking beyond what we see and attuning our senses to the other affective frequencies through which photographs register."[53] In addition, I integrate the recorded testimonies of those there, whether through formalized oral histories or informal chitchat gathered from commercial print media and artist memoirs. And I, in performance studies parlance, write *with* (rather than simply *about*) the luscious polyrhythmic soundtrack of the disco.[54]

After all, as novelist Justin Torres reminds us, the (gay) disco's imperative was the act of transformation it imparted on those who entered, allowing one to be "transfigured in the disco light. To lighten, loosen, see yourself reflected in the beauty of others."[55] My immersion in this audio archive—including Roy Ayers, La Lupe, Earth, Wind & Fire, Gwen Guthrie, Larry Levan, Cheryl Lynn, Herbie Hancock, and, of course, Grace Jones—has acted as a temporal gateway, enabling me to enter the recent past sonically. But it has also implored me to listen very closely to the details, "those bits of history that get skipped over or left unattended" and often "effect in flashes and refuse analytical capture."[56] Doing so has enabled me to hear the faint tempo of these main characters' steps as they circumnavigated the street, the studio, the disco, and the world. I, in turn, have carefully crafted prose whose cadence mimics the rhythm of these protagonists' artistic journeys while also attempting to capture that certain je ne sais quoi—a fleeting feeling, a sensation, a tactile hue—that punctuated their lives and permeates these pages. Here, we enter and exit stages where Black and Brown creatives are the leading players, orchestrating a beautifully rendered portrait of the seventies where style is the tool at hand for forging a better world.

I always want to know what's new; that's why I love the street. I get so many ideas just walking around New York or Paris.

ANTONIO LOPEZ, *VOGUE*

MUNDANE MADE SPECTACULAR

Antonio Lopez

In 1983, Antonio Lopez showcased his energetic visual language to New York City's Fashion Institute of Technology students. In this lecture and drawing demonstration, one of several he offered at various design schools during the first half of the 1980s, the Nuyorican fashion illustrator invited audiences to witness his kinetic drawing method as he sketched a live model.[1] These were far from typical drawing lessons. To recreate the stimulating energy of his studio, where models drifted in and out and music was on a constant loop, Lopez played mixtapes created by graffiti artist Bill "Blast" Cordero. Occasionally, Cordero (who later became one of Lopez's models) upped the ante by DJing live during these presentations. And, in a final flourish, the feisty members of the South Bronx–based Rock Steady Crew, frequent visitors to Lopez's studio at the time (and artistic subjects for him), breakdanced to the same soundtrack. They adeptly modeled breaking's developing role as a "public showcase for the flamboyant triumph of virility, wit, and skill. In short, of style."[2] The lesson Lopez and his collaborators implied was clear: fashion illustration was more than technical proficiency. Instead, it was a high art form that was revitalized when sharing space with—and mutually informed by—putatively low cultural forms, such as breakdancing and DJ culture. These Black and Brown "expressive repertoires" were indebted to the percussive cacophony of the street and the body heat of the nightclub.[3]

These disparate elements survive in a brief clip documenting Lopez's FIT demonstration, which I saw at a 2016 retrospective of Lopez's body of work at El Museo del Barrio on the (very) northern edge of New York City's Museum Mile. Lopez's model for this lecture was Angelo Colon, an artist in his own right, who served as Grace Jones's body double in several of her films and was also a peer of Stephen Burrows. Acting as a muse, Colon sits patiently in a chair while Lopez stands to his right before a large sheet of white paper on an easel. Dressed in red pants and a white button-down shirt, back to the camera, Lopez swiftly applies swaths of color to the paper with oil pastel crayons, like a painter. He glances back and forth at Colon as he draws. He steps back briefly, and we see, for the first time, a simulacrum of Colon's angular face carefully outlined in black strokes, turned slightly in profile, which Lopez has partially colored in with brown. Lopez's portrait-in-progress emphasizes Colon's high cheekbones, highlighted in bright orange, while exuding an undeniable aura of coolness. As Lopez sketches, the unmistakable, chant-like chorus of Grandmaster Flash's "White Lines" booms in the background. "White Lines," an early hip-hop anthem released in 1983, serves as a timely and unexpected musical backdrop; it transports the percolating energies of the South Bronx into FIT's Manhattan classrooms. Lopez demonstrates his seemingly effortless ability to harness hip-hop's brash sonic energy and compress it into dense lines and color; at one point in the clip, Lopez's drawing speed accelerates to match the feverish intensity of the song's crescendo. Not coincidentally, Lopez's skill as a fashion illustrator was described by a close friend as "dancing on paper," hinting at Lopez's dexterity in imbuing the two-dimensional drawn body with the energy of live dynamic movement. It is also an apt description of his life.

Lopez was born in 1943 in Utuado, Puerto Rico, but grew up in East Harlem, also known as Spanish Harlem or "El Barrio," where his family migrated in 1950; his father was a mannequin maker, and his mother was a seamstress.[4] "I came to America by the age of eight. It was always my dream to come to America," he said in a 1983 interview. Lopez could freely pursue creative pursuits at home, but the outside world—his neighborhood—was another story: "I was like the school vice president for two years, and these boys didn't even know I could draw. Outside was a different life altogether. I was working with my father making mannequins in the summertime, helping my mother make dresses. I had a collection of dolls, but if my friends ever found out, they would have killed me."[5] Elsewhere, he expounded further on the social dynamics of his urban environment: "It was tough growing up poor in Spanish Harlem. At P.S. 77, I found out that you *had* to be a member of a gang for self-preservation, so I ended up as 'war counselor' of the Comanches."[6]

Nonetheless, Lopez's early talent took him on a different path from his peers. He attended high school at the prestigious School of Industrial Art, now known as the High School of Art and Design, graduating in 1960. Photographer Gerard Malanga, a classmate who later became one of Andy Warhol's assistants, noticed Lopez's evident skill: "It was a terrific school. Calvin Klein was doing costume design, Antonio Lopez was doing fashion illustration—a field he would revolutionize. When Antonio showed me his portfolio, my jaw dropped. I thought, Wow, you're going places! He was quite amazing."[7] According to Malanga, Lopez also brought his collection of 45s to campus, entertaining his peers in the cafeteria during lunchtime: "We would have a ball. Chuck Berry, Fats Domino, that sort of thing. Antonio also had mambos and cha-chas, which he taught me how to do."[8] Lopez subsequently enrolled at FIT, where he learned technical drawing skills and became an art editor of the college yearbook in 1962.

Through a placement program tied to his studies, Lopez gained experience at Fairchild Publications, which ran the trade journal for the American fashion industry, *Women's Wear Daily*. Staff in the millinery department of WWD liked his drawings of hats; publisher John Fairchild, in turn, offered him a job, prompting Lopez to drop out of FIT. Lopez recalled in a 1986 interview, "I was very lucky because right after FIT, John Fairchild hired me for womenswear, and at the age of seventeen, I was, you know, working with all the top people, so it was a break. It was those years—the 1960s—when anything was possible."[9] Within four months of his first credited drawing on May 1, 1962, Lopez had produced nineteen editorials with his name attached; as Alistair O'Neill has noted, this feat was "considerable for a starting junior position."[10] After six months, Lopez was offered a freelance position at the *New York Times*. After accepting the job and publishing his first piece, he was fired from WWD.

At FIT, Lopez met Juan Ramos, a fellow student in interior design; the chance encounter would have lasting ramifications. Ramos, like Lopez, was born in Puerto Rico and grew up in Spanish Harlem; he designed hats and freelanced as a window dresser. They had a brief fling (their romantic relationship ended in 1968) and started a lifelong collaboration across various artistic enterprises. Together, they rented two floors in a townhouse in the West Village on Thirteenth Street and, in 1967, moved to the Carnegie Hall Studios on Fifty-Seventh Street, renting one space to live and two to work. In those years, they established a lasting template for their working relationship: Lopez "drawing at his noisy studio amidst a crowd of friends or at the places he had helped to create or had discovered" (such as Studio 54 in New York City or Club 7 in Paris), while "Juan was creating the setting for his drawings."[11] Strikingly, I could not locate any direct quotations from Ramos or joint interviews with him and Lopez. Absent his photographic presence, Ramos is strangely muted in the archive—we can only speculate whether that omission was by his design and whether he ever tired of his background role. A mutual friend of Lopez and Ramos, fashion designer Charles James, further clarified. In his words, Ramos was the "invisible engineer, without whose knowledge of graphics, the perversities of editors and art directors, the miracle work of his partner in crime could never be processed…and, if desperately late, delivered in time for the presses to roll."[12]

If Lopez's early success seems too easy, attention to his physical labor—especially his breath—belies this interpretation; it suggests instead his effort to make it *appear* effortless. Model Pat Cleveland met Lopez at *Vogue* in 1970, and he sketched her at the Carnegie Hall studio on numerous occasions afterward. She describes Lopez's heavy breathing while he sketched, as though he were trying to extract something from deep within himself and transfer it onto the page. In her words, "he would suck in air, as though taking energy from the entire universe" when he drew. Once finished, Lopez appeared physically drained, "as if he had been riding a wild horse and had just let go of the reins. It seemed to take him a minute to come out of his trance."[13] While Cleveland perceived this intensity as evidence of spiritually ordained artistry, Lopez jokingly dismissed the notion.

Lopez's characteristic playfulness was camouflage for the undeniable work ethic he must have had to survive and flourish in the fashion industry, especially as a young queer Puerto Rican illustrator. This labor is symbolized by his search for more and more air. His gulps of oxygen suggest endurance.

Juan Ramos (*left*) and Antonio Lopez at their studio, 31 Union Square West, 1978 (1 and 2 of 3). Courtesy of the Estate of Antonio Lopez and Juan Ramos.

Juan Ramos (*left*) and Antonio Lopez at their studio, 31 Union Square West, 1978 (3 of 3). Courtesy of the Estate of Antonio Lopez and Juan Ramos.

Sandra Ruiz argues that endurance is intrinsic to Puerto Rican subjectivity, or *Ricanness*, which she identifies as a collective attempt to breathe.[14] Breath sustains a Puerto Rican body made to bridge the gap between the island and the mainland, between American citizenship and being "foreign in a domestic sense," as the US Supreme Court termed Puerto Rico's ambiguous status in 1900. Lopez's heavy breathing, I suggest, also indexed his continual navigation between whiteness as a norm and the cultural vitality of Brownness.[15] This straddling, while seemingly a fait accompli, was sweaty work. Hence, while hidden, Lopez's durational labor—his breath—haunts his extant corpus.

By the late 1960s, he was a successful fashion illustrator, working both in New York and Paris, with a palpable aesthetic vision; he treated the body as sculpture and fashion as art—all the while effortlessly straddling downtown and uptown, the popular and the avant-garde. He became well-known for resuscitating a staid Eurocentric artistic form and transforming it into one brimming with Pop Art sensibilities. At the time of Lopez's professional ascent, fashion illustration rapidly declined. The practice was swiftly being supplemented by photography, in part because such renderings were typically "stiff" and "Waspy," to use Lopez's adjectives—"very Lord and Taylor." Lopez modernized the form, injecting these drawings with (as he would describe his work years later) a "feeling of sensuality, feeling of movement, feeling of sex, being outward."[16] Moreover, he centered women of color and gay men in his work, producing what two scholars called "minoritarian affirmations that are proud and unapologetic," a recurring theme in what follows.[17] Eventually, for all these reasons, Lopez was later referred to colloquially as the "Picasso of fashion illustration."[18]

Across three decades, Lopez's confident and breezy drawings repeatedly showcased a facility with the human anatomy's intricacies, how bodies moved in space, and how fashion acted as a visual signifier of one's personality—undoubtedly a lingering trace of his parents' professions. Lopez's colorful and spirited drawings drew on visual cues from psychedelic art and youth cultures in the 1960s and later (alongside his photography) disco, s-m subcultures, and queer sensibilities in the 1970s and early 1980s, while reflecting Pop Art's affection for the quotidian and commercial. His artistic subjects—celebrated portrayals of women and lesser-known representations of men—radiated a magnetic self-possession that infused these drawings with undeniable sex appeal. He wryly referred to himself as the "Puerto Rican Henry Higgins" (referencing the fictional professor character in the 1964 film *My Fair Lady*) for his similar skill in molding models, particularly women, into icons.[19] But Lopez's favorite artistic stimulus was the streets, whether it was the majestic boulevards of Paris or the noisy sidewalks of New York City, where a momentary glance at a well-defined physique or an exceptional mix of accessories could serve as fresh sources of inspiration.

Lopez was a central player in, and documentarian of, New York's downtown scene of the 1970s and 1980s; simultaneously, he flitted in and out of the orbit of an eclectic artistic network with an outsize influence. Lopez and Ramos lived, collaborated, and socialized alongside an amoeba-like web of artists, models, fashion editors, photographers, and performers, like the extensive networks Grace Jones and Stephen Burrows circulated in, as we will see in chapters 2 and 3. They worked in proximity to or alongside photographer Bill Cunningham; graphic artist (and Union Square neighbor) Jean-Paul Goude; fashion designers Charles James and Issey Miyake; Club 57 stalwarts and performance artists Joey Arias and Klaus Nomi; and a glamorous and ever-evolving circuit of models, including Donna Jordan, Tina Chow,

Jerry Hall, Pat Cleveland, and Grace Jones. Lopez shared models with photographer Robert Mapplethorpe and traveled to Jamaica in May 1975 with fashion editor Grace Coddington for a British *Vogue* shoot focused on Lopez and the leggy Hall. And he partied with Jones, Cleveland, and the statuesque Potassa de la Fayette—a glamorous Dominican trans woman and Warhol model Lopez also photographed—at the Queens disco Enchanted Gardens;[20] he once arrived there in a rented bus from his studio with fifty guests in tow. The product of these extensive artistic collaborations is what we will explore here: seemingly haphazard in their organization yet formal in their aesthetic principles; art-making that was fun and improvisational while also elegant and cosmopolitan; works that merged art-historical references, commercial design, and Nuyorican street sensibilities.

Lopez is primarily thought of as a fashion illustrator. Still, he was also a pioneer in the realm of photography and a blend of art direction and fashion design. Reconceiving Lopez as all three necessitates a shift in our typical perspectives on his work. It requires us to realign all his work along a horizontal axis rather than a vertical hierarchy. Lopez's fashion illustrations are part of a broader continuum of artwork spread across mediums and disciplines, which share equal billing and build off one another. Lopez surfaces as an inherently restless artist, constantly searching for newfangled and elastic forms that could satiate his voracious creative appetite. Consequently, as we will see, Lopez unapologetically pivoted to whatever medium was best suited for expressing his ideas, whether hip-hop-inflected sportswear or lush photography.

However, this merger also prompts a consideration of work that still needs to be explored in scholarship about post-1960s American art. This neglect is startling and not entirely surprising, given that the contributions of artists of color in the United States remain minimized in our mainstream narratives. Still, Lopez's complete absence from historiographies of Pop Art, for example, is deeply troubling. And it speaks to a broader occlusion, or minimization, of the historical exchange between American and Puerto Rican aesthetic cultures.[21] Despite his immense influence, Lopez stubbornly remains a footnote in the stories of Andy Warhol, Fiorucci, or Studio 54. This glaring omission in the narratives we continue to tell about the confluence of race, visual art, and Pop sensibilities in the 1970s is heightened by the persistent erasure of Lopez's skills in multiple artistic arenas and his gleeful disregard for the putative boundaries between them.[22]

Potassa de la Fayette, Sterling St. Jacques, and anonymous models, New York City, November 1974. Kodak Instamatics. Courtesy of the Estate of Antonio Lopez and Juan Ramos.

Here, we will dive deep into a brief period of rapid innovation, from 1975 to 1978, when Lopez's acumen in photography, window displays, and fashion design were seemingly in full bloom. The story I tell unfurls in three parts. First, I discuss Lopez's transition to the Kodak Instamatic camera and the photo series he began staging with friends-turned-models in showers, broom closets, and other locales—both while living in Paris and then upon his return to New York City. Focusing on *The Ribbon Series* and its relatively unknown male models, I aim to contextualize Lopez's work alongside other gay male photographers exploring erotic desire and the themes of representation and censorship that attend to such images. Second, I examine the *Candy Bar Wrapper Series*, a riff on Pop Art and advertising campaigns featuring voluptuous women seemingly exploding from life-size candy bars. I distill the *Candy Bar Wrapper Series*—an exploratory series that prominently featured Grace Jones—as a mash-up of performance art, Pop Art, and photography. Finally, in the last section, I examine the hip Manhattan department store Fiorucci, where Lopez and Ramos acted as in-house consultants. I reveal Lopez's multiple roles—commercial photography, clothing design, and curation of the store windows—while highlighting his influence in merging uptown commerce and looser downtown sensibilities. In doing so, I underline the various artistic communities that Fiorucci connected, while framing Lopez's artistic endeavors as also symptomatic of this collective ethos. I hope to cast a magnifying lens on a significant and overlooked body of work and its conditions of possibility—immense friendship, limited resources, and boundless creativity.

INSTAMATIC PHOTOGRAPHY, DESIRE, AND THE MALE MODEL

Antonio Lopez likely didn't know it then, but when he first picked up a new toy—the Kodak Instamatic—in a Parisian storefront in 1973, he was ushering in a decisive shift to his work. Inexpensive (his first one cost less than twenty dollars), easy to load, and highly portable (later versions were even pocket-size), the Kodak Instamatic was a mass-produced camera that was wildly popular in its heyday; more than fifty million were sold in its first nine years on the market.[23] This ease of access also appealed to Lopez. In a 1976 interview, he was asked why he preferred the Kodak Instamatic over pricier brands like Nikon. After all, the interviewer implied, wouldn't more expensive equipment produce higher-quality, professional-looking photographs?

"I hate gadgets and mathematical things. I like to press a button and have things happen," he remarked, adding that the aptly named Instamatic was "the perfect camera for the simple person like me."[24] As friend Paul Caranicas recalled, "Determinedly low-tech, Antonio preferred the Kodak Instamatic (one step up from the Kodak Brownie camera of the 1940s and 1950s). Natural light and the flash attachment were all he needed or wanted—no backdrop, no special outfit, unless that was part of the concept."[25] Lopez began referring to the numerous photographs he shot with the camera not simply as snapshots or pictures but as "Instamatics," a capitalized title that implied he was developing a new artistic form.

But perhaps just as important, the camera's technical simplicity and instantaneous images belied the rich, bold color it could produce. The Instamatic, while cheap, summoned vivid hues that were, in Lopez's words, "Perfect! Beautiful, beautiful color. Instamatic color."[26]

This chromatic saturation is evident in Lopez's early use of the camera. Lopez lived with Juan Ramos in Paris, where they had moved in 1969 (and were soon joined by aspiring models Grace Jones and Pat Cleveland); he began staging photo shoots with friends soon after buying his first Instamatic. He organized these shoots around a particular theme, collating the specific photographs under a named series. One of the first was called the *Red Coat Series* (1974), in which seminude Tina Chow, Jones, and Jessica Lange coyly posed in a black-and-white-tiled shower wearing a puffy, bright red "coat"— which, in reality, was a sleeping bag. Another was known as the *Blue Water Series* (1974–75), in which Cleveland and Jones preened for the camera while nude in a pool of sudsy, electric-blue water. He called these photographic series "conceptual," implying they were each intentional and exploratory experiments—an idea expressed through poses and props. Models, in particular, were seen as the artistic embodiment of a concept. Indeed, the lush liquidity of the *Blue Water Series*, for instance, suggests Lopez's world-making power and his astute ability to coax and transform his models—many of them virtually unknown at the time—into striking aesthetic subjects.

During his time in Paris, other themed series would quickly follow; they were eye-catching for their sophisticated, studio-like quality—created in his apartment with minimal funds—but more so for the sultry sex appeal of his models. The faint eroticism of the *Plastic Series*, in which seemingly incandescent models posed inside and alongside the unlikely prop of a large plastic bag, contrasted the synthetic and the organic. Meanwhile, the often-homoerotic

Café Society Series included Jean Eudes Canival, a reportage photographer Lopez met in Paris in 1973 (and briefly dated), dressed like a real-life Tom of Finland character in head-to-toe black leather. The sensuality of Lopez's subjects, overt in some photographs and more subtle in others, is a prominent theme that would continue to imbue the multiple Instamatics he later created once he returned to New York City.

Contrary to expectation, Lopez was a bit shy about discussing the process of eliciting this eroticism in his models; in a 1976 interview, when asked what kind of situation he tried to get people into when photographing them, Lopez merely replied, "Sexy," and then laughed.[27] Paul Caranicas, luckily, offers a bit more insight into Lopez's technique. "Often," he remarked, "the person being photographed took off clothing as the session progressed because Antonio liked to close in on his subject, literally and psychologically."[28] Lopez's Instamatics, Caranicas suggests, are not just closely cropped photographic stills but also psychic portraits. They underline Lopez's careful establishment of trust, friendship, and even romantic relationships with his models (most notably, Jerry Hall) that resulted in the shedding of not just clothes but also layers of psychological armor. Unsurprisingly, given that music was always playing in Lopez's studios (Sly and the Family Stone was a favorite), this mutual understanding frequently came via dancing.[29] Lopez noted as much, likening the act of eliciting vulnerability in his female models to a process of following and leading.[30] This linkage between dancing and creating resurfaces throughout *Mavericks of Style*, exemplified by the disco-ready fashions Stephen Burrows concocted in this milieu. Lopez's skill in obtaining his subjects' surface energy and subterranean emotionality echoes Andy Warhol's astute observation of Lopez: "Above all, he has a journalist's eye. He sees more than others."[31]

In 1975, Lopez, Ramos, and Caranicas—an art student by day and DJ by night who met the duo in Paris in 1971 and began dating Ramos in 1972—moved back to New York City together. They settled into a vast loft at 876 Broadway on the northwest corner of Union Square, near Warhol's Factory.[32] By this time, Lopez noted in a 1976 interview, "I've even been able to use the Instamatics in my work. Last year, I had ten pages of Instamatics mixed with drawings in Italian *Vogue*. I also had ten pages in *L'Uomo* and another eight pages in *Gentlemen's Quarterly*. I've also done a lot of editorial work in Japan with Instamatics."[33] Meanwhile, Lopez's Instamatics continued to proliferate and expand in scope. The most notable shift was that he began to arrange them in action-oriented grids. Lopez placed nine images in a three-by-three grid, encouraging the viewer to read them together as a cohesive narrative and an art object. As Phillippe Garner notes, Lopez's "cinematic sequencing" of these photographs was crucial for their efficacy: "The flow of pictures recreated a real-time sense of the session, an evidently compressed burst of activity, a high adrenaline moment of image making, seemingly lasting no longer than a disco single and just as packed with energy and excitement."[34]

Lopez carried his Instamatic everywhere, and the nine-image series became his default way of arranging the results. Viewing them now, we can see the more casual photographs he took, documenting the antics of his inner circle—Jones, Cleveland, Ramos, Coddington, and Cunningham, for example—as well as his interactions with the diffuse networks of fashion, music, and art-world luminaries he ran with. These included supermodel Beverly Johnson (and a bevy of other lesser-known Black American woman models); Chloé head designer Karl Lagerfeld conversing with *Vogue* editor in chief Diana Vreeland; actress Liza Minnelli and fashion designer Halston posing together at a party attended by Andy Warhol; and funk siren Betty Davis (Miles Davis's wife at the time), whom he worked with repeatedly. The nine-image sequence also became the preferred format for the experimental and often humorously named series he seemed to rapidly generate, including the *Men in Showers Series*, the *Broom Closet Series*, the *s-m Series*, and the *Shoe Series*, in which Lopez zeroed in on the feet of women (and occasionally men) in high heels.[35]

Lopez also used the grid format for the Instamatics that appeared in an August 1975 special issue of Andy Warhol's *Interview* on Puerto Rico that he and Ramos guest-edited, yoking them to a critical celebration of their shared ethnic heritage. Lopez designed the color cover image, featuring *West Side Story* actress Rita Moreno in a drawn dress of hot pink–edged frills that segue into the Puerto Rican flag. The reverse page was a black-and-white photograph of palm trees by Robert Mapplethorpe titled "Puerto Rican Palms." Similarly tropical, Lopez's nine-image grid comprised portraits of individuals framed by the beach and palm fronds, their first names written in script across the bottom edges. A muscular man in a swimsuit, identified as "Tino," occupies the top row by himself. Lopez referred to the photographs as "Los Instamaticos" in the Spanglish table of contents. His imagery added to the savory, curated mix of commissioned interviews, illustrations (of course, done by Lopez), photographs by fellow Nuyorican Charles Tracy (whom we meet again in chapter 3), and even traditional recipes. The issue, Alistair O'Neill emphasizes, acted as a "detailed mapping of a country's contribution to the broader Latin American influence at play in the mid-seventies, impacting music, fashion, art, food and sport."[36]

Given their prominence in many of Lopez's Instamatics, especially the nine-image grids, it is remarkable how little attention has been given to the carnal and often risqué imagery of Lopez's male models. This is perhaps because Lopez was (and is) more regarded as an illustrator than a photographer. Moreover, many women he worked with became household names, whereas his male models did not achieve that same level of notoriety. For instance, model and friend Victor Fernandez, who later worked for Stephen Burrows (himself featured in a nine-image grid from 1975, coincidentally), appeared in several of Lopez's named series of photographs. Described in the Puerto Rico issue as "smooth, shy, svelte Victor Fernandez, stalking the city in basketball sneakers, painter's pants, and a sweatshirt," the athletic Fernandez was a frequent muse; he posed for the *Broom Closet Series* in 1976, partially exposing his buttocks, and the *Shoe Series* in 1979. In the latter, staged at Fire Island (the Long Island, New York, queer haven), he jumped into a pool fully nude except for a pair of cherry red women's high heels. And, as I momentarily discuss, he was a prominent model for the *Ribbon Series*. And yet, he remains a minor figure. Similarly, a nude John Stavros appears in the *Blue Water Series*, taken in New York City in 1975, and two years later in a sexy boudoir-themed shoot with Betty Davis, where he lays naked, face down, on a red satin sheet. A mutual friend of Warhol and Charles James, Stavros remains marginal and unremarked on.

This erasure also stems from the fact that these images are not well-known: Magazines and newspapers often censored Lopez's photographs and illustrations, either due to explicit nudity or because they were deemed too homoerotic. (The irony, of course, is that censorship heightens and reproduces the very fantasies it attempts to suppress, as would soon be the case with the controversy surrounding Lopez's peer Mapplethorpe.)[37] Nude portraiture of men was especially ripe for scandal. Full-frontal male nudes, after all, were illegal until 1962, when a Supreme Court decision declared that magazines consisting primarily of nude, or nearly nude, male models were not obscene. As art historian Phillip Gester explains, "The male nude was, in the 1970s, still a relatively scandalous subject, particularly in photography," since any such depiction was "in itself tantamount to homosexual longing."[38]

Pat Cleveland and Victor Fernandez, New York City, November 1974. Kodak Instamatics. Courtesy of the Estate of Antonio Lopez and Juan Ramos.

Moreover, while there were undoubtedly plenty of gay and lesbian artists in the 1970s New York art world, art historian David Getsy argues, "few made work overtly *about* their queer experience, and even fewer were allowed to exhibit it in the late 1960s and early 1970s."[39]

As a result, much of Lopez's editorial work luxuriating in male physicality—most of it photographic, some of it illustration, and nearly all of it emphatically erotic—was never published. This was true even when male and female models were featured together. For instance, *Gentleman's Quarterly* censored an eight-page spread of sketches featuring Ramos and Jerry Hall in a motorcycle fashion layout in 1973.[40] According to fashion historian Michael Langkjaer, the editors thought they were "too hot."[41] They eventually ran in the S-M issue of *Blueboy* magazine in 1976, while sketches from the same motorcycle series (but ones that only featured men) were published in the April 1976 issue of gay magazine *Mandate*.[42] For this reason, Lopez accepted commissions from adult magazines—including *Playboy*, *Oui*, and *Viva*—as well as gay publications like *Blueboy* and *In Touch*, which agreed to publish his work uncensored.[43] He also was able to get his work published in artists' magazines that welcomed overtly sexual imagery, including cheeky male nudes. For example, several of Lopez's Instamatics and illustrations (credited to "Antonio") were reproduced in Steve Lawrence's *Newspaper*, an underground periodical featuring drawings, photographs, and found images contributed by artists, all published without the threat of censorship.[44] (Circulating by mail, in spaces like Max's Kansas City, or hand-delivered by Lawrence, it was not sold on newsstands.) Lopez's Instamatic grid of model Jerry Hall, posing suggestively next to an unidentified male model with his ass out, was printed in color for the cover of the July 1975 issue. A racially diverse cast of male models, in various stages of undress and arousal, posed for Lopez's camera, wearing an assortment of plastic masks, black leather accoutrements, and miscellaneous sports memorabilia (jockstraps, helmets, football gear, and boxing gloves)—the latter evincing a "sort of sports fetishism beyond the purely commercial."[45] Shot in arid broom closets and damp showers, the male models in Lopez's often-steamy nine-image grids enacted a dual function: They knowingly mock heteronormative notions of machismo while performing them in an eroticized manner.

Lopez's editorial work in the 1970s, Mauricio and Roger Padilha emphasize, "took on a more blatant sexuality that put him in the forefront of a new movement in fashion photography that included Chris von Wangenheim,

Guy Bourdin, and Helmut Newton, one that placed fashion in a S&M context."[46] (Unsurprisingly, these same peers shared the fearless Grace Jones as an artistic subject.) Lopez's edgy, lo-fi Instamatics, however, pushed further than his peers, perhaps because they appeared much less glossy and manufactured, making them more dangerous in their "realness." (After all, in addition to using a modestly priced camera, Lopez never hired a hair and makeup person: "He did it himself or had Way Bandy, then the best, do it for fun.")[47] Indeed, several of Lopez's named series reference—sometimes implicitly, but often explicitly—sexual subcultures and taboo practices, such as erotic asphyxiation (the *Plastic Series*), sadomasochism (the S-M *Series*), and foot fetishism (the *Shoe Series*). They playfully toe the line between the pornographic and the artistic as his models drench themselves in water, grab their erect penises, or strike poses in slid-down sweatpants and open trench coats. These male models are framed by Lopez's photographic gaze as aestheticized objects of desire, while they are also subjects who actively perform for the camera.

Hence, viewed from our historical vantage point, these visual representations require an ambivalent interpretation. This ambiguity is not simply contained "inside" these often-titillating and playfully rendered pictures. Instead, as art historian Kobena Mercer insists, it is "something that is experienced across the relations between authors, texts and readers, relations that are always contingent, context-bound, and historically specific."[48] The electric circuit of queer desire that circulated between Lopez and the men who deliberately self-objectified themselves is one example. We can only speculate about whether their suggestive poses roused Lopez's (sexual) pleasure, their own, or both. Likewise, any tension that surfaced in their roles as muses, a theme explored below, is also unknown. The erotic charge between the image and the viewer also requires multivalent perspectives.

Moreover, this ambivalence was heightened by Lopez's deliberate embrace of color photography, a curious decision considering the debate and derision the form incited in the 1970s. In an essay on photography published in 1969, American photographer Walker Evans declared, "Color photography is vulgar."[49] While the advances of the 1960s—the era of Pop Art, color television, and standard color movies—began slowly changing the perception of color in commercial media and artistic representations, color photography was still viewed with acute suspicion.[50] Black-and-white photography, its proponents argued, "transformed the visible world into a monochromatic field of darks and lights, signaling an image of documentary and/or artistic intent," while the excesses inherent to color photography were more nefarious; color converted the world into "a 'colorized,' make-believe version of reality," one synonymous with Hollywood more than high art.[51] In short, it was "an undistinguished practice reserved for uninspired advertising campaigns and the increasing numbers of amateurs who took to the Kodak Instamatic."[52] Lopez knew of this distinction but preferred color: "I respect black and white, but for myself, I love color."[53] He purposely chose an instrument (the Kodak Instamatic) and a form (color photography) regarded as the provenance of the masses and their putatively low sensibilities. And he manipulated color photography's ambiguity—the inability to perceive the photographer or discern meaning, as its critics alleged—to his advantage, creating mundane yet dreamlike worlds in which color was gloriously abundant, threatening to spill past the edges of the image.

Lopez's sly and sensuous framing of male beauty also materializes in what is undoubtedly the most conceptual and infectious of his series, the *Ribbon Series*, which began around 1976. I have not been able to locate the exact number of pieces in the series, but to my knowledge, only two male models posed for it: John Stavros and Victor Fernandez. Nonetheless, all usually start from the same premise: a tightly composed shot of a model's upper body, centered on their face, while they sit or stand in front of a blank wall. Lopez's choice of camera format was flexible; he alternated between Instamatics and Polaroids. His experimentalism was perceived in the sheer number of images: most are a three-by-three grid, but some push past that limit and are over twice as big. In the first image of the grid, one (or sometimes a few) strips of what look like brightly colored ribbons were draped somewhere across the model's body. Additional strips of differing colors would slowly accumulate throughout the photographs. Eventually, the model's face or body would become completely obscured, engulfed underneath a Technicolor profusion of yellow, hot pink, bright green, and red tape approximating the decorative material.

The use of the three-by-three grid to imply a sequence of events was ideally suited to Lopez's aim here, as implied by the sharp visual contrast between the first photo of a bare, or barely decorated, body and the ninth photo, where the body's outline is sometimes not even perceptible underneath the abundance of ribbons. Occasionally, he deliberately produced even more photographs to lengthen the duration of the action. Model Jane Thorvaldson, a studio regular whose face (with its strong jawline) was used

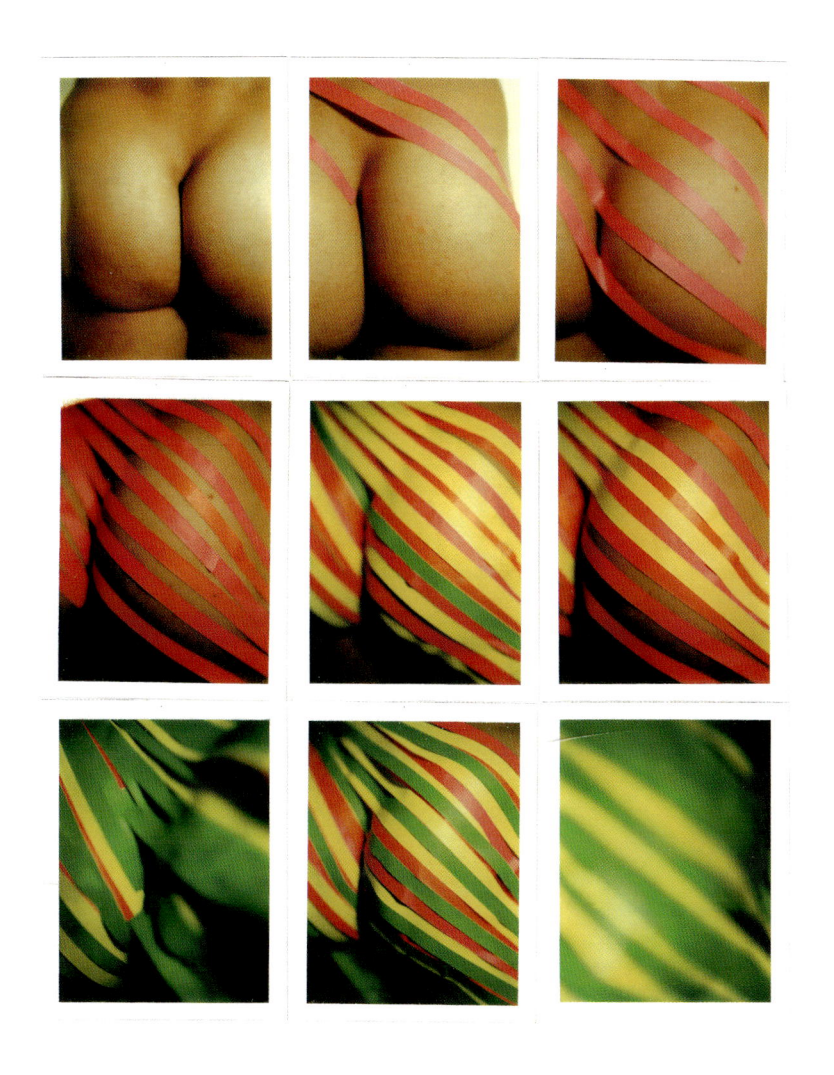

Ribbon Series, John Stavros, New York City, 1977. Kodak Instamatic. Courtesy of the Estate of Antonio Lopez and Juan Ramos.

Ribbon Series, Victor Fernandez. New York, December 1975. Kodak Instamatic. Courtesy of the Estate of Antonio Lopez and Juan Ramos.

frequently in Lopez's drawings for Bloomingdale's and Saks Fifth Avenue, is the subject of one of these series that has been elongated to a double grid of eighteen images.[54] The largest two I have seen, featuring Fernandez, have thirty-four images each; the sheer quantity of frames makes them almost akin to stop-action photography.[55]

Moreover, the *Ribbon Series* is rare because it is one of the few extant photography series not solely credited to Lopez but is a joint effort with Ramos. Specifically, Lopez took the photographs while Ramos, as art director, devised the visual concept of the ribbonlike material entering, covering, and retreating from the frame.[56] Ramos, who usually sourced art-historical references and thematic influences for Lopez's work, helped arrange the ribbons. A photograph from 1977 confirms this division of labor. In it, we see Ramos holding up the ends of a handful of ribbons, attached to a tall mount, which extend across model Nina Gaidarova's entire face and the upper half of her body in a diagonal pattern. (Gaidarova, a model in Paris when Lopez met her, moved to New York City in 1976; she posed for the *Plastic Series* and the *Broom Closet Series*.) The flouncy "ribbons," likely sourced by Ramos, have been meticulously applied to the body to give the sticky adhesive the appearance of weightlessness. Indeed, throughout the *Ribbon Series*, the tape-turned-ribbon floats effortlessly in space, even when its manipulation is visible. At the same time, it almost lovingly adorns the body with buoyant strips of delicious color.

And yet, in concert with Ramos and Lopez's deft touch, the *Ribbon Series* also exudes a dazzling play: The images abound with the sensory qualities of texture, shine, surface, and depth. These visual themes are particularly salient in the stretched-out versions with Victor Fernandez and John Stavros, which are even more remarkable given that these specific sessions occurred over just a few weeks. (In contrast, Lopez developed each series with several models over two or three years.) Lopez and Ramos seemed dedicated to quickly working out ideas in visual form. Without stated objectives from the artists, we must turn to the photographs for subterraneous clues about what the pair may have been trying to work out or explore.

For instance, these images diverge from others in the *Ribbon Series* in Lopez's technical use of close cropping, often zooming in on specific body parts amid a colorful transformation. We glimpse, for instance, the slope of Fernandez's shoulder or the curvature of Stavros's ass, embellished with the intensely hued "ribbons" that fill out the frame. Lopez's camera zooms in so closely at times that the tactile surface of the skin is rendered in almost forensic detail. Moreover, when isolated as individual images, the body seemingly disappears entirely from several photographs. Lopez centers a wavy mass of undulating color with palpable layers of shadow and depth in these renderings—suggesting that color itself, as a visceral phenomenon, is the focus. In others, we have what some viewers would call "bad" photography—hazy, blurry colors that make clear the camera lens is out of focus. In those cases, each photograph's inclusion in the more extensive series is the only indication of what you are perceiving, particularly when the body of the photographic subject is absent. When viewed sequentially, the resulting photographs sometimes exact a reverse anthropomorphism, transforming a human being into something that, despite having the outline of a body, is seemingly something else. While mysterious in their artistic intentions and indeterminate in their meanings, these more extended series present a fascinating set of aesthetic explorations—a palimpsest of "natural" and inorganic surfaces, an interplay of bright color and the more matte tones of the skin, off-center and tightly framed glimpses of the male body, portraits of fleeting ribbons that shift in and out of focus…all of which linger long after these photographs have been viewed.

This close cropping of aestheticized male body parts in the *Ribbon Series*, whatever its intents, indexes a nascent sensibility among gay male artists in the late 1970s, even as Lopez's photography eventually pushed toward divergent ends. Robert Mapplethorpe, who shared bodybuilder/model Lisa Lyons with Lopez and had his first major exhibition in 1977 in SoHo, noted the emergence of this art world phenomenon as it was happening. In a 1979 interview published in the magazine *Manhattan Gaze*, he underlined the emergence of a new "energy" around what he derisively termed "faggot art." Was Mapplethorpe alluding to the rise of gay-owned galleries in New York City, five of which operated in Manhattan alone by 1980?[57] Or was he perhaps thinking of the frank depiction of gay sex and male genitalia in Andy Warhol's *Sex Parts* (1977)? After all, Warhol used models recruited from clubs and gay bathhouses by his assistant Victor Hugo, a Venezuelan window dresser (who also served as an interviewer for the *Interview* Puerto Rico issue). Nonetheless, the artistic imperative of Lopez and Ramos in the *Ribbon Series* differs from the flashy sheen of Warhol's sexually explicit Polaroids or Mapplethorpe's more elegant bondage-based portraits, despite their shared lusty portrayal of male models.[58] Unlike their peers' work, the *Ribbon Series*

Ribbon Series, New York City, December 1977. Kodak Instamatic. Courtesy of the Estate of Antonio Lopez and Juan Ramos.

steers away from the strictly representational or overtly homoerotic, arriving at the abstract as the destination.

Lopez and Ramos foreground their artistic style in these photographs: a determined play with the aesthetic principles of light and shadow, texture and form, and color. Style, of course, is often seen as frivolous and inconsequential. Yet, as sociologist Dick Hebdige exhorts, it is of immense cultural import. Subcultural groups, he argues, repeatedly express themselves *obliquely* through style by engaging in a process of bricolage: utilizing readily accessible commodities to scramble and subvert meanings, ultimately creating something new.[59] We will see this practice throughout our immersion in the 1970s. Grace Jones, Stephen Burrows, and their cohorts repeatedly harness it for their respective ends. Likewise, Lopez and Ramos redeploy inexpensive, easily procured tape in the *Ribbon Series*, transforming it into an aesthetic prop far exceeding its use value. On a more macro level, we can also consider Lopez's manipulation of the modestly priced Kodak Instamatic itself—a determinedly lo-fi means of production—and the incredibly assured and formal photographs he could wrest from the apparatus. They easily rival the photographs of Warhol and Mapplethorpe from this period, now canonized and regarded as high art, while the *Ribbon Series* remains obscure.

Performance theorist José Esteban Muñoz has urged us to consider the quotidian and ornamental as aesthetic forms, particularly for glimpses of what he refers to as queer utopian aesthetics. Mass-produced items, he argues, can hold a surplus value beyond their practical function, "a kind of potentiality that is open, indeterminate, like the affective contours of hope itself."[60] Likewise, Lopez and Ramos tap into this forward-dawning energy by repurposing banal materials to probe aesthetic concepts and push them to their limits. And in these seductive journeys in form, where fidelity to bodily representation takes a back seat to abstracted physicality, Lopez and Ramos eschew what art historian Kobena Mercer denotes as the "burden of representation" often foisted on queer and artists of color.[61] Put differently, as Ann Cvetkovich suggests in a different context, they "use photography in ways that don't fall into conventional identitarian politics or positive images."[62] In this way, instead of seeking to locate glimmers of their queer Nuyorican sensibility in more typical and politicized representations of the self, we must enact a different viewing practice. In doing so, we come closer to perceiving how Lopez and Ramos refract their sexual and racial identities, like a prism, through the ornamental, in the dynamic interplay between luminescent color, cutaneous skin, and queer masculinity.

But I wish to briefly return to Lopez's insight about his preference for the Instamatic camera, especially its fertile color, as an entry point for a final rumination on these photographs. I first saw the lengthened-out *Ribbon Series* at Lopez's retrospective at El Museo del Barrio. Positioned inside a long rectangular white frame, thirty-four grainy, low-lit Instamatics of Victor Fernandez from 1977 formed a linear narrative arc, as one flirtatious ribbon gracefully falling over the left side of Fernandez's face slowly grew into a distended mass. Upon seeing these curated glances at Lopez's archive of illustrations and photographs, my curiosity was immediately piqued. Who was this person I had never heard of? And how had this ridiculously sublime body of work been ignored for so long?

Several years later, when I visited the extensive archives of Lopez and Ramos's artwork as a researcher, I came across photographs of Stavros from the *Ribbon Series* for the first time while listening to one of Lopez's beloved mixtapes. I was intrigued by the images' subtle sexiness and jolted by their swaths of high-intensity color. Perhaps because of the rhythms coming through the tape deck, it felt like an invisible switch was suddenly turned on; the images began reverberating and speaking. If listening to images involves hearing their subtle vibrations, as Tina Campt implies, I started to hear not a set of voices but rather a location: the electric atmosphere of Lopez's Union Square studio, where friendship and art-making coincided. In short, the chaotic vibrancy of 1970s New York City as a setting and inspiration for Lopez's photographic experiments came rushing into the present.

As Elspeth Brown and Thy Phu state, "That we feel photography can hardly be doubted. Photography excites a spectrum of feelings."[63] Roland Barthes famously describes the punctum, or "prick," in photographs as these first felt impressions, revealing the uncanny way photographs provoke affective responses.[64] He was especially attuned to the various affective reactions generated by our subjective experiences with them, including desire, suggesting a theory of photography predicated on *feeling* rather than thinking. In other words, long before my intellectual scrutiny of these photographs, I felt entangled by them; the magnetic affective pull I felt (and continue to feel) from them and their intoxicating, almost hypnotic color informed my need to understand them.[65]

If color is fundamental to how we see the world, the intricacies of how our eyes process and distinguish between colors remain primarily imperceptible. Our sensitivity to colors is complex and highly subjective; seeing color is a product of the dynamic interplay between material objects and the wavelengths of the visible color spectrum, all filtered through the elaborate apparatuses of our eyes.[66] Let us recall that Warhol mused that Lopez saw more than others. Perhaps, then, the luxuriant hot pink, tomato reds, sumptuous greens, and warm yellows we happen upon in these meticulously produced conceptual portraits serve an explicit purpose: They coat our retinas in an exuberant wash of color to retrain us how to see, to view the world that he saw in the way he perceived it. In this "wish-landscape," the tape-turned-ribbon is a line of thought and feeling, an energy-filled "act of transfer" across time and space, momentarily activated when we meet its beckoning glance.[67]

FRIENDSHIP, REHEARSAL, AND PERFORMING CONFECTION

In the late 1970s, while English punk band X-Ray Spex was brashly decrying the deadening effect of consumer culture in its 1978 song "Plastic Bag," Antonio Lopez and Juan Ramos embraced one of the most ubiquitous mass-produced items in American culture: the candy bar. The *Candy Bar Wrapper Series* (1976–78), also referred to as the *Candy Bar Series*, was made across the same two-year time span as the *Ribbon Series*. In it, their photographic props and deliberate staging became more developed and performative. Meanwhile, they continued a practice of bricolage. They gathered miscellaneous items from art supplies and sporting goods stores, converting them into fulcrums for their increasingly ambitious conceptual photography. And like the *Ribbon Series*, it is credited to both Lopez and Ramos, who once again worked together as art director and photographer to bring their collaborative vision to fruition: injecting a sugary confection with a dose of Pop Art flair, sprinkled with the signature eroticism of their models.

Luckily, a surviving set of preliminary sketches on vellum paper (four in total, dated 1976) serve as blueprints that, despite their hastily drawn lines, lay bare the design and modeling of Ramos and Lopez's bold concept. In each "fashion study," a series of topless women are situated inside what appear to be life-size cylindrical tubes with scribbled writing on the sides. Each model, captured in various poses, is fanned by a flame-like swirl of orange scribbles emanating from their body's upper half, suggesting a fiery visual eruption.

Despite their slapdash abstractness, the sketches convey a palpable kinetic vivacity. In each, with the individual model's name written in blue below the drawn figure, Lopez tinkered with how space, perspective, and proportion would work within the frame. For instance, he conveyed a salient degree of depth in two of the four drawings, with the respective models—"Jane" (Thorvaldson) and "Anita" (last name unknown)—appearing to lean against a wall inside a sizeable cube-like structure. They imply that the models are dynamically arranged inside a setting resembling a three-dimensional environment, instead of posing in front of a static two-dimensional background. These sketches indicate a more theatrical version of self-presentation that seems closer to performance art than fashion photography, with the body as art object exhibited in a space resembling the white cube of a gallery.

Ramos and Lopez's lengthy prep work for the *Candy Bar Wrapper Series* utilized professional and romantic relationships, as well as proximity to commercial arenas where source material could be quickly acquired. First, Ramos designed a "movable stage" for the models. In a pencil rendering by Paul Caranicas, we see the spatial particulars of Ramos's design; he stipulated an enormous box on wheels, ten feet in width, depth, and height. Open in the front, the box tapered down to eight feet in the back, as the sketch's side view makes evident. Carpenter and artist Michael Thiele, Lopez's boyfriend and the studio manager at the time, built the stage and the cylindrical tubes the models posed in, following Ramos's specifications. Lopez and Ramos then drafted the colorful candy logos—occasionally riffing on the model's name and using it as a starting point for the design—and meticulously hand-painted the tubes with acrylic. Meanwhile, at some point in 1978, Lopez and Ramos rented half the tenth floor at 31 Union Square West, where the upper floors had recently been converted into loft apartments, transforming half of it into a second place to work.[68] The new studio, an additional two thousand square feet of space that was a quick jaunt from 876 Broadway, was also near Paragon Sports, a huge sporting goods store. There, Ramos and Lopez purchased "space blankets," highly reflective insulated emergency blankets first developed by NASA in 1964, taking advantage of the shiny material's close resemblance to the layer of aluminum foil typically found underneath a candy bar wrapper. When seen in photographs, it becomes clear that the foil-like appearance of the space blankets achieves the intended visual effect of the orange swirls in the sketches, as if the voluptuous models had suddenly erupted from the ripped-open tops of the life-size candy bars. In Alexandra Vazquez's words, we again perceive "techniques of making-do with the at-hand and how this making do is aesthetically mobilized by the dispossessed."[69]

But this series was only possible because of the larger-than-life presence of the models themselves; like trained performers, they theatricalized the assorted candy bar fittings and staged themselves as seemingly edible objects of desire. We can glimpse this in the various photographs from the series, several of which have been reproduced in books dedicated to Lopez's oeuvre. These photographs also circulate on Pinterest boards created by fans, attesting to a fascination with the series despite its esoteric nature. Most of the models are unknown; a partial list I obtained of fifteen models includes a few names that have surfaced throughout this chapter, such as Jane Thorvaldson and Nina Gaidarova. (Both also posed for the *Ribbon Series*.) Despite their relative anonymity, the models' animated faces and bodily expressivity attest to Lopez and Ramos's artistic direction, namely their ability to spur displays of beatific seduction in these photographs.[70]

In short, these models are not avatars of icy glamour. Instead, the *Candy Bar Wrapper Series* models share an overt confidence in their fleshy physicality, which is remarkable given that most appear to be posing while fully nude. This is conveyed through their agile bodily poses and ecstatic, almost postcoital faces. The visual effect of the tapered ceiling at the back of the portable stage makes it seem like the models are larger-than-life, not only bursting out of the candy bar wrappers but also pushing against the walls that box them in. This photographic emphasis on the models themselves and ostensible encouragement to *reveal* rather than mask their personalities operated in tandem with a more significant paradigm shift in the modeling world that began in the 1960s. Due to the influence of youth culture, historian Elspeth Brown explains, modeling's previous focus on stiff couture was discarded in favor of looser, street-influenced clothes, fashion boutiques, and "the erotic circuit between the model and the photographer." As a result, fashion photographers began to deemphasize the clothes and instead "honed in on the women wearing the clothes—the models—as well as their movement and sexuality."[71] Alva Chinn, a Black American model who also became a favorite of Stephen Burrows, confirmed that Lopez was unusual in that he "was drawn to models with more character.... He liked that we were atypical, that we led interesting lives, and were interested in learning about different things in fashion. Because he loved teaching. He loved turning you onto things that you knew nothing about."[72]

The series' visual format and bright colors are greatly indebted to the realistic figure paintings of little-known 1960s Pop artist Mel Ramos (no relation to Juan Ramos). While studying in Sacramento in the early 1960s, Ramos was the pupil of painter and Pop artist Wayne Thiebaud. Known as a "cheerleader of the Bay Area Figurative School," Thiebaud created pastry-themed canvases that evinced Pop Art's obsession with low culture and were a big hit with the New York City art crowd in 1962.[73] Between 1962 and 1964, Ramos's first paintings of the decade centered on comic book superheroes, another source for Pop artists. However, his most notorious works were his paintings of nude white women posed suggestively alongside, astride, or emerging from life-size replicas of everyday commodities: Cuban cigars, Wrigley's gum, Coca-Cola bottles, Velveeta cheese, and candy bars. These works merged visual cues from pinup culture, epitomized by the painter and *Playboy* illustrator Alberto Vargas (whom Mel Ramos was likened to), and Pop Art's creative reuse of mass culture. Some critics interpreted these paintings as pointed critiques of the sexist underbelly inherent in commercial advertising, even if Ramos partly contradicted that view.[74] In 1975, Playboy Press published a book of his pinup drawings, titled *The Girls of Mel Ramos*; we have no direct evidence of this, but it wouldn't be surprising if Juan Ramos ran across this book while sourcing materials.

Two photographs from the *Candy Bar Wrapper Series* became magazine covers in France. Virginia Shaddick MacGregor, a *Cosmopolitan* cover girl whom Lopez met in New York City in 1977, was featured on the February 1978 cover of *Photo*, a monthly publication dedicated to photography, in a special issue titled (in translation) "New in New York."[75] The gold-colored cover complements the copper metallic-like interior of the candy bar wrapper, while the topless Shaddick MacGregor preens against a blue background. (Inside, the magazine published a spread of at least seven other models from the series, each identified by their first name.) By June 1979, Grace Jones had transitioned from model to recording artist and appeared on the cover of *Lui*, a monthly adult magazine oriented toward men. It anointed her as (in translation) the "new sex symbol of disco." A smiling and topless Jones, both arms full of stacked metal bracelets, tilts her head to the side, one hand tugging her earlobe. Her other hand rests on the bottom edge of the seemingly torn-open candy bar wrapper, its silver foil-like interior fanning out behind her.

The ambiguity of these images and the lack of written or oral testimony from the women who posed for them—or from Lopez and Ramos—makes

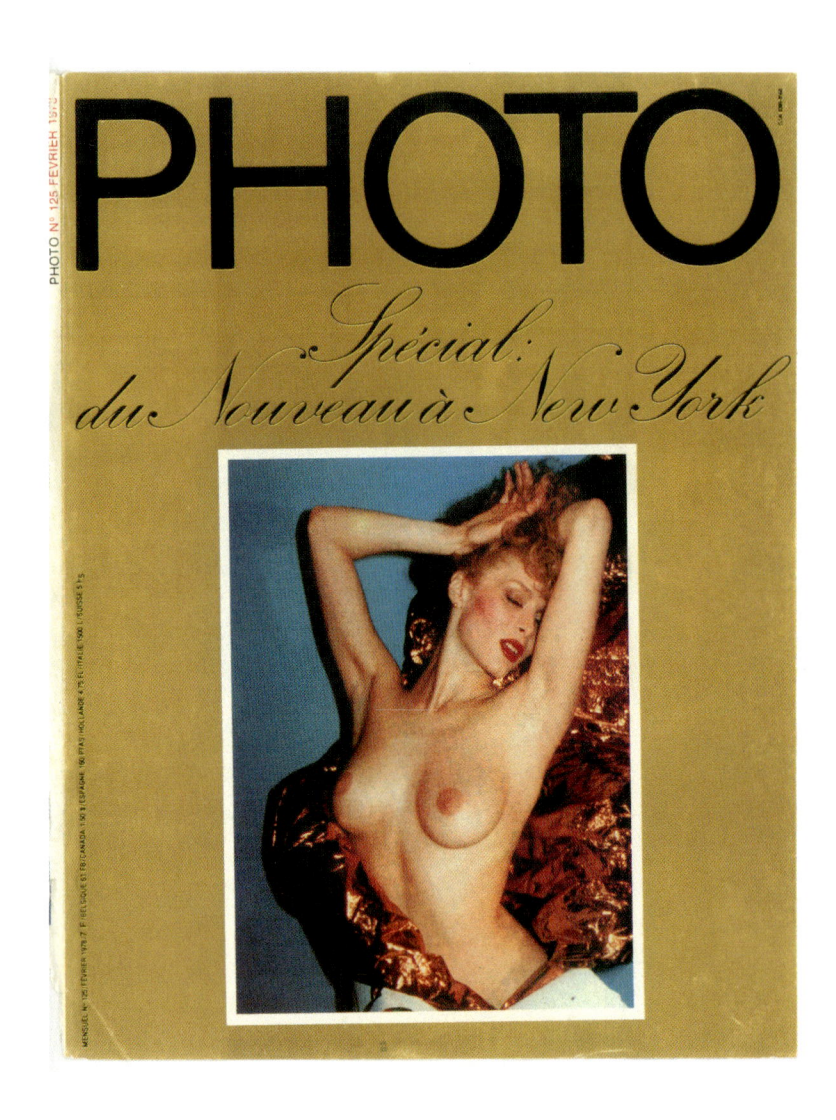

Photo magazine featuring Virginia Shaddick MacGregor, February 1978. Courtesy of the Estate of Antonio Lopez and Juan Ramos.

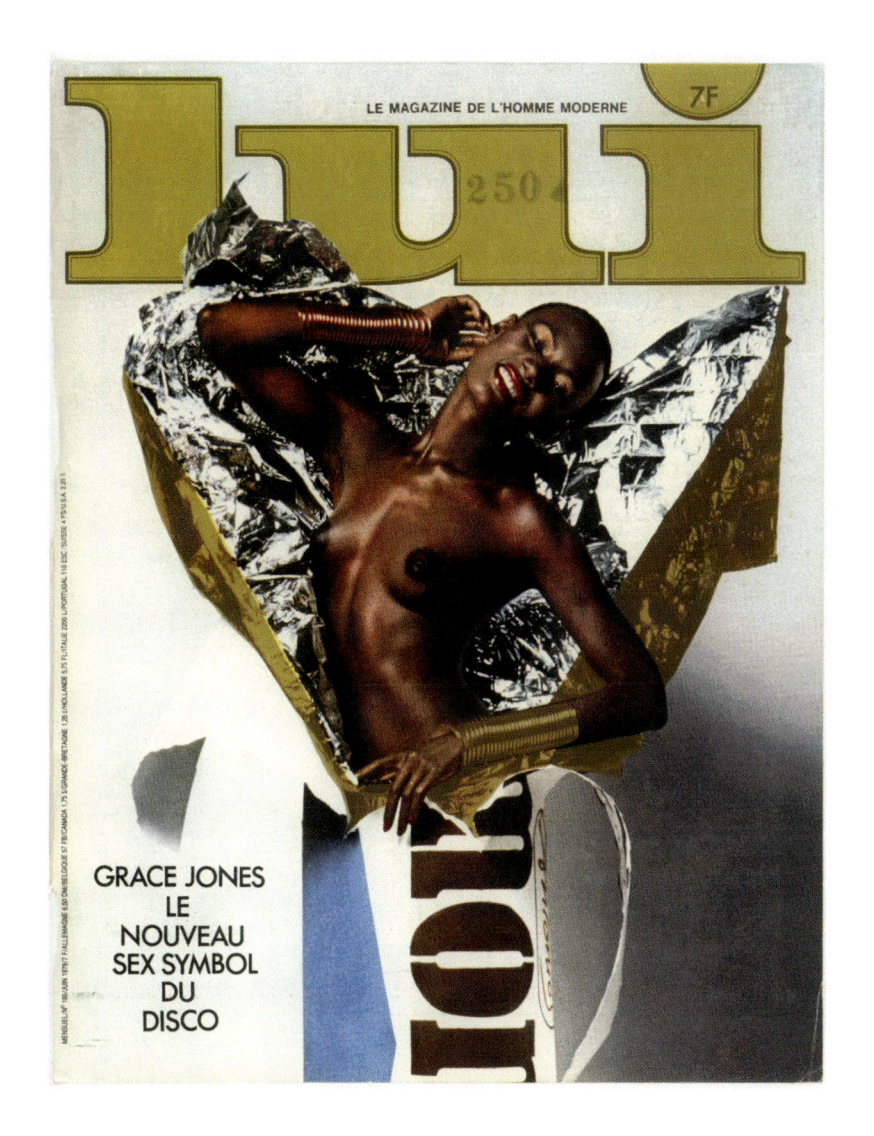

Lui magazine, Grace Jones, June 1979. Courtesy of the Estate of Antonio Lopez and Juan Ramos.

it challenging to decipher their meanings; some contemporary viewers may interpret these models as performing a playful and purposeful self-objectification, while others may see the opposite. The latter audience may conclude that Lopez deliberately sexually objectified these models, making them objects of consumption for the prurient appetites of men. That perspective, of course, has good company. The construction of beauty ideals in the late 1960s and 1970s—from advertising campaigns to beauty contests—became an increasing target for white second-wave feminists; these representations were seen as the instruments of a "male-dominated mass media" promulgating "an inauthentic representation of American womanhood."[76] These activists, therefore, advocated for a more "natural" and less overtly sexual depiction of women. In hindsight, the irony of this well-meaning critique was its narrow focus: shielding middle-class white women from a sexually predatory white male gaze. In contrast, Lopez and Ramos were *neither white nor heterosexual* (Ramos was gay, and Lopez was bisexual). Their models for the series (one of whom was male) were a multiracial cast who seemed to delight in their spectacularly unnatural eroticization of a candy bar–human assemblage. Thus, the multiple and even polarizing affective responses this series provokes may be part of its artistic aim.

In other words, what if we attempt to wrestle more fully with the complex and unanswered, rather than attempting to untangle its messy roots? We should aim not to resolve this difficulty but acknowledge that it is intrinsic to the work, as Jennifer Doyle reminds us.[77] Moreover, L. H. Stallings highlights ambivalence as a Black feminist strategy, urging us to consider "fresh contradictions and paradoxes," especially concerning sexuality. As they argue in a different context, "we might have to think of performances" such as the *Candy Bar Wrapper Series* "as something other than pornographic or exploitative."[78] Granted, there is a gendered and racialized dynamic implicit in the relationship between the typically male artist and the female muse, just as the performed objecthood of the model can cross over into overt objectification.[79] (I explore both themes in the next chapter.) However, we must be careful not to project unverifiable assumptions, such as coercion, onto the ultimately unknown when faced with sexualized imagery.

Moreover, we gain a more nuanced assessment by taking a panoramic view of the *Candy Bar Wrapper Series*. If we include an unpublished set of outtakes that I ran across in the archives—impromptu photographs from 1977 capturing Jones in costume and documenting the presence of others as they collectively prepare for the shoot—we might not assuage feminist concerns. But, in return, we gain a broader sense of the project's possibilities; we see both the inchoate process of "getting ready" and the "takes" that often end up on the cutting-room floor. In these numerous close-cropped photographs, Jones in costume strikes an array of poses. Sometimes, she acts mischievously, playfully sticking her tongue out at the photographer (Lopez, we can assume). In others, we see her acting more seriously, modeling for a different camera outside the photograph's frame. In several, Lopez's first name is written in red cursive on the outside of the wrapper (two fingers point at it in one of the photographs). Riffing on their names and Hershey's Almond Joy candy, the wrapper spells out "Antonio's Almond Jones." In another photograph, an unidentified Asian American man in a white shirt is seen in the background, standing behind Jones. Juan Ramos is prominent in the foreground, glancing at the camera while holding onto the top of her candy bar costume with both hands. Jones, meanwhile, looks coyly at the camera, only the top half of her face visible above the wrapping, while her arms are arched above her head. In contrast to the abundant color and formal composition of the *Ribbon Series*, these photographs are decidedly unvarnished. Some are lit by natural light, while others suggest the additional glow of an unseen spotlight. What appears to be plywood is visible in a few of the photographs, possibly part of one of the unfinished walls of the stage. In another photograph, we can see a tall metal ladder propped next to a long pipe, most likely used by Lopez to stand on while he photographed. Jones poses seductively in front of the ladder, holding an empty wine glass.

When put together and set against the more polished photographs from the *Candy Bar Series*, these little-seen, more candid shots illuminate the collaborative labor that transforms the sourced items and fabricated setting into a coherent, sophisticated *look*. The work required in this type of shoot— from the model to the set assistants to the art director to the photographer—is rarely revealed. Indeed, even if such labor is understood within the industry, a vital part of fashion's appeal to the public is its seemingly flawless, prepackaged feel. Ladders and props along the edges puncture that carefully wrought image. Yet Lopez seems to insist on doing just that: to show the work, to reveal the process. These behind-the-scenes moments of Jones thus provide a different perspective on the photographs from the series published in *Photo* and *Lui*. Such "B-sides" show us that each model's individualized expressions and choreography are not simply the product of Ramos and Lopez's coaxing

Candy Bar Series, Grace Jones, New York City, August 1977. Kodak Instamatic. Courtesy of the Estate of Antonio Lopez and Juan Ramos.

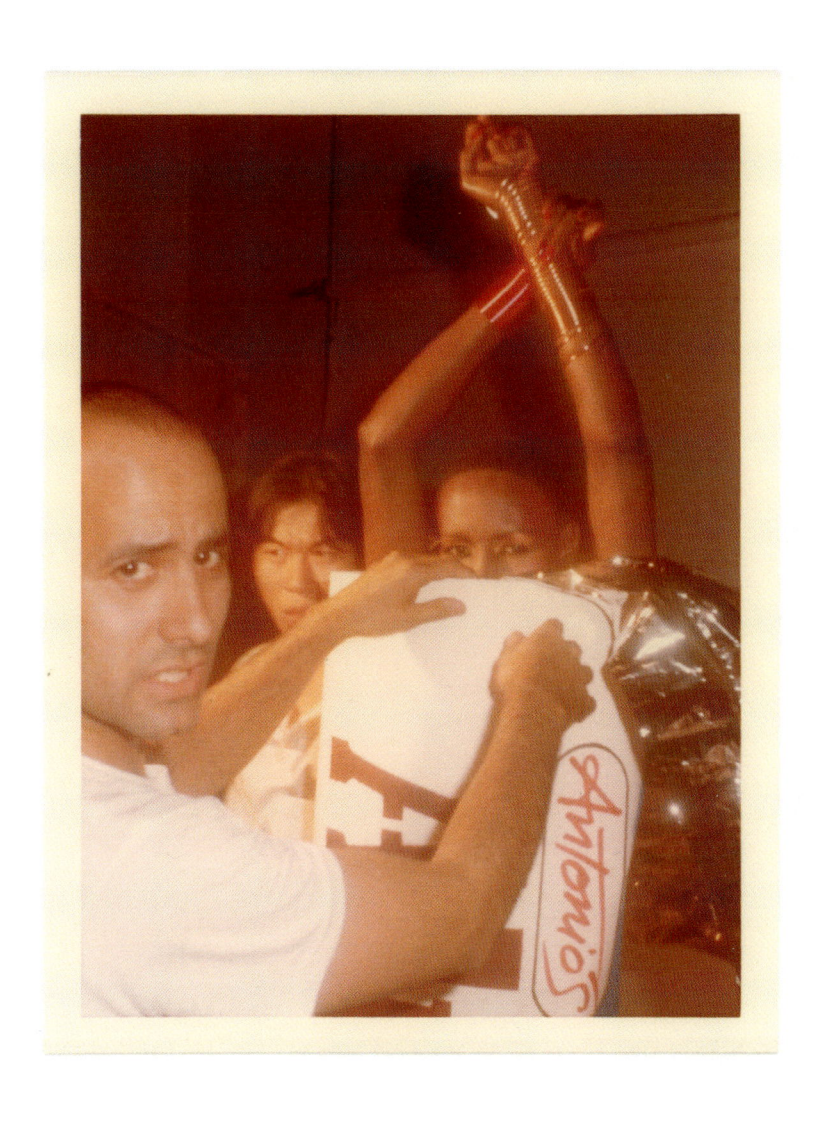

Candy Bar Series, Grace Jones and Juan Ramos, New York City, August 1977. Kodak Instamatic. Courtesy of the Estate of Antonio Lopez and Juan Ramos.

Candy Bar Series, Grace Jones, New York City, August 1977. Kodak Instamatic. Courtesy of the Estate of Antonio Lopez and Juan Ramos.

behind the camera. Instead, we see that the final product is indebted to the deliberate efforts of many. It includes the models themselves, who seem to relentlessly experiment with what their bodies can do and how to properly calibrate themselves for the camera lens. It also includes these unknown aides, who are adjusting the light, repositioning the models' costumes on the stage, or perhaps turning the volume up on the stereo. While the formal series implies that these models are seemingly ready-made, these obscure photographs pull back the proverbial curtain to unveil a "fashion becoming"—the process of embodying an artistic ideal.[80] And in this manner, what we sense here is a type of freedom, one that functions less like a right that one possesses or a definitive point of arrival and more like an intangible *"something* to be collectively improvised, produced, and made" among this motley assembly of models, artists, and friends.[81]

    I highlight these behind-the-scenes images to point us toward more significant interconnected themes in the *Candy Bar Wrapper Series*—specifically, friendship, rehearsal, and a more expansive vision of the artistic act. These photographs allude to the multiple hands at play in creating these images and the scripting of these models as creative subjects. In her memoirs, Jones used the word *love* to describe the act of Lopez drawing her.[82] Love and friendship are typically not emphasized in art-historical scholarship. And yet many of these artists, living and working together in the 1970s, underline friendship as a bulwark that enabled their work to flourish. This is particularly true of women and artists of color, who frequently lacked the institutional recognition from museums that their whiter, more noteworthy peers enjoyed.[83] As a result, many of these artists formed and worked within collectives. Coalescing around "asymmetrical lines of association," these loosely organized groups resisted the narrative of single authorship fetishized by museums; instead, they fused their "shared anxieties about their social and political context into open-ended, often participatory artworks."[84] Again, there is much we do not, and cannot, know about the making and taking of these images, so much that remains ambivalent and even problematic. Still, what is undeniable as we gaze around the edges of these photographs is that a community of peers was essential in their construction.

    Moreover, the haphazard scenes in Ramos and Lopez's studio, captured in these on-the-fly images, illustrate rehearsal. Our scholarly discussions often minimize rehearsal as something typically seen as a mere prelude to the main event. Yet here it becomes the star attraction. A counterintuitive focus on rehearsal, rather than the formal product of that action, indexes what Michelle Stephens calls a "haptic notion of the artistic act." This enlarged idea of the artistic process highlights the various stages inherent to producing an image or performance, viewing the creation process as an ongoing "interaction-in-the-making" between the artist and subject. The energy flows between the camera lens and the corporeality of the model and back again, rather than merely constituting "an action with a terminated end."[85]

Such an interpretative move may also include what we *cannot* see, such as the various lubricating agents that helped these women become full-throttled versions of themselves. Perhaps red wine was poured into Jones's empty goblet, a joint was passed around, or someone played the just-released 12-inch remix of R & B singer Loleatta Holloway's "Hit and Run," gloriously lengthened to a then-unheard-of eleven minutes.[86] These visible and unseen elements ignite the electrifying visual frisson of the *Candy Bar Wrapper Series*. In these photographs, a group of bold models—several of them people of color, many known to us now only by their first names—pointedly refused the more "positive" images of women advocated by white second-wave feminists or the harmful effects of advertising that X-Ray Spex lamented in song. Instead, they irreverently oozed their nude bodies out of torn-asunder candy bar wrappers, boldly resignifying their fleshy physicality as a cloying confection gone awry. This hybrid of performance art, fashion photography, and Pop Art animates a more horizontal notion of art-making, a working together, where a tasty Technicolor iconicity is produced out of networks of reciprocity and imagination.

UPTOWN FASHION MEETS DOWNTOWN COOL AT FIORUCCI

If you were a savvy teenager or even a jaded New Yorker strolling by the window of the curiously named Fiorucci on Fifty-Ninth Street in 1978, surely you would have done a double take. Because there, inside the trendy fashion retailer's large window, a leggy Black model was dancing. Hard. Instead of continuing onto the N/R/W subway stop down the block or entering the natural tranquility of Central Park, perhaps you temporarily stopped to take in this enthralling theatrical display. Indeed, you were not alone; a group of passersby were gathering, delighted and confused. *Who* was this woman, and *what* exactly were we witnessing?

That wacky model was Pat Cleveland. And for a onetime solo event in 1978, Antonio Lopez invited her to perform in the store's windows—to be a thrilling avatar of the typical store mannequin. Cleveland "disco-danced in the windows, attached to a chain that was suspended from the ceiling" while using it as a dramatic prop, writes performance anthropologist Sara K. Schneider. She "transformed the chain into first a belt, then a sash, then a tie, then a tube top, as she danced."[87] Cleveland's amusing antics indicated a new commercial phenomenon in which the borders between the stage and the street—as well as fashion, music, and art—seemingly evaporated overnight.

In what follows, I build on the momentum of Lopez's chromatically lush Instamatic photography and his work with performer-model Grace Jones in the *Candy Bar Wrapper Series* to consider his collaboration with the fashion emporium Fiorucci. This now-defunct department store left an indelible impression on New York City. As we will see, Fiorucci shared Lopez's disciplinary porousness, and both actively assembled an aesthetic vocabulary using fashion as an energizing property. Though Fiorucci's heyday was brief (the Manhattan branch closed in 1984), Lopez found a way to flex his artistic skills in a creative and immersive retail environment where breaking the rules and privileging fun was the modus operandi.

Fiorucci opened in April 1976 at 125 East Fifty-Ninth Street, between Park and Lexington Avenue, the first US-based outpost of Elio Fiorucci's eponymous Italian fashion brand. The nine-thousand-square-foot Upper East Side department store was a mere stroll from Bloomingdale's. (Lopez, coincidentally, also had a professional relationship with that upscale department store.)[88] Yet its "neon, plasticized, Italian, hyper-graphic studio" sensibility couldn't have been more different.[89] Italian architect (and Memphis Group founder) Ettore Sottsass designed the New York store; he aimed to recreate a simulacrum of the distinct decor and festive spirit of the Milan flagship, where Italian consumers encountered "unique interior concepts and creative windows" in a youthful space decorated with "bold-colored prints, stickers, posters, and flashy lights."[90]

The two-story Fifty-Ninth Street shop differed from most retailers in the uptown fashion area primarily due to its smooth design and funky ethos. For the former, Fiorucci's spacious and uncluttered interior, its "almost non-use of space" with clear sight lines, differed from the more typically small and overstuffed boutiques of the 1960s. Moreover, it modeled a "sleek modernity" with movable aluminum fitting rooms, aluminum fixtures for hanging merchandise, a waxed oak floor, track lighting more typically found in an art gallery, and "neon tubes of mauve and blue."[91] Unlike the Milan store, the New York City space was intended to be "even more flexible and more suitable to stage performances." Creative director Franco Marabelli, who worked with Sottsass to design the store's concept, said, "We could remove all furniture, host a party at night, and then put everything back in place for the next morning."[92] The laid-back atmosphere was further established by its fashionable staff, a house DJ (often spinning "New York disco music"), and "an espresso bar serving coffee as you walk in. The look might seem campy at first, but it simply represents a youthful, anti-establishment, fun attitude towards clothing and shopping," a 1977 trade publication noted.[93] The *Times* concurred in a November 9, 1976, story on the "handsome two-story shop" titled "A Tongue-in-Chic Boutique Revives the '60s." As the newspaper asserted, "It's a reincarnation of the youth explosion of the last decade—loud rock music bouncing off the walls hung with tongue-in-cheek posters, a counter for theatrical makeup, another for cookies. And mostly, lively clothes designed for and beamed at the young—which over-30 oldsters also buy."[94]

Elio Fiorucci invited Lopez and Ramos to the brand-new store shortly after opening, according to Paul Caranicas, which was unsurprising given the prominence of Lopez's illustrations. While not recalling how exactly the relationship began, Caranicas offered insight into what may have attracted him to Lopez and Ramos: "The three of them shared an appreciation for the avant-garde, and Elio was enthusiastic about their drawings, their diverse experience, and their global mindset."[95] Fiorucci's invitation indicates how much Lopez's downtown cool had pervaded the uptown world of fashion and commerce. Lopez was living and working downtown, and the energy of his immediate surroundings was reflected in his creative practice. Using Alexandra Vazquez's words, Lopez, Ramos, and their friends used their shared location as a calling card "to live and do beautiful things."[96] But Lopez was also known to the fashion establishment uptown because he worked as an illustrator for Bloomingdale's and *Vogue*. (Diana Vreeland, the editor in chief at *Vogue* until 1971, was a friend and photographic subject of his.) Essentially, Lopez was already straddling the line between uptown and downtown. We can speculate that Fiorucci offered Lopez, with Ramos by his side, the chance to collapse that schism more concretely within a store space. Again, we can surmise that while Lopez's transition into commercial fashion may appear effortless and inevitable, the high stakes involved in partnering with a brand and assuming a new role were laborious—it must have required the same deep breaths and concentration that animated his drawing practice.

Soon after their initial meeting, Caranicas states, the pair became "the in-house 'consultants,' with biweekly meetings at the Fifty-Ninth Street headquarters."[97] Fiorucci's penchant for ordinary apparel dyed crazy colors—a men's dress shirt in Day-Glo orange or pink, for instance, or boots in "fluorescent shades of red, violet, turquoise and blue"—was a glove-like fit for Lopez's proclivities toward aesthetic excess, his embrace of *too-much-ness*.[98] (Cleveland recalls, for instance, Lopez "wearing three freshly pressed shirts, one layered over the next, pointy collars turned up. That, too, was pure Antonio.")[99] A 1979 photograph attributed to Lopez, used for Fiorucci's often-risqué marketing, evinces this. In it, a female model in lilac-colored lingerie is wrapped in cellophane; as Matteo Guarnaccia put it, this image exemplifies how "the decadent and erotic art of Antonio Lopez defined an era."[100] Lopez designed fanciful acrylic mannequins for the front window (a nod to his father's vocation), while he and Ramos arranged the large glass windows on the ground floor as living tableaux; they used the dramatic talents of Pat Cleveland and a rotating cast of model-friends to perform in the vitrines playfully. In doing so, they underscored Lopez's belief that the "live" windows, reimagined as stage sets, should highlight fashion's dynamism to perambulating urban denizens. However, the ever-creative Lopez was not content with creating publicity for the store; he decided to dabble in clothing design, specifically women's wear. A popular design was a tulle skirt that came in multiple colors, edged in metallic rickrack, and worn over a swimsuit.[101] (Grace Jones and Pat Cleveland both danced while wearing them.)

Lopez, Ramos, and their model friends were part of a phalanx of downtown artists who exhibited art, worked at, or performed in the front window, collectively transforming Fiorucci into the "hippest store in Manhattan."[102] Several of these figures were stalwarts of Club 57, an East Village orbit of "arty-farty misfits."[103] They included graffiti artist Keith Haring and painter Kenny Scharf (whose work was exhibited in the store in 1979), fashion designer Maripol (who became the store's art director), performance artist John Sex (who performed in the store's window in 1982), and singer Klaus Nomi (a former pastry chef at the World Trade Center).[104] Lopez and his multiracial cohort were decidedly *not* part of the Club 57 ecosystem, preferring more inclusive venues like Queens-based Enchanted Gardens over Club 57's racial

Fiorucci window display, mannequins by Antonio Lopez and Juan Ramos, circa 1977. 35 mm Kodachrome slide. Courtesy of the Estate of Antonio Lopez and Juan Ramos.

homogeneity. And yet, at least one of Fiorucci's salespeople—Joey Arias—was an exception to this stark division, freely circulating in Lopez's glamorous network while also associating with Club 57's more DIY aesthetic.

Arias was a recent West Coast transplant who wore dramatic makeup and had an even more exuberant personality. He eventually became known for his quirky fashion sense and robotic window dancing. In a segment aired on NBC's *Real People* in 1979, he, Nomi, and other coworkers dazzle a group of tourists who stand outside the store's windows; Arias is shown dancing in a slow, mechanical movement. A singer and performance artist, Arias became a fan of Lopez's while living in Los Angeles, where he saw Lopez's drawings in *Interview*. He recalls a day when Lopez appeared at the store, about six months after it opened: "I freaked out when I saw him and stayed behind after the store closed so I could help him with his designs. He said he liked my energy." Calling his work with Lopez the "highlight" of his time in fashion, Arias would later visit Ramos and Lopez at their studio. Lopez eventually

Pat Cleveland at Fiorucci, New York City, circa 1977. Courtesy of the Estate of Antonio Lopez and Juan Ramos.

Donna Jordan and Pat Cleveland at Fiorucci, New York City, circa 1977. 35 mm Kodachrome slide. Courtesy of the Estate of Antonio Lopez and Juan Ramos.

sketched him, and Arias attended Lopez's parties, knowing that "there would be creativity everywhere."[105]

Arias's suggestion—that various forms of artistic creation were emerging from a gathering of like-minded creatives, albeit in a nontraditional art space—is part of a larger pattern, namely the "flourishing of alternative venues and opportunities for artists outside of the commercial art system" in 1970s New York City.[106] That flourishing, as we know, primarily happened downtown, in neighborhoods like SoHo and the East Village. Fiorucci, therefore, may appear an outlier in this genealogy, a department store situated on the tony Upper East Side, a world apart from the nonprofit art galleries (like Artists Space) and the artist-run studio and exhibition spaces (like 112 Workshop / 112 Greene Street, later renamed White Columns) that proliferated several miles south. However, it is more accurate to consider Fiorucci as one example among other sites in *Mavericks of Style* that, while more profit-driven and polished, thrived and even capitalized on the aesthetic vibrancy below Fourteenth Street. Foiling long-standing schisms between downtown and uptown, low culture and high culture, the offbeat artists inhabiting Fiorucci's commercial space suggested that "a progressive blend of punk, feminist, and queer messaging was escaping from downtown."[107] Moreover, while this "artsy, Mudd Club–type crowd" was attracted to the store for its themed interiors and the references to street art refracted through its window displays, they also lent the store an aura of "fashionability" that prompted Fiorucci's arguably more important audience—those everyday consumers, at least some of whom were deep-pocketed Upper East Siders—to purchase its jeans, accessories, and housewares.[108]

Fiorucci was notable for bringing "the dance party out of the nightclub and into the shop" while asserting the "dynamics of style influence, in which appropriation goes both ways, between styles of the street and the halls of high fashion."[109] As Joey Arias recalled, "I'd bring the Downtown people Uptown, and I used the place as my office, or my gallery, for myself. It was a very important place for New York."[110]

Arias was not merely boasting: Fiorucci's showroom was a hive of artistic activity. It was a source of aesthetic inspiration. It was a laid-back environment where visual and performance artists met one another, exchanged ideas, and brokered collaborations. It was an unofficial gallery where these same fledging artists displayed work or performed "happenings" in the windows, right alongside dancing models. Fiorucci, therefore, was not only a dynamic nexus point between polished uptown retail and downtown art-school energies but also a pulsing locus that constantly rendered the quotidian vibrantly anew.

While Fiorucci was colloquially referred to as the "daytime Studio 54," Lopez's designs for Fiorucci also extended to Studio 54 itself. A former opera house and CBS-TV studio at 254 West Fifty-Fourth Street, Studio 54 opened as an exclusive, chic nightclub on April 26, 1977. "Although a late arrival onto the disco scene, the club created New York's most powerful trifecta of music, celebrity, and fashion," Sonnet Stanfill writes.[111] And its environs—like Fiorucci—were exquisite. Studio 54's ethos was ultrasophisticated, replete with high-end interior design, including a brass bar, waterfall, and state-of-the-art lighting and sound systems installed by Broadway specialists and design virtuosos. Open for a mere thirty-three months, Studio 54 hosted over-the-top celebrity birthday parties, record launches, fashion shows, and film premieres. If Studio 54, as Tim Lawrence remarks, represented "the climax of the downtown dance network continuum," the endless publicity it garnered also stoked the imagination of a broader national public, as its anything-goes reputation and splashy vibe captured the period's zeitgeist.[112]

Lopez wore multiple hats concerning Studio 54, but his most impactful role was designing the costumes worn by the prestigious Alvin Ailey American Dance Theater's dancers at the club's opening night performance.[113] The extant sketches of Lopez's costumes reveal his ability to yoke energetic colors to dance-friendly streetwear. Each set of layered drawings featured an in-color outline of the specific dancer in the full costume (often drawn on envelopes), along with attached fabric swatches, smaller sketches of specific garments and their intended colors, and written notes on graph paper that included detailed bodily measurements. In several of them, the dancer's first name appears on the garments themselves, spray-painted on the back of a sweatshirt in graffiti-like typography or outlined in color on the back of a long-sleeved T-shirt. While the designs run the gamut from informal to formal, at heart, they are sportswear garments—headbands, kneepads, and leg warmers are abundant. Most involve a combination of sweat shorts and cropped sweatshirts (worn off one shoulder by the female dancers) with FIORUCCI or NYC emblazoned on the front.

Lopez's predilection for sportswear themes infused the football helmets and gear worn by models in the series *Men in Showers*, let us recall, and the commercial fashion illustrations he executed for brands, magazines, and department stores. The proximity of Paragon Sports to Ramos and Lopez's Union Square studio—the same place they purchased space blankets for the *Candy Bar Wrapper Series*—undoubtedly influenced their return to this theme again and again. Such preferences influenced how they dressed, too, as the pair traded in tailored suits for athletic leisurewear upon their return from Paris. "The 1970s were very much focused on the care of one's body and personal appearance—with clothes to match," fashion historian Michael Langkjaer emphasizes.[114] Lopez concurs in a page from "Antonio NYC 78," an editorial in the November 1978 issue of GQ magazine writing, "Healthy, in good shape—to survive, stay fit!" The toned bodies and athletic fashions in Lopez's various drawings, Langkjaer writes, reflect the "increased involvement of both sexes in sporting activities, the proliferation of fitness centers and discotheques, body-conscious fashion styles, and New York as an erotic and hedonistic metropolis through the 1970s and into the 1980s."[115] Many sultry designer dresses worn to Studio 54 emphasized this less-is-more trend, including backless silhouettes paired with high-cut legs or halter necks. These fashions filled the growing desire for chic, colorful clothes that could *move*. The results were abundant, from Stephen Burrows's flowy chiffon numbers in candy-colored hues, as we'll see, to the gold lamé unitard and leggings, with matching cape, that Norma Kamali designed for Grace Jones for her New Year's Eve performance there in 1977.

On the same page from Lopez's "Antonio NYC 78," he wrote "From Union Square to El Barrio—Shades of Thomas H. Benton—Reginald Marsh—Edward Hopper," above illustrations of three brawny male figures in sporty outfits with red accents, their backs to us, one with what appears to be a radio or small boombox resting on his shoulder. *New York City* is spelled out across their coordinating shirts. On the right side of the page, he jotted, "The street—a strong fashion influence." Lopez's entry implies that the athletic wear he witnessed daily, from Fourteenth Street to 125th Street, echoed visual motifs in these three "American Scene" painters, an art-historical reference possibly stoked by Ramos. He goes further in an entry from the visual diary he kept, also from 1978, inserting reproductions of two Marsh paintings—*Subway Station* (1930) and *Twenty Cent Movie* (1936)—and then recording coordinating captions for each: "Uptown Past 96 Street" and "Downtown Bowery." Above this, he has inserted sketches of three figures in the Alvin Ailey costumes. Here, Lopez links some of high art's curiosities—the physicality and mundanity of urban life—with their low complement: the forward-thinking Black and Brown dwellers on the periphery of the fashion world who began popularizing sportswear, turning the streets of New York City into their makeshift runways.

Lopez's musings also suggest the influence of developing hip-hop cultures in Harlem and the South Bronx on the sportswear-inspired designs he customized for the Alvin Ailey dancers. His uptown-past-Ninety-Sixth-Street costumes echoed the attitude of the various subcultures in the South Bronx—breakdancing, graffiti, and DJing—evolving into hip-hop. The Rock Steady Crew, a breakdancing collective formed there in 1977, is one key example. (Lopez befriended them in 1981.) His Alvin Ailey designs also reflected the visual energy of graffiti, the putative urban menace defiantly displayed on New York City's labyrinth of subway cars. Lopez made this point explicit when he took Polaroids of three Alvin Ailey dancers in costume, posed against a backdrop decorated with graffiti. Spray-painted lettering on the dancers' cropped T-shirts and sweatshirts echoes the kinetic calligraphy behind them.

Lopez's synthesis of Fiorucci, Alvin Ailey, and Studio 54 illustrated his defiance of the barriers that had long separated culture's high and low realms, while also bucking assumptions that commercialism hindered creativity. Seemingly at ease placing sportswear, disco, and Black dance together in the same context, his colorful, spunky costumes helped choreograph this cross-disciplinary conversation. Like his other clothing designs and window displays for Fiorucci, Lopez's commercial endeavors furthered his artistic impulses rather than hindering them. His approach, welcoming cross-fertilization across the arts and drawing from the raw energy of the street, was also echoed by his peers, such as Black American clothing designer Willi Smith. Smith, the lead designer of the New York City–based sportswear label WilliWear (which he founded in 1976), also crossed into the domain of Black dance. He designed costumes for *The Deep South Suite* (1976), which premiered at Ailey's Duke Ellington Festival. Later, he hired Ailey dancers as models for one of his shows.

Again and again, Smith and Lopez (and others in their overlapping networks of friends and collaborators) envisioned a more horizontal relationship to art-making across fashion, dance, and visual art disciplines. These mavericks

"Antonio NYC 78." GQ magazine editorial, November 1978. Mixed media. Courtesy of the Estate of Antonio Lopez and Juan Ramos.

Visual diary, 1978. Mixed media. Courtesy of the Estate of Antonio Lopez and Juan Ramos.

perceived such aesthetic spheres as mutually coconstitutive, refusing the more typical hierarchical ordering of disparate artistic fields. They suggested art was not an entity made in isolation from external stimuli. Instead, it was the product of a dialogue created when fashion designers, choreographers, dancers, and visual artists attempted to speak across their respective wheelhouses, working, living, playing, and loving together. In doing so, as we'll continue to see through this story, they insisted on artistic style as both a collective and solo endeavor. They also reiterated that style was a goal unto itself, an entity as valuable as any one work of art.

Lopez is emblematic of this exploding aesthetic purview that fundamentally altered and took root in 1970s New York; his enormous body of work moves so adeptly and elegantly between artistic categories that are usually distinct. As we have seen, these included fashion illustration, photography, mannequin design and art direction for Fiorucci, and costume design for Black and Brown dancers. Suppose we perceive Lopez's inclinations as those of a conceptual artist, a polyglot who jumped to whatever medium best suited his creative impulses. In that case, his intrepid moves across various genres of expertise suggest a broader vision. As such, Lopez repeatedly pulled from and was conversant with a grab bag of seemingly incongruous sources—including Pop Art, Bauhaus, and hip-hop—that he adroitly recombined to create inventive and often invigorating forms. He transformed fluorescent tape into body-adorning ribbons, reconfiguring bodies into sculptural forms. He converted an assortment of miscellaneous bric-a-brac—space blankets, painted cylindrical tubes, and a makeshift stage—into dynamic props to be brought to life by the seductive Grace Jones. He designed clothes and coordinated kooky performances in a department store that introduced pedestrians to a frothy mixture of outré fashions, bouncy music, and Italian graphic design. A worldly flaneur and future-oriented visual artist, Lopez took inspiration equally from the banal and the high-minded, infusing photography, fabrics, or drawn lines with a dense force field of contagious energy, brilliant color, and undeniable swagger.

Moreover, Antonio Lopez's artistic genius was also the act of surrounding himself with a network of equally motivated and highly inventive peers in 1970s New York City. These fellow travelers labored, like Lopez, to traverse the seemingly oceanic divide between downtown and uptown, pushing against the categorical distinctions between art, fashion, and nightlife; this effort required physical and mental stamina—like Lopez's inhalations of more and more air when deep in his creative zone. Collectively, they were constantly choreographing new selves, whether it was Pat Cleveland's performance art in Fiorucci's windows or Grace Jones's eroticized embodiment of a life-size candy bar. Perhaps they also perceived themselves differently based on how Lopez reimagined them, such as the dynamic sketching of Angelo Colon to Grandmaster Flash's song "White Lines" that opened this chapter. In doing so, little-known historical figures (like Lopez's frequent male model Victor Fernandez) were elevated into artistic subjects. Together, they wielded fierce forms of style as elastic "expressive equipment," cleverly reconfiguring the mundane into the utterly spectacular.[116]

2

I am very stubborn, and I was always looking for the new, even if it makes life difficult for me. The new, or nothing.

GRACE JONES, *I'LL NEVER WRITE MY MEMOIRS*

NEOPHYTE TO MUSE

Grace Jones

In 1976, Grace Jones performed at Enchanted Gardens, a disco in Queens, with some help from her friends. Steve Rubell, one of the owners, introduced her to the venue's elated audience. In the grainy black-and-white footage, we first see a disorienting close-up of a large mass of balloons as we hear his nasal voice over the microphone. After a few seconds, it becomes clear that the balloons are rotating on the ceiling, like a disco ball, as the blurry outlines of the disco's patrons become visible below it. The minute he says, "Miss Grace Jones, everybody," we hear the schmaltzy string arrangement of her single "That's the Trouble" as the crowd cheers. The camera swiftly pivots to the dance floor, showing a crowd of clapping spectators standing, and then quickly zooms in on those seated on the ground as Jones enters. We see the bottom half of her body first, specifically her long ruffled skirt with a metallic-like fabric on its edges. It is one of the tulle skirts that Antonio Lopez designed for Fiorucci, which she is using as a theatrical prop. She holds one end in her right hand and boisterously swings it as she prances around the stage, revealing its layers of fabric. She is wearing a camisole with slinky straps that keep slipping off her shoulders, partially exposing her breasts, and a head covering that appears to be a cross between a hood and a stocking cap. She twirls around, happily lip-synching before someone (presumably Rubell) passes her a microphone, which she pretends to sing into; she appears blithely unconcerned with verisimilitude. Full of energy and sass, she demonstrates an evident glee in performing for the benefit of others.

Almost three and a half minutes into the video, Jones gets rid of her mic and feverishly spins around in a circle. She is then joined on the dance floor by Pat Cleveland, Sterling St. Jacques, Potassa de la Fayette, and others. Cleveland appears to be donning a version of the same skirt Jones is wearing, and she also uses its flouncy fabric for theatrical effect. St. Jacques, who was dating Cleveland then and was her dance partner when they appeared on *Soul Train*, also spins around in a circle on the floor. The regal de la Fayette, wearing a long skirt, strapless top, and long gloves, strolls out while holding balloons in one hand. She begins whirling around in a circle too. The record abruptly skips, but no one seems to notice. They all are too busy enjoying their roles as backup support for Jones and as dancers, hyping up the crowd...and each other. Multihyphenate Jones dances with her peers in the middle of the dance floor while her record plays, suggesting how her artistry—as a model, recording artist, and wild performer—was continually invigorated by the art of friendship.[1]

Jones was born in 1948 in Spanish Town, Jamaica. Like Lopez, she later immigrated with her family to the United States; when she was twelve, they settled in upstate New York—Syracuse, to be exact. As she remarks, "My father was a minister. It was a very religious family, so the people I went around with...fashion wasn't their world."[2] After high school, she enrolled at Onondaga Community College. She initially thought she'd become a Spanish teacher, then she dabbled in theater, and after a year, she dropped out. Here, what we might consider a more recognizable Grace Jones begins to emerge. Over the next few years, she would pursue an eclectic set of occupations and experiences—including a brief stint as a nudist, a go-go dancer, and a resident at a rural hippie commune outside Philadelphia with other societal misfits. It was at the latter that she first experimented with LSD, the psychedelic drug then widely perceived as a tangible threat to the social order.[3]

Still from *Anton Perich Presents: Grace Jones*, filmed concert at Enchanted Gardens, Queens, New York, 1976. Courtesy of Anton Perich.

Somewhere amid all that experimenting, Jones moved to New York City to pursue modeling. Looking back on her life in 1982, she told an interviewer, "When did I come to New York? When I was eighteen, nineteen…something like that. I can't remember. I wanted to be a model."[4] She recalls someone in the theater world encouraging her to pivot to modeling "because it would give me the freedom of still looking for theatre work and films and stuff like that. I took advantage of what was there and used it. That's basically what I did."[5] Jones's intrepid waywardness exemplifies, in Summer Kim Lee's words, "desirous and desiring ways of turning toward oneself in order to be inclined differently toward others."[6] A desirous inclination toward difference seems like a very apt description for all we'll explore below.

Grace Jones and Antonio Lopez had a formative encounter—on the dance floor. She explained that she had been modeling in New York for two years and met Lopez while dancing in the city: "I think I was dancing with someone else when we met, but he liked the way I was dancing, and I liked the way he was dancing. That's how we got together."[7] Lopez and Jones developed a friendship and a productive working relationship. She reminisces that "every time Antonio drew me, it gave me a clue about how to do my make-up and work on different looks, different ways of shading and shadowing."[8] Later, when she arrived in Paris to further her modeling career, Lopez was already there; they partied at Club 7, and he introduced her to photographers and his friends. "I started hanging out at Antonio's apartment when Jerry [Hall] started living there. That's where he did that series of Polaroids of me in the bathroom—that was fun," she recalls, most likely referencing the *Blue Water Series*.[9] In what follows, even as we shift our focus to Jones and her work with other artists, Lopez's influence will continue to reverberate, particularly in her galvanic rebirth as a disco star in the second half of the seventies.

Jones is part of a continuum of artists—like her peer Lopez—whose restless search for refreshing sources of inspiration led them, again and again, toward cutting-edge artistic productions. They continually flouted prescriptive notions of what they *should* create along the way. Jones was part of a network of creatively inclined individuals breaking from aesthetic traditions; they straddled the line between commercial and high art, exploiting the thrill generated by the juxtaposition of disparate materials. "I was moving with artists who really were underground—known, even successful, but rooted in the avant-garde, experimental," she emphasizes.[10] Jones adds an artistic dimension to the multivalent term *underground*.[11] In the 1970s, its multiple meanings included the subterranean network of clandestine loft parties and word-of-mouth private events frequented by these artists. The pinnacle of these efforts was David Mancuso's "Love Saves the Day" party at the Loft downtown, which Jones attended. There, participants were elevated to a collective high by a combination of LSD and carefully curated music.[12] Jones's wording conveys the porous boundary between the art of partying and the act of artistic creation, a hallmark of *Mavericks of Style*, where gatherings in nontraditional art spaces often led to sui generis visual art, performance, and fashion. These group exercises in unruly noncompliance jettisoned the familiar and instead luxuriated in the unknown and aesthetically exhilarating. Jones is an intrinsic figure in any thorough understanding of the American avant-garde, even as the "delusion of whiteness" that animates it continues to position her as an outlier.[13]

Jones, much like Lopez, had a gravitational pull so strong that a cluster of highly inventive individuals constantly revolved around her. She was a charismatic figure who worked and played with a vast creative crowd: fashion designers, stylists, graphic designers, visual artists, and fellow models. Several of these names appeared in the previous chapter—former *Esquire* art director

Jean-Paul Goude, Jones's onetime boyfriend and a Union Square neighbor of Lopez and Juan Ramos; Club 57 habitué and School of Visual Arts student Keith Haring; and Pop Art impresario Andy Warhol, whose Factory at 860 Broadway was proximate to Lopez's studio at 876 Broadway. Models Pat Cleveland, Jerry Hall, and Toukie Smith shared space and runways, often working with the same designers and artists. Her ambit included former *Interview* receptionist and emerging fashion journalist André Leon Talley—who described her as "the clergyman's daughter converted into a Parisian *sine qua non* of sophistication"—and fashion designer Issey Miyake.[14] As we'll see again and again, Jones's commanding air—her theatrical energy, sleek looks, and uncanny ability to inhabit and energize radical aesthetic forms—catalyzed these creatives as they jointly reached toward the "new."

While the previous chapter detailed the various forms of community and collective art-making animating Lopez's aesthetic endeavors, this chapter is tailored to distilling changes to Jones's self-presentation via her artistic collaborations. This makes sense, given that Lopez primarily focused on his models' styling and aesthetic portrayal or the environments he helped mold, such as Fiorucci. While Lopez's charm and peacocking are well-documented, he did not appear as interested in being the center of attention, gladly ceding that space to figures like Cleveland and Jones. In contrast, as a seemingly elastic medium of artistic expression for others, Jones herself was the art object. To paraphrase sociologist Stuart Hall, she harnessed her body as a form of cultural capital, as if it were her most valuable resource.[15] Grace Jones did not create a painting or a sculpture; the masterpiece she created was Grace Jones. To quote Gwendolyn Brooks in another context, "That was the offering, the bit of art, that could not come from any other. She would polish and hone that."[16] And this cultivation of herself as a tabula rasa for aesthetic innovation is the famous image of Jones we have now: the larger-than-life icon, sporting oversized shoulder pads and a sharply angled crew cut; the endlessly fascinating personality; and the aggressive visual persona that was also unapologetically Black. The ever-mutable Jones was the nucleus of a sprawling set of connections between peers in art, fashion, and performance. In other words, it is not that notions of communal creativity do not apply to Jones. Instead, they are harder to discern when, to quote Jennifer Brody's words in a different context, "her own body (as artist/object) is implicated in her work."[17]

Thus, in this chapter, I attempt to defamiliarize Jones; I aim to render her acts of creation and the peers she worked with more apparent by focusing on lesser-known interlocutors and the atypical arenas where her style was forged. And I gesture toward the tensions inherent in her artistic development. My instinct in doing so is to recast that which now seems seemingly effortless as labor, highlighting the skill required in modeling while foregrounding the specific difficulties she (and others) faced as a Black woman in a predominately white industry. Moreover, Jones draws our attention to the nefarious underbelly of the artist-muse relationship—one can become just an object. She complicates that working relationship, exposing how a dynamic that appears elsewhere in these pages as an equilateral exchange can morph into something more one-sided.

First, I turn to Jones's early days as a model and her friendship with fellow model and photographer Ming Smith. I track the former's self-development, as perceived in photography, and unravel the latter's unconstrained interdisciplinarity and skillful talent as a budding artist. I also introduce a hair salon that, like other spatial sites in *Mavericks of Style*, was a resourceful zone of imagination and self-expression. In the late 1970s, Jones moved away from modeling to become a recording artist. The second half of the chapter makes a similar shift, focusing on commercial artist Richard Bernstein, who devised her colorful disco album imagery. I detail how his visual work with Jones is more of a collective enterprise than it may first appear and discuss the multiple implications of Jones as his "muse." I close by meditating on her baby shower at the downtown disco Paradise Garage, a chic and colorful extravaganza that was also, unsurprisingly, an art-family affair.

Jones's navigation of the vast gulf between slick uptown environs and more laid-back downtown hangouts was not a fait accompli; it required a skilled pivot between distinct worlds and the aid of her fellow striving artists. Likewise, her transition in the 1970s from a novice in the modeling world to the multihyphenate performer we know today was a steep learning curve, but one abetted by the deftness of others. Thus, in this chapter, I offer a B-side of Grace Jones, illustrating over and over how friendship and love sustained and contributed to the development of her artistic style, as she and her coconspirators pushed to widen the lens of what was considered a work of art. To use Tina Post's words, we witness the "aesthetic field as a place where power's organizing relations play out" as Jones and her peers sought to challenge what counts as legitimate artistic forms while also radically stretching the bounds of beauty itself, that quintessential aesthetic property, to include Jones.[18] As we see below, Jones constantly manipulated style as her preferred medium of artistic insurrection, shapeshifting and blurring the edges between discrete categories like modeling, performance, photography, and fine art.

PERFORMING GLAMOUR IN MIDTOWN

Ming Smith, who photographed Grace Jones on multiple occasions in the 1970s, is a fascinating character in her own right, yet another strand in this web of collective art-making. After graduating from Howard University with a degree in microbiology, she moved to New York City in 1973, intending to become a model and artist. She lived briefly on Central Park West and in Chelsea but eventually settled in the bohemian West Village, a queer enclave whose denizens embraced her: "They were about free spirit and being free to be you. And I loved that. I LOVED that in the Village."[19] She began taking photographs, often roaming the streets with a Rolleiflex camera. The Young Lords, a Puerto Rican group of radical community organizers, was one of her early subjects, as was the novelist James Baldwin, her neighbor. And she took fly-on-the-wall snapshots of fashion designer Stephen Burrows and his showroom model, Bethann Hardison. (She also owned a dress by Burrows, which she described to me as "navy blue but with red thread trim.")[20] Meanwhile, she cultivated her burgeoning craft among peers, becoming "acquainted with all the Black fashion photographers."[21]

During this period, Smith became affiliated with the Kamoinge Workshop, a group of Black photographers with the bold mission of producing "significant visual images of our time."[22] This was a lucky by-product of her professional relationship with the commercial photographer Anthony Barboza, who also worked with Jones. Barboza, who lived in the West Village as well and did work for *Essence*, had a studio on 10 West Eighteenth Street. In a 2021 interview, he recounted his first encounter with Jones there: "One day this girl named Grace Jones came up to show her portfolio. She had some photographs but not enough. She hadn't done any jobs before, so I decided to test her."[23] In her memoirs, Jones recalls that Barboza was a "hardworking photographer, as well as a historian and artist, and he really liked me. He said that I wasn't a classic beauty, but had a very interesting face." Barboza "took photographs of me to study my face, but he had time only in the morning to do some tests before his day job."[24] Soon after, in 1971, he featured her in an *Essence* magazine spread with the Chambers Brothers, a psychedelic soul group.[25] "They said I could use a female model to pose with them, so I called

Stephen Burrows, New York, 1974. Courtesy of Ming Smith.

Grace and another model. That turned out to be her first job. She was all excited and she tore the studio up."[26] Smith, too, was sent to Barboza's studio on a modeling job: "While I was waiting in the lobby, I overheard some men talking—or rather, debating—about photography: was it an art form or just nostalgia? I was fascinated."[27] Louis Draper, whom she met at Barboza's studio, invited her to join the collective, a pseudouniversity.[28] Just a few months after she arrived in New York, she became the sole female member.

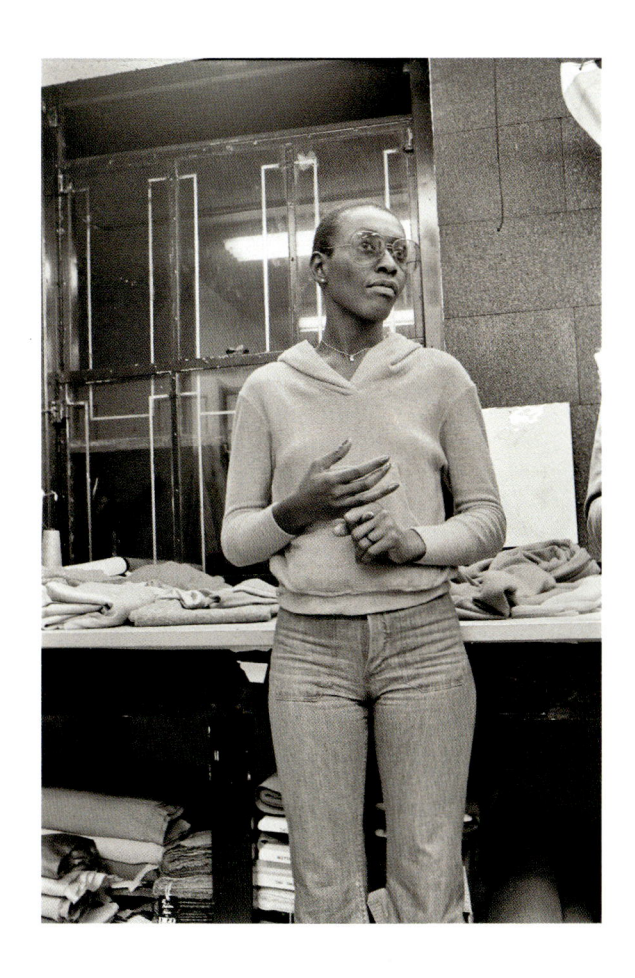

Bethann Hardison, New York, 1974. Courtesy of Ming Smith.

Smith and Jones officially met each other not at Barboza's studio but through another place they had in common: a leading midtown Manhattan hair salon that was a crucial node in their social and artistic orbit. Smith explains, "When I was modeling, I met a hairdresser who worked at Cinandre at 57th Street and Fifth Avenue. Now, you're saying like, 'What does that all have to do with everything?' Well, it was like a cultural hub; there were makeup artists that were working for *Vogue* and *Harper's Bazaar*—that's

Self-Portrait at Cinandre, New York, 1974. Courtesy of Ming Smith.

where I met Grace Jones—pioneers. We were all new, we were all striving."[29] Cinandre opened at 21 East Fifty-Seventh Street in 1969, catering to a vanguard of models and young professional women. It was co-owned by Andre Martheleur, a young Belgian turned New Yorker with shoulder-length blond hair. He eventually became the salon's sole owner and a widely respected celebrity stylist. Cinandre was two blocks from upscale Bloomingdale's and, importantly, a mere three blocks from the eventual location of Fiorucci.

Andre Martheleur at Cinandre, New York, 1974. Courtesy of Ming Smith.

Four years later, on July 19, 1973, the trendy salon expanded from its increasingly cramped space into an "airy two-floor arrangement at 11 East 57th Street." The *New York Times* reported that the "crisp, white salon, with touches of blue and red," was "not only handsome" but strategically "devised so that traffic moves freely without the bottlenecks of the former shop." The profile featured a candid image of Martheleur tending to a patron's short coif. A smiling Jones stands beside him, looking off to the side.[30] While Cinandre was, in Smith's words, "the VIP number-one hair salon," it was also where she met up with friends, including different makeup artists. It seems that chic Cinandre, like its whimsical counterpart Fiorucci, was a bustling forum for creative personalities and shared artistic energy. There, a network of models, hair stylists, and makeup artists collaborated in the art of dynamic self-expression—hair was being cut, but style was being made.

Jones and Smith initially bonded over the obvious—neither fit into the modeling world's narrow ethos at the time. Jones very briefly worked for the Black Beauty agency but left after a month because she was told her facial features did not fit within "Black beauty" standards: "They said, *Your face doesn't fit. You are really black and your lips are big but your nose is too thin and your eyes are slanty. You won't get the catalog work that brings in the big bucks.*"[31] Both were also initially passed over by Wilhelmina Models, opened in 1967 by Dutch-born model Wilhemina Cooper, presumably because neither was potentially marketable in Cooper's eyes. But perhaps even more fundamental, they both felt an urgent desire for aesthetic freedom. "It was a much more conservative time," Smith said. "We didn't fit in as regular models. We were too exotic, too light, too dark." Jones concurs, remarking that she was perceived as "too black for the white world, not black enough for the black world."[32] Smith adds that Jones was often perceived as "too much," code for either her unconventional, exotic look or her gregarious personality. They shared a lot of the same friends in the industry and, as struggling models, were both attempting "to find our way, to express ourselves." Smith used modeling to pay for her photography, while Jones considered trying her luck as a singer. In addition, they had similar liberal viewpoints, especially regarding sexual orientation: "We didn't judge. We were open to the times. We were not trying to put people in a box." But ultimately, when contemplating their friendship, Smith recalls being drawn to something more ephemeral: "I love her spirit, then and now."[33]

Smith attempted to capture this elusive essence when she photographed Jones at Cinandre in 1974. Wearing a two-tone tutu and holding ballet shoes in her hands, Jones faces the camera head-on with a demure look. Her hair is in a closely cut, short Afro, her hairline shaved high above her forehead. Jones's profile is reflected in a long mirror on her left, above a row of outlets and under illuminated lights, which cast a warm glow on the left side of her face. The profile of an unidentified man in a light T-shirt and dark pants is also reflected in the mirror. His ink-colored arms and head are almost indistin-

Grace Jones at Cinandre, New York, 1974. Courtesy of Ming Smith.

guishable from the wall he is walking past. Smith recalls that Jones came to the salon wearing the outfit she was photographed in, presumably from a previous modeling shoot, and that the photograph was not planned but rather happenstance. She remarked on this destiny elsewhere: "When I photographed Grace Jones at the hairdresser, I was there to get my hair done too."[34] Smith's resulting photograph, *Grace Jones at Cinandre*, is somewhat surprising in its straightforward rendering of Jones, who appears overtly feminine in her attire and almost muted in her facial expressivity. The black-and-white image portrays a rarely seen side of Jones, particularly in the 1970s: quiet, even a bit withdrawn, minus the overt embellishment or palpable confidence we see later in the decade. This is, perhaps, because "Grace Jones wasn't Grace Jones," Smith emphasized—not yet a star, but rather a relatively unknown model trying to break through.[35]

Smith's choice of black-and-white film may seem at odds with Jones's colorful personality, yet it was consistent with the artistic hierarchy of the era, as we have seen. "Black and white was the preferred art form," Smith told me, a sentiment shared by the other members of the Kamoinge Workshop. Black-and-white film and its "great gradation scale," she said, was perceived as the domain of a "true artist," while color photography was interpreted as "commercial or even whorish."[36] Indeed, we saw how Antonio Lopez, keenly aware of this divide, chose the cheap Kodak Instamatic camera precisely *because* of the buoyant color it could solicit.

And yet, while Smith was a black-and-white believer, she seemed uninterested in portraying Jones as a proper art-historical subject or an explicitly political one. If anything, it was an economic decision, one of "making do" with limited resources. Color film had to be sent to a lab to process, making the total cost five times more expensive than black-and-white film, Smith told me.[37] By situating Jones as a photographic subject within Cinandre's voguish environment, Smith accomplished something else: Her portrait frames the artistic labor of women of color in producing beauty—in front of *and* behind the camera. We can imagine the reciprocity between Smith's photographic gaze and Jones's carefully held pose as they recognize each other's skill and subjectivity on both ends of the camera lens. In short, their friendship became the fulcrum of this fruitful and spontaneous encounter. In the midtown hair salon, rather than Barboza's studio downtown or a more traditional art space uptown, it was another instance of subverted expectations about *where* collaborative and edgy art-making occurred. Finally, while the photograph ostensibly lacks color (despite its interplay of soft gray, white, and black shades), it is a reminder that color, regarding race, was the basis of Jones and Smith's marginalization in the fashion industry. In other words, while color was aesthetic, in the artistic sense, it was also profoundly politicized, an unending marker of racial difference—and also, for Smith and Jones, of mutual support and determined connection.[38] As José Esteban Muñoz reminds us, by way of W. E. B. Du Bois, "feeling like a problem is also a mode of belonging, a belonging through recognition," which is a perfect description of their shared commonality.[39]

Several years later, in 1978, Smith photographed Jones again at yet another fashionable site: Studio 54. By this time, Jones had become a singer (with two disco albums to her credit) and a breakout star: her 1975 single "I Need a Man" became her first number-one on *Billboard*'s Hot Dance Club Songs chart when it was rereleased in 1977, attesting to its popularity with nightclub DJs. The occurrence of the photograph was, again, sporadic. "She called me and said, 'Bring your camera!'" Smith said. Fresh from Paris, where her modeling career had taken off, Jones was "returning to New York as a success."[40] That sense of triumph was evident in the photographic magic Smith and Jones conjured. In *Grace Jones, Studio 54*, Jones is seen in profile, artfully staging herself. She is wearing sunglasses, piles of metallic bracelets on each arm (the same ones, it seems, she wore while posing for Antonio Lopez's *Candy Bar Wrapper Series*), a Lurex-like camisole, and a coordinating long scarf, which rests on her head. At the same time, its ends are held in each of her hands. Light reflects off her skin at various contact points—collarbone, neck, cheekbone—and her mouth is slightly ajar. If you look closely, two oblivious Black patrons are visible behind Jones on the right side of the image. However, the hip setting of Studio 54 is not visually apparent because Jones's elongated scarf takes up most of the photographic space, becoming a pliable aesthetic object.

In contrast to the aspiring model that Smith photographed in Cinandre, this incarnation of Jones is closer to the disco diva who still stimulates our imaginations, the perpetual performer who flamboyantly wields artifice. After all, as writer Ramon Lobato reminds us, excess is a quintessential component of Jones's body of work, where the "abundance of style becomes the work's substance."[41] Jones's adept self-staging in Smith's photograph also suggests how Jones learned "key devices for subversive performance during the 1970s in the worlds of Parisian fashion and New York disco," art historian Miriam Kershaw writes. These dramaturgical strategies included how to "give movement and costuming maximum visual impact," reinventing the self through "rapid modifications of external appearance" and enthralling audiences with "artifice and constructed effects."[42] Jones's configuration of herself here also illustrates how "the medium of photography necessarily relies on the performance of the photographed subject," as Joshua Javier Guzmán and Iván A. Ramos succinctly put it.[43]

Yxta Maya Murray, who argues that Smith's photographs also drew "from her life as an aestheticized and objectified woman of color," interprets the photograph's glimmering elements as evidence of Jones's manipulation of glamour and Smith's alliance of dance and photography.[44] "Less posing than unfurling herself before the camera" is Murray's apt description. In the interplay of light bouncing off the various metallicized finishes of Jones's accessories and clothing and her skin, we see glamour as a "weapon and power source that Jones embodies with her seemingly unvanquishable gift for movement. Indeed, Jones's almost flamenco contrapposto speaks to Smith's lifelong interest in

Grace Jones at Studio 54, New York, 1978. Courtesy of Ming Smith.

dance."[45] Specifically, Smith began taking dance classes in New York City after learning about choreographer-anthropologist Katherine Dunham, whom she cites as one of her artistic forebears. Smith has also described the quick adjustments employed while walking down a runway as identical to trying to grab that decisive moment in the frame.

Smith, like Antonio Lopez and his compatriots, and like Grace Jones more and more, ignored disciplinary boundaries. Instead, she imagined—and *willed*—a loose continuity between modeling, dance, and photography. Hence, we can interpret Smith's photograph of Jones in Studio 54, the preeminent site of the get-down, as hovering between these different mediums of artistic expression. This improvisational approach between Jones and Smith, working together in the spaces between seemingly distinct art forms, is another example of horizontal art-making. We can speculate further that Smith's cross-disciplinarity urges viewers to engage the portrait through a movement approach rather than a strictly ocular one, perceiving it as dancing in place. Indeed, it is no surprise that Smith masterfully renders a fleeting sense of Jones's dramatic movement since Smith is adamant that photographs constantly shift, even when they appear static: "The image is always moving, even if you're standing still."[46]

Furthermore, Smith's skill in showcasing Jones's theatrical wielding of glamour was influenced by her shared experience as a model. Smith was versed in conveying allure through gestures and facial expressions in front of the lens and on the runway. However, the "white world of fashion and advertising" in the late 1960s and early 1970s limited the opportunities of models of color, especially Black women, to *perform* glamour.[47] Naomi Sims, who studied at the Fashion Institute of Technology simultaneously with Stephen Burrows, was widely celebrated in the 1970s as the first Black supermodel. Sims and Beverly Johnson, the first Black woman to appear on the cover of American *Vogue* (in 1974), were part of the first wave of Black models who began integrating these industries.[48] Yet that select group, in the 1970s, was tiny. For instance, Pat Cleveland, a model for *Ebony* and *Jet*, the most successful Black publications, as well as the prestigious *Vogue*, said, "These represented two different cultures; they were like different sides of the railroad tracks, and I kept crossing over from one to the other."[49] Wilhelmina eventually reversed course and signed Smith and Jones. Smith became one of the agency's top performers, appearing in several advertisements for cosmetic companies. Meanwhile, Jones—whose exotic look was still unsuited for catalog work—outraged Wilhelmina when she shaved her head without permission; she was forced to wear wigs while her hair grew back. Who better than Jones to understand that, in an industry rife with racism and overt antipathy toward Black women models, boldly staging yourself as an object of desire, glamour, and radiant self-possession was the ultimate transgressive act?

Smith and Jones's joint aspirations in figuring out how to be themselves, frequently *through* their art, unites them with the broader constellation of characters permeating *Mavericks of Style*. This polyglot group shared an obstinate refusal to stay within the limits of recognizable forms.[50] Their creative exploration was often a search for the optimal form to articulate a thematic concept, such as Lopez's sudden switch to the Instamatic camera. However, Smith and Jones remind us that this inquiry was also about utilizing one's chosen medium to express oneself in the most expansive way possible, such as carefully held facial composure or the exacting drape of a piece of glittering fabric. It was an act of becoming—transforming into a bona fide artist or personifying an idea. In short, style was continually harnessed as a conduit for personal and aesthetic transformation.

This is particularly salient in Smith's second black-and-white photograph of Jones in Studio 54, almost identical to the first, albeit adorned with flourishes of orange and pink paint. Also titled *Grace Jones at Studio 54*, Jones—in profile—is pictured in the same outfit, still using her long scarf as a malleable tool, with one side falling to the floor and the other extending past the photographic frame. Her head is tilted back this time, and her eyes are closed behind her oversized sunglasses. Jones's angular jawline, much more prominent in this image, appears sculptural. She looks blissful, momentarily lost in the sublime rhythms of an unheard song. Around her, we can see glimpses of other bodies, someone's hand in the foreground on the image's left side, and another's face in profile. The most noticeable person, besides Jones, is another Black woman standing behind her, face visible over the top edge of Jones's outstretched scarf. While this woman's eyes are downturned, we can see the subtle smile on her face. One of her hands is suspended in the air; she appears to be snapping her fingers. The collective embodiments suggest that Smith's photograph was taken on the dance floor. Meanwhile, a faint circular orange swirl is painted above Jones's head, and hot pink brushstrokes, moving left to right, complement the stripes in her scarf and seem to undulate like waves.

An incredible tactile energy comes from Smith's pink brushstrokes, their bright hue and palpable texture adding a multisensorial element to the photograph, elevating it to another realm. These squiggly lines enhance the sense of Jones's corporeal movement, as they seem to emanate from her electrifying presence. Their "material surplus," to use Rizvana Bradley's language, is evident in the visible marks left by the paintbrush as it moved across the photograph's surface and in the warm intensity of the hot pink itself.[51] This effulgent shade also appears in Lopez's *Ribbon Series*. Smith's painterly sensibility imbues the photograph with a startling haptic quality; it calls us to see and *touch* it.[52] In this sense, its visceral hapticity gestures to the painted photograph's excess, how it spills out of the bounds of one sense and into another. This seems appropriate for the times, considering how the prototypical 1970s disco was repeatedly described as a venue that engaged multiple senses simultaneously. For instance, Roland Barthes visited the Parisian disco Le Palace in the spring of 1978, the same year as Smith's photograph. He marveled at its fantastic unison of "pleasures ordinarily dispersed," including dance, music, and "the exploration of new visual sensations, due to

Grace Jones at Studio 54, New York, 1978. Courtesy of Ming Smith.

new technologies"—an insight easily applicable to Studio 54.[53] Barthes's musing could also apply to Smith's artistic proficiency here. Her textured hot pink paint jars us out of passive spectatorship, using color to invite us into this elusive but sharply rendered world: aural ecstasy, chromatic excess, and haptic pleasure.

Moreover, Smith and Jones's friendship is evident in the ease with which they riffed off each other's energy, like musicians in an ensemble, as if Jones's fearlessness as a model and club fixture stimulated Smith's freewheeling artistic freedom. After all, Jones continued expanding her repertoire in this period, channeling her artistry into a newfound music career, where her "appearance, musical taste, and sense of fashion in many ways shaped the image and public perception of disco."[54]

Meanwhile, Smith experimented with painting and blurring her photographs—an instinct-driven, ad-lib method that differentiated her from her purist peers in the Kamoinge Workshop. In doing so, she developed a more poetic, dance-inflected approach to photography—driven by light, beauty, and energy—that has become her signature. Put differently, Smith has mastered "a singular and technically challenging style: Her images shake and soften the lines between the subject and its background, mimicking movement itself."[55] Smith and Jones's camaraderie underpins these portraits, an artistic duet in which they became their freest and most imaginative selves. And while Jones's breakthrough as a model occurred in Paris, Smith's big break was local: The Museum of Modern Art purchased two of her photographs in 1979. She became the first Black woman photographer to have her works acquired by the institution.

We have witnessed Jones's shift from a neophyte model to a more seasoned pro, as her respective representations have also become more layered and complex. Jones grew increasingly confident before the lens, starting with her incipient work with commercial photographer Anthony Barboza in the early 1970s. She began staging herself more theatrically, which has become her trademark. (Barboza photographed model Pat Cleveland, Jones's equally bubbly peer, in 1977.) The portraits taken by Smith, first at Cinandre and later at Studio 54, can be interpreted as "before" and "after" shots that visibly mark the transition in Jones's professional self-development. In this arc, we can see a simultaneous artistic change, from Barboza's photo-editorial work for *Essence* to Smith's elegiac black-and-white portrait at Cinandre, culminating in her exuberant, disco-infused hybrid of hot pink paint and photography at Studio 54. Smith and Barboza's straining of clear-cut delineations in their work—between color and black and white, or in Barboza's case, between commercial and fine art photography—mirrored Jones's intrepid traversal across genres and categorical imperatives.

For instance, the artsy filming of Jones's haircut in an obscure color video from 1978 showcased the morphing of the quotidian into a fresh performative event. The fourteen-minute-long video, titled *Anton Perich Presents Grace Jones, Haircut* (1978), opens with a close-cropped shot of hairstylist Andre Martheleur, standing in a light blue button-down shirt, before quickly zooming out to show Jones sitting in a salon chair beside him.[56] The camera zeroes in on her. She is wearing red lipstick, a gold chain around her neck, and a brown unzipped jacket, suggestively ajar, without a bra. She has the same closely shaved haircut with a high-cut scalp that we saw in Smith's photograph at the same salon. Over several minutes, Jones and Martheleur banter with each other in French while he applies what appears to be Vaseline to her forehead and uses a pair of small scissors to trim her scalp. Around eight minutes in, Martheleur takes out a small makeup palette and begins painting something on the back of her head with a small brush. At one point, the camera pivots down to show Jones holding a small microphone in her hand while wearing a jumble of silver bangles, presumably the same ones worn in Lopez's *Candy Bar Wrapper Series*.

Soon after, we see that Martheleur has painted a jagged, zigzagging gold line down the back of her head; he then starts painting one of her earlobes the same color. "You like to make me bleed…suffer for beauty," Jones jokes. Randomly, she says, "Willi Smith," before switching back to French. She name-dropped the Black fashion designer who pioneered streetwear in the 1970s and the brother of model Toukie Smith, a peer of Jones. Later, she tells an off-camera patron, "You look so different with your hair down." After the woman audibly responds with resignation, Jones exclaims, "Come on, get it up. Get it up." Jones laughs, playfully sticking her tongue out, amused by her sexually suggestive double entendre. When Martheleur finishes, she stands up, looks at herself in the mirror approvingly, and puts the microphone down. Then, after a quick pivot, she and Martheleur are seen standing against a wall talking, with evident mutual affection for each other, before she turns to exit the salon-cum-stage.

Regarding genre, this video moves beyond easy classification into something less defined and amorphous. While it certainly exceeds the simple documentation of Jones's haircut, it frustrates any further desire to categorize it. Is it video art, a salon-based "happening," or something else? There is no clear-cut answer, as it could be all those things. And yet, in the context of our discussion on the staging of glamour, *Anton Perich Presents Grace Jones, Haircut* reveals a type of fashion performance in which beauty is carefully calibrated and physically produced. In short, it becomes a verb, a *doing*, rather than a noun. Beauty is a performative act. It is often refined through the input of others, a fact embodied in the working relationship between Jones and Martheleur. After all, Jones has described his skill in artistic terms elsewhere, stating that he "created paintings in my hair" and "treated my hair as though he was producing a sculpture, with incredible attention to detail." She adds, "He was more than a hairdresser. He was an artist…very experimental."[57] The video captures an "interaction-in-the-making," to use Michelle Stephens's words—an unfolding event rather than a onetime occurrence with a finite endpoint.[58] Jones's quirky magnetism is so strong that she singlehandedly transforms the seemingly banal act of a haircut into a captivating

Still from *Anton Perich Presents: Grace Jones, Haircut*, filmed haircut with Andre Martheleur, Cinandre, New York, 1978. Courtesy of Anton Perich.

display of her charisma. And when we see her smiling face reflected in the salon's mirror as Martheleur gracefully touches up her hair, she reminds us that the performance of glamour is not simply a honed skill but also a site of joy.

AIRBRUSH, SURFACE ENERGY, AND THE FEMALE MUSE

Jones's switch from model to recording artist was not a deliberate decision, though her success in the former arena helped shape her nascent ascent in the latter. As Jones recounted in Antonio Lopez's 1982 book *Antonio's Girls*, she initially envisioned herself in much less formal terms: She and her raucous creative peers prized spontaneity and the art of partying. "I always wanted to be a performer but I never thought of being a recording artist. Honey, we *all* wanted to be performers. We all used to sing. Me and Pat Cleveland used to sing together at parties. We'd make up our own songs and change harmonies…but laughingly, not seriously. I got discovered that way, singing along with a record at a party—nothin' serious."[59]

Jones's shift to a different medium of artistic expression had more to do with chance encounters and luck than a hatched-out plan—it was a shift seemingly as improvised as her and Cleveland's impromptu duets. However, as she became a musical artist, what *was* intentional was how Jones was visually represented to audiences. The avatar of Jones that surfaced in Smith's Studio 54 photograph is a clue here: an undeniably dramatic appearance, the hint of performative skills, all in a collage-like hybrid of paint and photography. Jones was a force field of energy, a figure whose presence was so strong she could inspire other artists, like Smith, to elevate their craft to new levels, reaching across one genre and embracing another.[60] She was also at ease in discos, spaces that "owed much to a gay aesthetic. The discos of the period were amalgams of gay culture, dress-up, role-playing, and self-expression."[61] The task, then, was creating something that could harness all of this: Jones's fluidity in movement, her unusual appearance, her aesthetic affinity with queer club culture, and her ability to seemingly bend the energy of spaces (and artistic forms) to her will.

While Jones would practice and hone this harnessing for the next few decades, one stunning example is her artistic collaboration with commercial illustrator Richard Bernstein. Over the course of several years, Bernstein produced fizzy airbrushed visuals in high-octane color; this work gleefully collapsed the boundary between popular and high art sensibilities, pinballing between queer subcultures and mainstream celebrity. Jones and Bernstein were first introduced by her managers, Sy and Eileen Berlin. According to Jones, the Berlins knew Bernstein because he designed an album cover for their band Black Soul—the American debut of the seven-piece disco-funk group from France by way of Senegal—and thought he would be perfect for her. Upon meeting, Jones was confident that Bernstein "definitely understood the tone of my image," adding that they "became best, best, best friends immediately. He was just so creative, always coming up with things we should try and experiment with."[62] As a result, Bernstein was entrusted to create the cover art for Jones's single "I Need a Man," a queer anthem that later became a hit single, and her debut album *Portfolio*, released September 6, 1977.

In yet another example of the porous art-making of the era, it was Jones's previous work with other photographers in their loose network of peers that

Bernstein made the basis for his soon-to-be iconic airbrushed album covers. In her words, "I had some photos from Paris that Antonio [Lopez] had taken, and these were the ones Richard treated in the way he had treated Andy Warhol's *Interview* covers. Around that time, we also used photographs that the wonderful, incredibly modest Bill Cunningham took of me making my way around the streets of New York, long before anyone knew who I was."[63] Cunningham and Lopez, let us recall, were close friends and neighbors in the late 1960s, when Lopez and Juan Ramos lived in the artist studios above Carnegie Hall. Jones's subtle words suggest that Bernstein's embellished portrayals of Jones should also be interpreted as palimpsests, building on the largely invisible labor of other image-makers. (A Lopez photograph also served as the basis for the cover art Bernstein produced for her 1978 album *Fame*.) This idea of the palimpsest, a partial erasure and rewriting of a text to make room for another, is a valuable analogue for the collective art-making we find again and again. It suggests that sedimented layers of materials, meanings, histories, and friendships underpin all these representations. Moreover, it is a perfect metaphor for Bernstein's artistic process, which was built of literal layers—he applied collaged elements, gouache, colored pencil, and pastel to these photographs before the final flourish of airbrush. Hence, even the visual construction of Grace Jones—an arresting image if ever there was one—was only possible through a collaborative effort in which Bernstein's chromatically luminous aesthetic signature *enhanced* Lopez and Cunningham's preexisting photographs of Jones.

From this foundation, Bernstein's cover art for "I Need a Man" and *Portfolio* became critical forebears for Jones's evolving commercial image and harbingers of the visual mythmaking she increasingly became known for. For instance, the foreground of "I Need a Man" featured a frontal image of Jones with a soft gaze, complemented by yellow and pale blue eyeshadow-esque coloring around her eyes and magenta blush-like coloring on her cheeks. (Intriguingly, it also shares hair stylist Andre Martheleur's emphasis on colorful makeup for Jones.) Initially set against a solid black backdrop, the vinyl record cover shows Jones's facial portrait against a bright pink background, with her name and the song title listed at the top in looping curlicues, a barely legible cursive. Again, we see the recurrence of a vibrant hot pink as the hue of choice for our motley crew of artists, models, and performers—be it the tape-cum-ribbon gracing Victor Fernandez's face in Lopez's *Ribbon Series* or the wavy patterns of paint in Smith's Studio 54 portrait. To use

Cover design for Grace Jones's single "I Need a Man," 1976. Courtesy of the Estate of Richard Bernstein.

Roland Barthes's term, the punctum that bursts forth is Jones's slightly parted lips; they have a wet sparkle that seems to emanate from the cover, a lusciousness that feels tactile. Manufactured by Bernstein to mimic a lacquered patina—like a coat of freshly applied lip gloss on steroids—the shellac-like surface of these lips creates a trompe l'oeil effect. The fleshly materiality is undeniably synthetic. This aesthetic manipulation of shine, the medium through which the visual and sensorial merge, produces yet another haptic rendering of Jones that, in its excess, breaches the bounds of one sense and travels to another.[64]

Similarly, for *Portfolio*, Bernstein used a black-and-white photograph taken in the early 1970s while she was living and working in Paris. Lopez and fashion photographer Francis Ing took the picture for Jones's modeling portfolio. (The album's name is a riff on this.) Juxtaposed against a turquoise background, Jones's edgy graphic look is amplified again by airbrushing approximating makeup. Fuchsia and purple shading decorate her cheekbones, and subtle, sealike tones of blue, green, and violet line her eyes like smudged eyeshadow. Positioned in the foreground, Jones's disembodied face seems to erupt out of the bright blue setting. Jones is given the seductive sheen of commercial illustration in Bernstein's technological enhancement and recontextualization of the original photograph. The cover was accompanied by three more portraits: dual interior images of a front-facing Jones set against separate leopard-print and floral backdrops, and a profile shot of Jones on the back cover with her head tilted back and her tongue stuck out. Together, the four images played with the idea of Jones's multiple stage personae. They also presented Jones to consumers as a star emerging from New York City–based gay discos, with her malleable likeness being a site of otherworldly glamour and visual exuberance.

Bernstein's subsequent work with Jones for the rest of the 1970s reveals how they collaborated. Besides prominently featuring her in a 1977 Bloomingdale's poster he designed to celebrate the eponymous label Kenzo (Japanese-born fashion designer Kenzo Takada was also a peer of Jones), Bernstein created all the album art for what would eventually be a disco trilogy. In addition to *Portfolio* (1977), these included *Fame* (1978), released at the apex of disco's popularity; and *Muse* (1979), the latter's title an explicit nod to Jones's ostensible role for Bernstein. For all three albums, he also devised back covers and gatefold art. (Gatefold albums, which unfold into two panels, were often used as a larger canvas to present the imagery of a musical artist.) In addition, he fashioned the cover art for the 12-inch singles "Do or Die" (1978) and "On Your Knees" (1979). He also devised select pieces in Jones's stage attire during this period. For instance, according to Jones, when she performed her 1977 single "La Vie en rose" at the Met Gala, Bernstein "designed my show, dressing me up as a multicolored luminescent chandelier in a tribute to the artist Erté."[65]

However, even the delight of making art with your friends can become complicated, and their friendship, like most, was not without pauses or friction—whether due to the assumed dynamics of the artist-muse relationship or the

Original mechanical art for the cover of Grace Jones's debut album, *Portfolio*, 1977. Courtesy of the Estate of Richard Bernstein.

petty jealousies to which even great artists are not immune. Jones, for instance, was fully aware of her role as artistic fodder for Bernstein's inspired flights of fancy and certainly benefited from his expertise. But she was not always pleased by the assumption that came with it—that she was nothing more than a static aesthetic surface, lacking any expertise of her own, simply at the whim of the recognized male artist. I discuss this in more detail shortly. Moreover, in a rare example of peers *stopping* work with each other, Bernstein and Jones temporarily halted their collaborations when she became artistically

Inside gatefold art for *Portfolio*, 1977. Courtesy of the Estate of Richard Bernstein.

and romantically involved with Jean-Paul Goude, a graphic designer and former *Esquire* editor. We can speculate that neither Bernstein nor Goude wanted to share Jones as a muse. Perhaps due to this mutual possessiveness, the hiatus lasted until the late 1980s—not coincidentally, after Jones and Goude's romance had ended.

Still, the array of projects Jones and Bernstein collaborated on, while extensive, only hints at the depth of their friendship. Thomas Holbrook, manager of Jones's onetime paramour, actor Dolph Lundgren, states, "Richard was a dear, dear friend of Grace's and he gave guidance on virtually everything from costumes to inspiration to career advice. He was instrumental

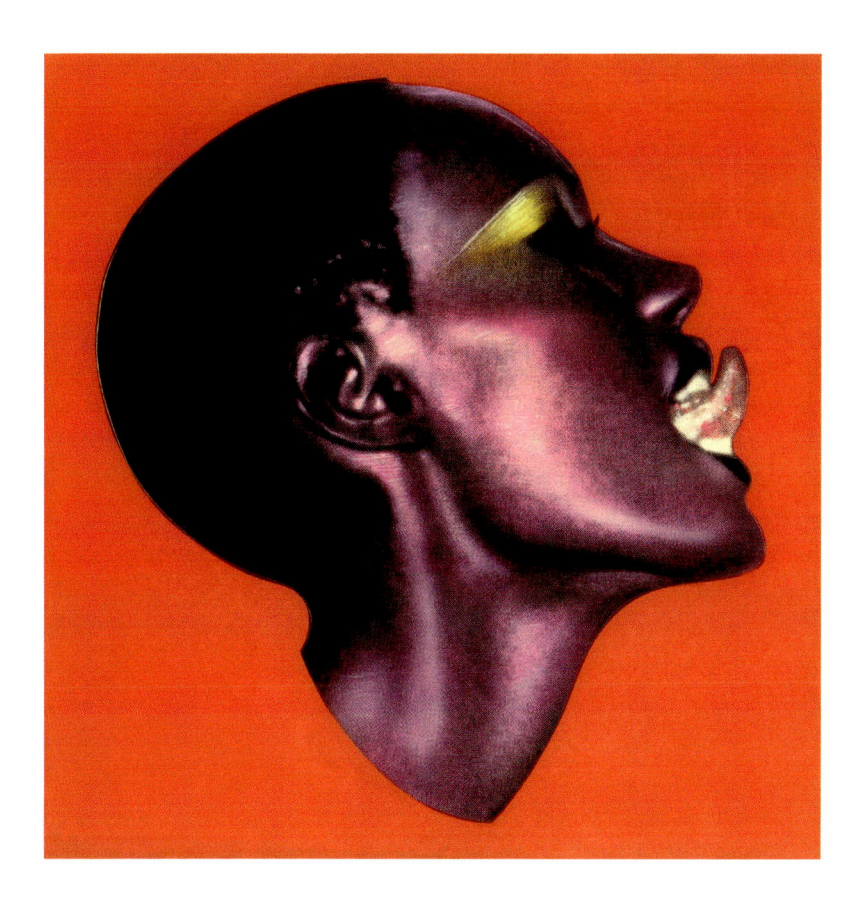

Original mechanical art for the back cover of *Portfolio*, 1977. Courtesy of the Estate of Richard Bernstein.

in everything she did—not just on the art of her album covers but everything."[66] This rapport was further exemplified by the fact that Jones served as Bernstein's unofficial and protective "art mother." She recalls, for instance, that she occasionally accompanied Bernstein to Warhol's Factory, at his request, because he'd be "nervous about showing his work there"—specifically his *Interview* covers, which had to be routinely approved by Warhol before their publication.[67] Subsequently, when Jones and Goude later had a child together, a son named Paolo, Jones named Bernstein Paolo's godfather and "art father." (Paolo's other "art father" was graffiti artist Keith Haring, Jones's close friend and occasional collaborator.) This minor detail belies its importance. It is illustrative of how the process of collective creating, so instrumental to Lopez's web of interlocutors in the previous chapter, is broadened out here, to the extent that Jones's cohort reinvented kinship terms *through* their aesthetic practices while extending that sense of an artistic collective to the next generation.

Given that Bernstein was instrumental in suturing Jones's exceptional looks to her burgeoning commercial image as a musical artist, their artistic partnership in the late 1970s is worth meditating on, especially since style was the engine of Bernstein's aesthetic enterprise. Following a primarily male tradition of image-based performers—such as the "King of Rock and Roll" Elvis Presley and his signature gold lamé suit of 1957, or glam rocker David Bowie's androgynous stage outfits created by Japanese designer Kansai Yamamoto for his 1973 Ziggy Stardust Tour—Richard Bernstein was instrumental in shaping Jones's visual image as an alluring disco diva. That Bernstein accomplished this with a dark-skinned Black diasporic woman is truly remarkable. In Nicole Fleetwood's verbiage, Jones became a *racial icon*.[68] As she argues, a racial icon often must perform a different kind of labor: They are perceived as a visual symbol of historical progress (especially regarding racism) while, often and without choice, being made a role model for their race. That elevation, however, does not insulate them from the harsh bite of racism, something Jones knew. Nonetheless, Bernstein's colorful airbrushed album covers are evidence of my larger argument about the power of artistic style, as just a few images helped make her phenomenally recognizable.

In contrast to the earlier, more "natural" portrayals of Jones, such as Smith's understated portrait of her at Cinandre in 1975, Jones's performances in the late 1970s—and Bernstein's resultant imagery—were pure "camp." Fundamentally reflecting a queer sensibility, Jones's shtick embraced the principal attributes of camp—self-aware irony, artifice, and detached theatricality.[69] Francesca Royster concisely characterizes what Jones was becoming: a "heady cocktail of glitter, camp, androgyny, and fear" and, for a white gay subculture, a "fitting muse for the space of the polyamorously perverse disco."[70] After all, Jones often performed in gay discos where her bawdy stage antics and lyrical sexual innuendos made her a club culture icon. Jean-Paul Goude first saw Jones perform at Les Mouches. She was topless and wearing a prom skirt: "That night she was singing her hit song, 'I Need a Man,' to a room full of shrieking gay bobbysoxers. The ambiguity of her act was that she herself *looked* like a man, a man singing 'I Need a Man' to a bunch of men. No wonder the fruit bars loved her!"[71] Music journalist Barry Walters describes a parallel dynamic in a 1977 performance at 12 West, a members-only gay disco: "Tough and lusty, Grace Jones sang 'I Need a Man' just like a man might, a woman who was not just singing to them, but *for* them, *as* them. Jones, an icon and cultural force, is as queer as a relatively straight person gets."[72] Thus, Jones employed camp as a vehicle for her flamboyant self-expression. Yet, as implied above, camp was associated with and recognized by queer subcultures, even if the link was not overt to more mainstream audiences. Jones's radicality as a performer, in part, was her flagrant disregard for social norms; she knowingly used a queer aesthetic sensibility to express her sexual longing while embracing her female masculinity. At the same time, she enabled gay men to speak to their lust for one another through her. In this sense, Jones also acted as a conduit for sexual minorities whose open display of same-sex desire was still verboten in many public places, as Walters implies.[73]

"But in its original and Blackest manifestation," Hafizah Augustus Geter writes, "Camp is a way of looking, one that shifts whose gaze has power as well as *who* can be at the center of the political project we call beauty."[74] This sentiment subtly critiques the perception of camp as an erudite sensibility whose assumed audience and progenitors were exclusively white gay men. But it also reminds us that Bernstein's disco album art framed Jones as an object of uncommon beauty. In this way, Bernstein's images are part of a continuum of visual representations—from Smith, Barboza, Lopez, Cunningham, and undoubtedly many others—that centered Jones as a commanding object of the gaze and a dashing figure. In the numerous images of her, she does many different things, but in all of them, she is implicitly or explicitly subverting narrow ideals of racialized beauty. Identical to Lopez and Smith's gravitation to punchy hot pink, Bernstein favored stimulating, artificially produced colors, shades "defying the 'natural' color codes of conventionality in order to highlight artifice, and hence exaggerate a sense of difference."[75] Jones concurs, noting that "Richard softened and sweetened me. For a while, looking at the disco sleeves and the way Richard colored me green, navy, blue, charcoal, you wouldn't have known what color I was."[76] Bernstein subtly displayed his skill at visually translating Jones's cosmopolitan fashion sense and campy histrionics into a buoyant, airbrushed fantasia led by the ever-stylish disco doyenne.

Moreover, his aesthetic portrayal of Jones echoed his work as the in-house illustrator for *Interview*, Andy Warhol's magazine. In the late 1960s, Warhol

Inside gatefold art for Grace Jones's album *Muse*, 1979. Courtesy of the Estate of Richard Bernstein.

urged Bernstein, an aspiring painter, to move exclusively into commercial work. The advice came during a formative exchange at Max's Kansas City, the artist hangout that, as we will soon see, was also frequented by Stephen Burrows and his posse. Bernstein eventually designed posters for Warhol's experimental films *Women in Revolt* (1971), *Heat* (1972), and *L'Amour* (1973). Meanwhile, as *Interview* shifted from its 1969 debut as a film journal to a breezy chronicle of celebrities in the 1970s, Warhol hired Bernstein to redesign the logo and create commissioned artwork for the covers. Those artsy covers featured a dazzling array of young pop stars, Hollywood actors, and models, all given Bernstein's airbrushed luster.[77]

Pat Cleveland—who was featured, holding a tape recorder, on one such cover in July 1972—recalled, "They had just started doing those color covers at *Interview*. Donna Jordan had the first color cover, and I had the second one. It was so *glamorous*. We were all partying together all the time, and work and play was the same thing."[78] Jordan, Cleveland, and Jones (who first appeared in the magazine in 1977 and then on the cover in 1984) were all part of Lopez's model cohort, nicknamed Antonio's Girls; Jordan also performed with Cleveland in Fiorucci's store windows. Cleveland fondly recalls the period, reminiscing that "we had such a hot gang of friends. Stephen Burrows and

Cover design for Grace Jones's "Do or Die" 12-inch single, 1978. Courtesy of the Estate of Richard Bernstein.

Halston and Richard Bernstein and Calvin Klein."[79] Interestingly, her words reaffirm the common perception of this era in New York City: a superficial in-group of young, physically attractive people who leveraged those qualities to socialize with others like themselves. Cleveland does not dispute this account even as she offers that, for her tribe, partying and art-making flowed into each other like a Möbius strip.

She further clarifies, "Richard Bernstein made those glamour covers. Andy didn't do the covers. Richard did."[80] This insight implies that Warhol may have wanted to get credit for everything related to his magazine.

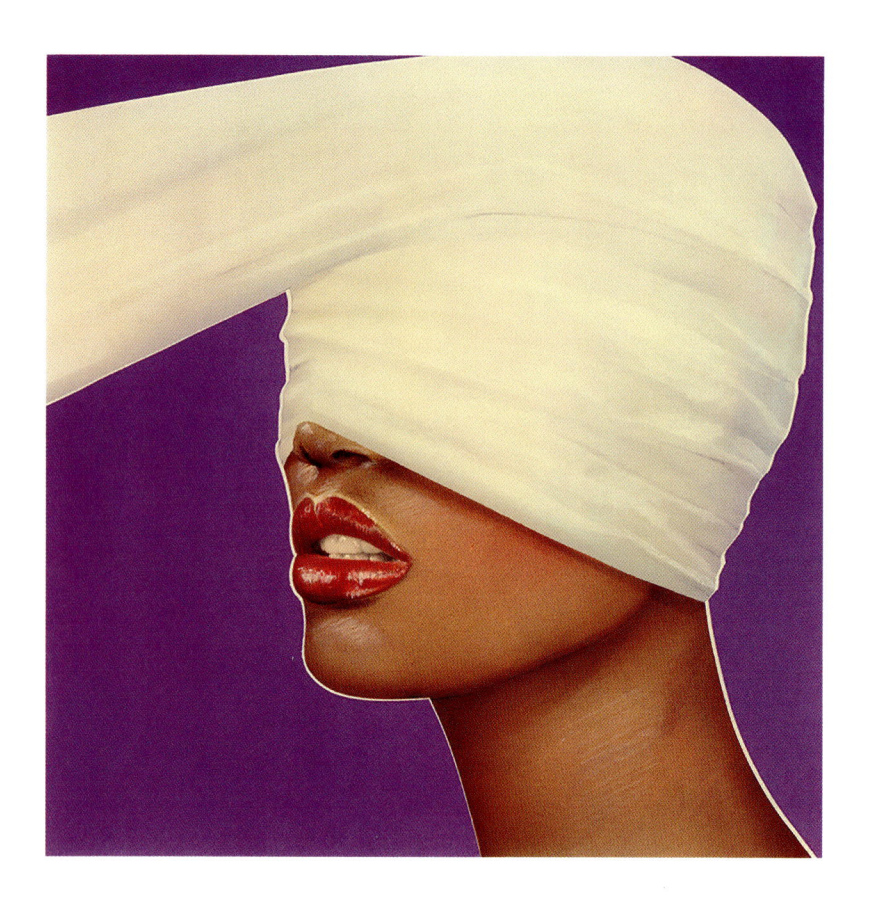

Cover design for Grace Jones's "On Your Knees" 12-inch single, 1979. Courtesy of the Estate of Richard Bernstein.

Cleveland's subtle words also suggest something more profound: that Warhol, the power broker of sorts, was *not* a part of the horizontal art-making collectives I focus on. After all, "*Interview* became both a vehicle *and* advertisement for Warhol," recalled Bob Colacello, who ran the periodical in the 1970s.[81] Warhol, in other words, was less than enthusiastic about the day-to-day particulars of operating a magazine; he was more intrigued at being a part of, or at the center of, the glitterati that *Interview* feverishly documented. Cleveland, Bernstein, Jones, and others had something different—they had a sense of community, stuck up for one another, were scrappy, and created

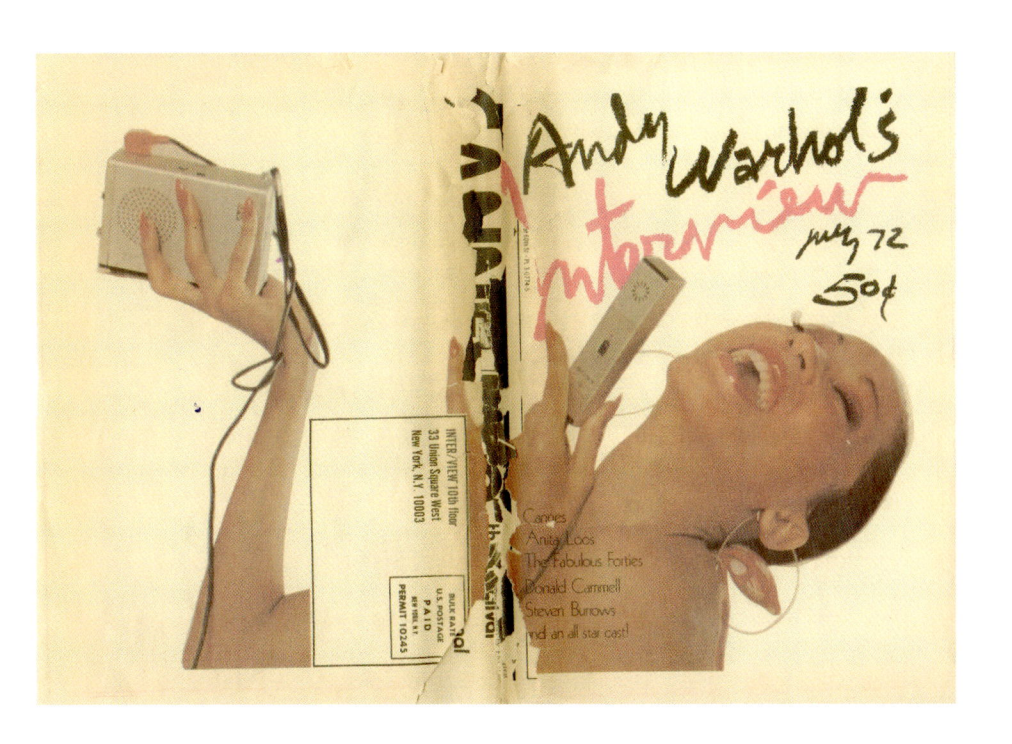

Pat Cleveland cover of *Andy Warhol's Interview*, July 1972. Courtesy of the Estate of Richard Bernstein.

together. And while some were more public-facing, others labored behind the scenes, like the shy Bernstein. But he was featured in the magazine in May 1973. Smiling casually in a black-and-white photograph, he was pictured with his tool of aesthetic innovation: his airbrush.

The surfeit of visual embellishment in Bernstein's portraits of Jones and other celebrities warrants more consideration, particularly in revealing the seemingly decorative as an atypical form of collective dissent. After all, "Stars are glossy to begin with. That's why they're stars—they shine a little bit brighter. And Richard made them shinier," his friend David Croland, a fellow artist and party regular, remarks.[82] As I discussed in the previous chapter, while style is typically understood as merely ornamental, it is often the medium through which subcultural groups speak, albeit more obliquely—such as via "loud" colors. "Style encoded political messages to those in the know which were otherwise unintelligible" due to their ambiguity, Kobena Mercer states.[83] In this manner, we perceive the politics of style. With the emergence of a distinctive avant-garde, art historian Thomas Crow suggests, a small group of artists and supporters become an oppositional public. As he argues, this subculture's "inarticulate and unresolved dissatisfactions" are reflected in the various discrete spaces that "though designed to contain them, also put them on display."[84] This rumbling discontent frequently manifests through style, whether it is rebellious forms of bodily self-presentation, a distinctive visual grammar, or a combination of both.

Put differently, if we see these horizontal networks as creating a community to reject mainstream sentiments, what if Bernstein's colorful, airbrushed faces are coded responses to the political tumult of the time? Jones suggests as much when she situates Bernstein's work, alongside Warhol's obsession with fame, as indicative of a need for diversion from the everyday newsreel of disaster, misconduct, and crumbling public trust. In her memoirs, she writes, "It was all part of the same sense of making entertainment for a world craving pleasure and escape larger, bolder, brasher, and more energetically enchanting. The unsettling growing chaos of the threatening, corrupt, and paranoid world out there, all the political scandals and indefinite war and crises, needed to be kept at bay. Presidents and governments were cracking up; people needed to look after themselves and create their own rules and customs."[85] Jones's description of an unstable political landscape seems opposed to these images' carefree tone. Their projected aesthetic qualities—a preoccupation with surface, color, and visual texture—align with the mostly young, hot, and fashionable people the magazine celebrated. In other words, this visual imagery seemingly takes pleasure in its superficiality and lack of meaning, as the elusive gleam of fame was the goal. However, Jones's alternative reading implies this picture may be more complicated. For instance, disco's swift decline in popularity in 1979 was coded as rejecting the musical genre's soullessness. The reality, however, was that the source of ire was the types of performers (i.e., racial and sexual minorities) who thrived in it. Admittedly, Jones's words may not be convincing to some present-day readers. While she, Bernstein, and some mutual friends circulated in a downtown orbit of young creatives, they also enjoyed unfettered access to a celebrity den like Studio 54 and its exclusive social networks. In short, these figures don't seem to occupy an oppositional public. Still, Jones's hint of a latent political underpinning implies that a pointed refusal of the present lurked within, or partly motivated, these images. The hazy aura of celebrity offered in Bernstein's Technicolor fantasies partly stemmed from this escapist urge, a reprieve from the "now" in exchange for the "new."

Jones's lengthy interpretation of Bernstein's artistic technique in her memoirs is insightful on multiple registers, particularly as we ponder the relationship between these subcultures and the mainstream. Jones recalls that Bernstein was the "link between old Hollywood glamour and the more subversive, nebulous glamour of the new underground art scene," suggesting how avant-garde artists often borrowed from low forms associated with popular experience.[86] By doing so, as Crow underlines, these artists skillfully manipulated this seemingly nonartistic material "to displace and estrange the deadening givens of accepted practice" and hence renew themselves.[87] Later, in her memoirs, when describing Bernstein's artistic style, she offers us an interpretative clue: "That was a different style of enchantment, reflecting the world as it was at the time in New York and Paris, in the clubs, in the night, in the world and Factory of Warhol, the unraveling of a very specific form of surface energy."[88]

While Jones's employment of the word *enchantment* is intriguing, with its suggestion of a kind of mysterious alchemy forged in Bernstein's studio, I am more interested in her concept of "surface energy." It is a suitable description of the record album art Bernstein produced for her, transforming her into a fabricated surface effect. Viewed collectively, Jones's disco album covers and gatefold art delight in overlays of textured surfaces that push at representational limits and proudly show their "visual seams."[89] Monochromatic color panels, images of Jones where her skin has been tinted a synthetic color, metallicized finishes that recall the gleam of custom car paint, and graphic typography all merge in his ebullient images of her. Meanwhile, the cover of her second album, *Fame*, was a visual representation of three colored pencils resting over Jones's drawn portrait, literalizing this idea of her as an artistic surface.[90] Bernstein's artistic flourishes produced a surface-oriented notion of the self. As I argued elsewhere, this counterintuitive understanding of surface can operate as a strategy; minoritarian performers, like Jones, manipulated bodily and synthetic surfaces to foil the demand for transparency and readability.[91] However, there is also the risk of something more complex and potentially harmful when Bernstein converted Jones, his aesthetic object, into a lavishly rendered surface. Depth and interiority were absent; instead, she became campy artifice, flatness, and sumptuous excess.[92] Jones was presented primarily as a spectacular technical *effect*. Her visual subjectivity arose in a highly aestheticized space, where her photographic image repeatedly served as the template for Bernstein's optical maximalism.

Jones retrospectively expresses irritation at both Bernstein's overt indication that she was his muse and its subtle implication: that she was a passive participant in a one-way artistic exchange. This sentiment emerges when she discusses her 1979 album *Muse*. In her words, "Richard wanted me to be his muse, no one else's. I didn't like the idea of a Svengali/muse thing. I wasn't a muse. That seemed so passive and uninvolved. It was Richard who named my third album *Muse*. I was amused to be a muse, and that was something else to try on, but it wasn't important to me to be one. I wanted to collaborate with artists on an equal footing. I was interested in being a part of the process, not simply a decoration to be manipulated."[93] Jones evinces full awareness of her perceived role in their artistic partnership, in which Bernstein was the recognized artist while she was the pliable object of his technical know-how. Her critique is partly a rebuke of the underlying gender dynamics of this relationship—the docile female muse who stimulates the imagination of the genius male artist.

Undoubtedly, there were racial tensions at play as well. After all, her "image and the draw of her black body are indeed the perfect inspiration for white male artists to enact their fetishistic fantasies," Ricardo Montez argues; Jones acted as "the perfect figure for their ideas of perfection."[94] Montez explicitly refers to Keith Haring and Jean-Paul Goude: both utilized her supple physicality as a screen, or a literal canvas in Haring's case, through which they projected their primitivist ideals. Haring and Goude hyperaestheticized Jones's racial difference, especially her dark brown skin. As a result, they toed the line between subverting racialized visual stereotypes and reinforcing them. In contrast, Bernstein's work aligned more with someone like Ming Smith, emphasizing Jones's chic nightlife glamour and the exquisite curvilinearity of her facial structure. His renderings merged Jones's savvy self-performance with his artistic competence, creating tableaus of riotous color and luxurious surfaces. But again, considering the muse-artist relationship between Jones and Bernstein as gendered and racialized gestures toward the dilemma posed by Black queer subjects "perform[ing] for and against the camera," to use Tavia Nyong'o's formulation, where the promise of the camera—as a means to visibility—can be illusory, and maybe even ultimately damaging.[95]

Our continued emphasis on the underappreciated role of community in the artistic process is vital here, particularly in recognizing the labor of models. With Antonio Lopez, we saw that a more horizontal approach to art-making, which recognizes his artistic work in different genres on equal footing, refutes vertical hierarchies of value. This sentiment is also true here. Models, visual artists, photographers, and stylists are commensurate participants in creative exchange. Therefore, perceiving modeling as an important, albeit underrecognized, form of affective labor is critical to a more balanced understanding of the artistic act. The embodied "work" of the model is not simply the artful act of posing or the adept manipulation of the body as a flexible corporeal medium. Models also produce feelings in their viewers, working in tandem with photographers, art directors, and copy editors. As we know, this transmission of feeling between models and viewers is explicitly designed (though not always) to advertise consumer goods. Nonetheless, this facility in summoning a range of affective responses in others is often the invisible labor of the model.

Peeling back the layers of Bernstein's disco imagery reveals the collective hands at play in their production: his airbrushing, Lopez and Ing's modeling shots, Cunningham's candid street photography, *and* Jones's prowess as a model. In short, an artistic community is the fulcrum of Bernstein's zippy visual reverie. What is less clear is whether Bernstein himself acknowledged this notion of community art-making or was more interested in the vertical hierarchies of value that Jones, Smith, and Lopez were refuting. For instance, did he talk explicitly about working with Lopez or Cunningham? Did he fully acknowledge how his airbrushing and drawing were layered on their photographs? Or did he subscribe to the notion of a singular genius often ascribed to and espoused by white male artists? Strikingly, I could not locate Bernstein's own words on any of these matters. Was this a willful occlusion? Or was it simply a historical circumstance—a failure to preserve the artist's testimony? Ultimately, we do not know, just as we can only speculate how his assessment of the collaboration with Jones would have differed from hers.

There is a surviving photograph from Studio 54, circa 1981, that may give a hint.[96] In it, Bernstein is seated in the middle of a long sofa, holding a wineglass and cigarette, facing a smiling Jones. Andy Warhol and Keith Haring are sitting next to Bernstein on the left side of the image. Lopez's face is seen on the far-right side of the image, one of his hands resting on the blazer of Michael Vollbracht, a fashion designer and illustrator who designed shopping bags for Bloomingdale's in the 1970s. Was *this* Bernstein's preferred artistic community? It's a mystery compounded by Jones being the only person in the image still alive. But we do know that, despite photographing Jones at Studio 54, Ming Smith wasn't part of that world; she noted as much in her discussion with me. Thus, even if Smith and Bernstein thought of themselves as participating in community art-making, there does not seem to be convergence between the groups they were part of besides Jones herself.

That dichotomy is mainly due to the difference between Jones and Smith's peer-to-peer relationship as Black models and Bernstein's more top-down approach, which Jones took issue with despite her obvious affection for him. Photographer Ming Smith, let us recall, understood what modeling entailed because she worked behind and in front of the lens. This instinctive comprehension of modeling's various skill sets is perhaps why the fraught word *muse* does not surface. Smith intuitively knew the microchoreographies implicit in modeling, such as quickly adjusting the tilt of one's head or shifting how one's face catches the light. Therefore, while Jones's quip relays her annoyance at Bernstein's failure to recognize her acumen, it also illustrates her fight to have her artistic contributions as a model of color recognized, especially when working with white male artists.

Jones's insistence on "being part of the process" is vague; still, her desire to recast the presumed roles of artist and muse—into a mutually beneficial and symbiotic relationship—is noteworthy. It hints at her gnawing trepidation that becoming a form of decorative "surface energy" at the behest of others may render her, to audiences, an inert muse "authored" by accomplished artists, but lacking any agency of her own. Jones was walking a proverbial tightrope in her performance of objecthood, consenting to be an aesthetic object while attempting not to succumb to total objectification. It suggests that, while she relished the aesthetic transformation that her peers imparted on her image, she viewed herself as an equal participant in shaping it. And she, too, viewed herself as an artist, full stop. Moreover, Jones's rejection of the role of a muse implies her wariness of a common misperception: that her subjectivity was completely evacuated from visual representations of her. Instead, she suggests that Bernstein needed to rejigger his limited understanding of the creative process. In doing so, he would scrap the artist-muse frame altogether and embrace a different approach, where the prototypical notion of labor was enlarged to include the more immaterial and elusive "doings" of the Black model.

SERVING DOWNTOWN ATTITUDE AT PARADISE GARAGE

In closing, I turn to a final example of Jones's labor as a model and the artistic community supporting it: her baby shower at the downtown disco Paradise Garage on September 25, 1979, jointly hosted by Andy Warhol and Blondie front woman Debbie Harry. The "disco baby shower," as the press dubbed it, began at 4:00 a.m. and celebrated the impending birth of Jones and Jean-Paul Goude's son, Paolo—their "rhythm baby," as Jones loosely referred to him in utero. Jones and her friend Keith Haring were frequent habitués of the Garage, the latter noting its spiritual significance. (In 1985, Haring also painted Jones's body for a performance there, photographed by friend-artist Tseng Kwong Chi.)[97] Paradise Garage, located at 84 King Street in SoHo, opened in January 1978. Guests entered the former parking structure by walking "in through a garage door and up a ramp with light bulbs on either side that looked like a runway or an old-fashioned marquee," recalled Juan Rivera, Haring's boyfriend at the time.[98] The vast, ten-thousand-square-foot industrial space housed an enormous dance floor, easily fitting two thousand partyers, a lounge, and a rooftop for revelers to relax. Instead of alcohol, the club offered abundant fruit and a punch bowl spiked with acid for its loyal tribe.[99]

The "legendary underground disco," affectionately dubbed the Garage, increasingly became known for the eclectic crowd it attracted; it was where "black and Latino gay youth, vogueing drag queen divas, straight-identified 'bangee' boys, and homeless and thrown-away kids stomped, sweated, and swirled with music business insiders and up-and-coming media celebrities," according to Arnaldo Cruz-Malavé.[100] Other attendees concur that it was a space of utter freedom and queer kinship. "Back then, it was still underground. Gay and trans people felt safe there—even on Fridays, which was the 'straight' night," said Michele Saunders, a photographers' agent who became part of a coterie of dancers at the club who met weekly in the Fashion District to select fabrics for their looks: "It was like a family, and once you were inside, you were free. You could do whatever you wanted."[101]

The main draw was its breathtaking sound system, arguably the best in New York City, and resident DJ Larry Levan, who spun records on Friday and Saturday nights and meticulously studied the disco's decor, acoustics, and audio equipment. Like Lopez and Jones's cohorts, Brooklyn-born and -bred Levan approached throwing a party as an art form; he made sure the floors were waxed and often shined the mirror ball himself, hoisting himself on a ladder.[102] A rebellious high-school dropout, Levan briefly became a dressmaker in the Harlem drag ball scene. It was there, in 1969, that he met his best friend Francis Nichols, who would become DJ Frankie Knuckles, the "Godfather of House Music."

Working alongside Nichols, Levan began his career as a decorator for Nicky Siano's SoHo disco, the Gallery, in 1972. It was a venue that Jones and fashion designers Stephen Burrows and Willi Smith attended and the first place Levan was invited to DJ. Soon after, Levan amassed a following as a DJ at the Continental Baths, SoHo Place, and Reade Street before arriving at the Garage. As Tim Lawrence argues, Levan became the first massive name among New York City–based DJs and introduced a sense of drama into nightlife.[103] And Levan's fierce and unpredictable mastery—expertly splicing disco, R & B, new wave, rock, and even gospel to create ecstatic highs—complemented Jones's equally bold intensity. "Everything Grace released was a hit at the Garage because she was the female Larry. She was crazy, she was wild, she was daring, and Larry was like that as a DJ," observed DJ David DePino.[104]

Levan was a sonic architect whose rapturous mixes defined the ethos of Paradise Garage, an incubator of the "new," where style was created and refined in real time by a Black and Brown, and primarily queer, cognoscenti. Elevated above the crowd in his DJ booth, Levan delivered wide-ranging sets that crested in surging aural waves over his audiences. He favored percussive rhythms, brash beats, and sassy soulful female vocalists, funky music full of attitude that created new social choreographies—what Lawrence describes as "unfolding relations of energy, force, and motion"—on the padded dance floor.[105] The music and liberatory environment were a glove-like fit for the expressive form of "voguing," a competitive queer ballroom practice dedicated to creating lines in the body that emulated postures seen in fashion magazines like *Vogue*. Paradise Garage, as a downtown sonic playground where Black and Brown innovation reigned, was the ideal venue for Jones, its unofficial mistress of ceremonies, to stage a fresh aesthetic breakthrough.

As Goude recalled, Jones needed to promote her new record *Muse* but was seven months pregnant, so he devised a solution to this logistic challenge: "the ultimate maternity dress."[106] In his words, "I decided to go to Antonio [Lopez] and ask him to design a Cubist, geometric, Japanese origami dress," a massive garment that ended up being ten feet tall.[107] Lopez's dress was built mainly using cardboard sheets covered in swaths of brightly colored fabric to form angular planes around Jones's protruding belly. At the same time, her torso was further obscured underneath a long column of black fabric.[108] A sizeable blue triangle jutting out past one of her shoulders was echoed by an oversized red, white, and yellow triangular hat adorned with a red exclamation point. The hat's visual punctuation was likely an allusion to the description of Jones coined by *Ebony* that year: "Grace Jones is a question mark followed by an exclamation point."[109] Goude recalled, "She looked just like a sculpture."[110] Intriguingly, with this description, we again see the tendency of Jones's white male collaborators to view her as an ornamental object. However, for maximum visual effect, he hoped to create the appearance of levity despite Jones's pregnant mass and the sheer size of the dress itself. To do so, he placed Jones on a platform and then had "the sculpture glide on rollers on the floor across the stage, the rollers and the bottom of the dress being hidden by a screen of dry ice. The effect was quite extraordinary."[111]

Surviving photo documentation of Jones performing in the garment beautifully evokes our theme of style.[112] Lopez's dress directly referenced Bauhaus, which emphasized geometric shapes and primary-color schemes, evinced by the toylike shades of red, blue, and yellow. Jones's splayed fuchsia fan added an element of feminine glamour and visual drama. Meanwhile, in a continuation from the last chapter, we see the recurrence of bricolage, or a "making do" with available materials, to produce a sum more extensive than its motley parts. Again, the readily accessible—cardboard and fabric—are elevated beyond their mere use value. Instead, they are reconfigured as hypercolorful surfaces, set at sharp angles, that attempt to emulate the craftsmanship of Japanese origami. Together, they present a striking bodily morphology of jarring juxtapositions and multiple planes of color that transform her into an iconoclastic living sculpture, echoing Goude's words. In short, Jones emerges as an unmistakably modern figure who effortlessly embodies a jumble of artistic references while merging Eastern and Western influences. Here, we gain a definitive sense of her style—or at least this iteration—since her style has changed repeatedly. This style reveled in the synthesis of the visually radical, hard-edged, and couture-like, melding exaggerated volumes that morphed, rather than naturally mimicked, the proportions of the body, with bright antinaturalistic colors and flat surfaces without depth. It took pleasure in its artificiality and overabundance while displaying an avant-garde downtown sensibility that favored rule-breaking over established tradition in its collapse

Grace Jones's maternity dress, New York, 1979. Created in collaboration with Antonio Lopez. Courtesy of Jean-Paul Goude.

of the lines between art, fashion, design, and performance. (A lyric from Jones's 1980 cover of the Pretenders' "Private Life" comes to mind: "I'm very superficial / I hate everything official.")[113]

Moreover, as Iván A. Ramos and Joshua Javier Guzmán remind us, the static medium of photography depends on the photographed subject's active posing or performance.[114] This sentiment is essential because Jones's calibration of her physical body helps create the illusion of monumentality captured here. In other words, her dynamic figure and adept ability to perform glamour, traits we explored above, unite the disparate elements of the dress into a coherent whole. Jones does not simply wear the maternity dress; she *activates* it. She enlivens it with her distinctive presence and showcases how her gifts as a performer and model, combined with Lopez's sartorial skills and Goude's graphic and set design talents, create art where, to paraphrase Ramon Lobato's argument, the excess of style is the work's substance.[115] Yet the venue of Paradise Garage has a particular and additional effect on Jones's staging of herself, even if it's largely immaterial. After all, as I noted above, attitude as an art form was perfected at the Garage. The mechanics of giving and receiving attitude, wielding one's body-in-motion as a veritable canvas to display attitude, was intrinsic to the Garage's thrilling setting. While Jones's stance of artsy nonchalance is on full display in photographs of the onetime event, what remains out of view but present nonetheless are the virtuosic poses of the Garage's inhabitants, who were equally deft at using style not to speak but instead to "mean in other ways," as philosopher Nelson Goodman discusses.[116]

Jones—the exotic provocateur alternating between chic sophistication and playful, tongue-in-cheek irreverence—was especially adept at maneuvering different aesthetic forms, genres, and spaces. She manipulated her slipperiness to her advantage, sliding in and out of visual representations like a model dons a garment, while energizing them from the inside out. She utilized an assortment of aesthetic qualities—surface, color, volume, texture, and angularity—to enhance her already striking presence and augment her visceral performances. She challenged standard notions of beauty through her androgynous and unconventional persona, creating a new template for what an image-based performer could look like, especially a Black diasporic woman. She spoke back as an artistic subject, dissenting from the perceived notion of the muse as a passive object fabricated by others, and instead perceiving herself as an equal player in the creative act. In short, Grace Jones was an aesthetic maximalist who enthralled audiences—whether live at a disco or viewers of a photograph—with her embodiment of style as art.

New York is color, music, food. New York is the world's heart. I cannot go away for longer than four days without suffering. New York is me, and I am New York. New York is a fantastic mixture; it's like an orgasm.

STEPHEN BURROWS, QUOTED IN MORERA, *STEPHEN BURROWS: WHEN FASHION DANCED*

COLOR THAT MOVES

Stephen Burrows

On November 13, 1976, Stephen Burrows appeared on the sixth season of *Soul Train*. Modeled after Dick Clark's *American Bandstand*, the Chicago-based, Black-owned, music-dominated television show gained national syndication in 1971 and quickly became known for its flashy dancers. In the short clip, host and executive producer Don Cornelius wears a sharply tailored brown suit, a pristine button-down shirt, and a perfectly coiled pocket square. Because it is 1976 and Cornelius is ever dapper, the lapels are oversized and the necktie is wide. He faces the camera, microphone in hand, and superimposed on the screen in front of him is the show's instantly recognizable logo: a cartoonish illustration of a gray locomotive spewing psychedelic-like streams of yellow, pink, orange, and red steam out of its smokestack. Above the spits of smoke, the show's title emerges in light green lettering. Once the music fades, Cornelius introduces his eager audience, nearly all Black, to a still off-screen person. Stephen Burrows, he tells us, is a "very special person" worthy of our attention. In his measured, almost-professorial cadence, Cornelius continues: "A few years ago, I would have had to introduce him as one of the top Black fashion designers in the business. But as it stands today, at this stage of his career, we have to call him one of the top fashion designers in the world, who just *happens* to be Black. His name is Stephen Burrows."

While the in-studio audience claps, a suave and boyish Burrows walks onto the stage, one hand loosely tucked in the pocket of his tan slacks. His ivory button-down shirt is unbuttoned at the neck, and his eyes are obscured by his trademark round shades. He shakes hands with Cornelius. After some short banter—in which Burrows clarifies that his clothes are available in every major department store in the United States, but not really the whole world, and gives a quick rundown of his career—Cornelius introduces another guest: "Also, with us is one of the top fashion models in the world...and she's wearing one of Stephen's outfits. How 'bout it for Pat Cleveland?" As the audience claps again, the camera moves to the dance floor, where a smiling Cleveland stands among the *Soul Train* dancers. She playfully swings herself around, pivoting on her heels, as she deliberately shows off her outfit before approaching the stage. She models what Burrows describes to Cornelius as a pair of "jodhpur pants with one suspender and a baseball jacket with fake suede trimming on it." She also wears a red cowl neck sweater, the same shade as her glossy lipstick, with her ponytailed hair tucked under a coordinating pageboy cap. Cornelius, who seems awkward in the presence of Cleveland's bubbly exuberance, asks her what Burrows's strongest point as a designer is: "Well, his colors, the fabrics. And the way you can wear the clothes when you're dancing. Here's his thing: They're designed for the dancer." Cornelius thanks them both and dedicates the next song to them. KC and the Sunshine Band's "I Like to Do It" begins to play. Burrows and Cleveland are no longer the focus as the camera pans around the cavernous, multilevel space to showcase the various *Soul Train* dancers, who swing their hips and arms in time with the earthy funk music, with Afros, bell-bottoms, and leather boots in abundance.[1] Amid this ecstatic collective display—soulful rhythms, jostling bodies, and funky clothes—Burrows recedes into the background, and yet the collective itself is a peek into Burrows's sartorial style—a vision of sporty, intricately designed garments, setting alight their wearers on a crowded dance floor.

Stephen Burrows was born in Newark, New Jersey, in 1943, just thirty minutes away on the commuter train from midtown Manhattan. Both his maternal and paternal grandmothers worked as sample hands in the garment industry, a behind-the-scenes laboring lineage not unlike that of Anthony Lopez. Burrows was a self-described "arty" (and asthmatic) kid, drawn to music and dance. With four siblings on the city's West Side, he grew up in a pre-riots Newark that was nearly suburban. Fashion historian Robin Givhan writes that Newark "was vibrant and lively, and his neighborhood was a diverse mix" of Black, Italian, and Latinx residents.[2] His maternal grandmother owned a Zigzag sewing machine; at age eight, a precocious Burrows created his first garment as a gift for a neighbor. But his primary passion was dance. He was briefly enrolled in the Fred Astaire Dance Academy due to the generosity of his grandmother, a fellow dance aficionado. (This was to his mother's chagrin; she worried it would make him fey.) Burrows eventually became, in his words, a "mambo freak" in high school. He began traveling on Sunday nights to dance at a popular Latin ballroom in Manhattan called the Palladium, colloquially called "the home of mambo."[3] "It was on 52nd and Broadway. I don't know how we got in.... We were only 15 years old! We went there every Sunday. We loved to mambo," he told *The Fader* magazine decades later.[4]

This experience piqued his curiosity about fashion, and he began sketching designs for his female partners to wear. Nonetheless, after graduating from Newark's Arts High School, a performing and visual arts magnet institution, Burrows enrolled at the Philadelphia Museum College of Art in 1961. He intended to become an art teacher rather than a fashion designer, a practical choice eerily like Grace Jones's initial goal to become a Spanish instructor. Serendipitously, Burrows later stumbled on a room in the economics department full of inanimate dress forms. That chance encounter occasioned a decisive shift: He decided to become a fashion designer. Burrows dropped out and saved money to attend fashion school by doing grunt work at Bamberger's (which, in the 1980s, would be rebranded as Macy's), a massive department store spread over 1.2 million square feet that occupied an entire city block on Market Street in downtown Newark. Its business—selling mainstream apparel and fine jewelry to moneyed customers—was, undoubtedly, a training ground for Burrows's budding career.

In 1963, Burrows transferred to the Fashion Institute of Technology in New York City, where he would have just missed Antonio Lopez, who dropped out the year before. Later, while living in an apartment on East

Seventh Street that he shared with his FIT classmates, Burrows commenced crafting outfits for his friends to wear for their nocturnal excursions. Ruminating on these informal gatherings, he explains, "I was into leather and jersey, so all these people wanted clothes, and they would come over to the house, and we ended up with twenty people in my house putting on my clothes and then we'd all go out."[5] Burrows's anecdote is instructive given that fashion designers are typically expected to be heavily referential, visually citing sartorial precedents. In contrast to this more typical approach to fashion history, Burrows's initial designs were primarily motivated by the casual collective in his living room. This group took the art of dressing up seriously, seeing it as a necessary prelude to fun. "That's how these designers (especially Stephen Burrows) became designers—by dressing themselves and their friends for the night," writer and downtown fixture Glenn O'Brien recalls.[6]

After graduating from FIT in 1966, Burrows's senior co-op job at Weber's Originals, which specialized in women's blouses, became full-time. "I was making $125 a week. That was a fortune back then," he recalled.[7] However, in his off-hours, he continued designing clothes for his friends to party in, a side hustle that became so financially lucrative that Burrows quit his job after a year and a half. He started selling his clothes to New York City–based boutiques, such as linen dresses to Outrageous in the East Twenties and feather vests to Allen and Cole on East Fifty-Fourth Street.[8] He acquired confidence (and customers) as a budding designer.

Burrows, whose garments continued gaining traction with select consumers and eventually with the gatekeepers of the fashion industry, became a highly influential women's wear designer in 1970s New York City. He was a "visual creator" whose primary aesthetic inspiration was the dancing body itself. Once dubbed the "Fashion King of the Sexy Cling," Burrows seemed to be stimulated by the lilt of R & B and disco, creating sexy second-skin clothes that adorned models gliding down the runway to Sly and the Family Stone's "Family Affair" or, later that evening, confidently strutting their stuff to Alfredo de la Fé's "Hot to Trot" at Studio 54.[9] Women of color, especially Black women, were the consummate models for his vivacious garments, conjuring personality and dynamic movement on typically subdued (and lily-white) runways. As a result, fashion journalists frequently interpreted Burrows's body-conscious clothes as symbolic of the joy of Black life, a common, if overly simplistic, characterization that Burrows distanced himself from.

Stephen Burrows, Fire Island Pines, New York, 1969. Courtesy of Charles Tracy Archive.

Burrows, like Lopez, had an exuberant fashion sense and youthful appearance that masked his steely determination to succeed, making both him and his designs a topic of curiosity for some writers. In 1977, one writer devoted a whole paragraph to it. She wrote, "He still looks the way he did 10 years ago—a shy, almost fey, boy-man. His walk is as quick and erect as a dancer's; his voice skips an octave whenever he wants to make a point; he often dresses in Wrangler jeans, washed-out navy sneakers with orange laces and a multicolored shirt of his own design. All help along the impression of boyishness and shyness. But underneath is a self-confidence that comes from an ego so strong it doesn't have to show off."[10]

In 1977, the *New York Times* dubbed him "the brightest star of American fashion" and noted, "He did things with clothes that had never been done before and he did them with style and panache."[11] Burrows envisioned fashion as a form of imagination, ultimately seeing the designer's role as one of "suggestion," as he told *Interview* in 1976. He treated fashion design as an artistic enterprise and himself as an artist. "The fabric is the medium, the clothes are the canvas," he aptly noted. Burrows, moreover, was perturbed by those who failed to perceive this synergy between inhabiting *style* and making *art*, an insistence he shared with his peers Antonio Lopez and Grace Jones: "Everyone says clothes are not an art. I say, Why not? They should be."[12] And he was known for his sartorial approach in the already innovative early 1970s, a peak period of fashion during which a growing number of designers became outright celebrities.

Burrows was widely described as the guru of zesty "color of the crayon-bright variety."[13] He expertly wielded the chromatic intensity of punchy reds, shocking pinks, sunny yellows, verdant greens, and tranquil turquoises—"hot equator colors," as one journalist described them—in shades so audacious that they were akin to an optical assault.[14] Burrows's flamboyant use of tropical-like shades was partly inspired by "Pop Art's graphic boldness," as Tanya Danielle Wilson Myers suggests, with an eye tuned to color combinations that prioritized the surreal and "artfully abstract" while shunning anything banal.[15] In doing so, he mirrored the shared inclinations of Lopez and Jones for radiant synthetic colors, be it the Technicolor profusion of the former's *Ribbon Series* or the Bauhaus-inspired shades of the latter's maternity dress.

I continue to chart the unlikely but meteoric rise of Stephen Burrows by constructing a spatial cartography of his artistic development in New York City and beyond. We see again how youthful downtown energies percolate up to midtown and eventually across national borders. Burrows morphs from a local designer dressing fashionable Manhattanites and celebrities to one recognized in Paris, the global fashion capital at the time, as a preeminent ambassador of American fashion. If Antonio Lopez, alongside his collaborator Juan Ramos, imbued his illustrations and photographs with the gritty energy of the metropolis, Burrows translated this same affective charge into luxurious dresses in vibrantly colored shades that loosely draped over the curvilinearity of the female body. Granted, he wasn't a polymath pinballing between genres like Lopez and Jones—his primary working material was fabric. Yet, as I suggest below, Burrows executed changes *within* the medium of fabric, switching textiles based on which was best suited to display the sensual body in motion. Like Lopez and Jones,

Burrows was supported by a meshy network of creative peers—including models, fellow fashion designers, leather-makers, photographers, magazine editors, and stylists—who quickly shifted back and forth from the shop floor to the dance floor.

Unlike the design of the previous two chapters, alternating between analyses of discrete works of art and particular locales where art-making flourished, I organize my discussions of Burrows below exclusively by place while progressing chronologically from the late 1960s to the late 1970s.

Such a narrative and place-driven approach, rather than an object-based inquiry, is reflective of the material I researched to tell this story; those sources tended to focus less on specific friendships or pieces he designed and more on the geographic sites and sensorial zones that inspired his work and where his designs proliferated. Ironically, while the sense of community is more emphasized in these pages, the *intimacy* of those deep friendships—or romances—is not as present here as in the previous chapters. This is not to say it didn't exist. Instead, its lack of prominence seems indicative of the discretion of Burrows's peers and Burrows himself.

I first take us to Fire Island, a weekend getaway frequented by New York City's queer creative class that served multiple roles for Burrows and his fashionable kinfolk. Next, we travel to O Boutique, a scrappy operation near Gramercy Park that briefly served as Burrows's first clothing storefront in New York City and epitomized the spirit of working together. From there, we enter the 1970s and bask in the olfactory and tactile delights of Stephen Burrows World, his eponymous boutique inside the midtown department store Henri Bendel. We then decamp to Burrows's participation in the now-legendary American fashion showcase at the Battle of Versailles and the theatrical role of his mostly Black models. Our last site is Studio 54, where, after a minor blip in his career, Burrows returns to prominence as his disco-ready fashions circulated and sizzled on the dance floor. Burrows is, along with his sultry clothes, often lovingly described as the fashion designer who best captured that elusive je ne sais quoi of the 1970s, especially the sultry vibe of the Studio 54 era. If there was ever a fashion designer capable of making chiffon or the sheerest of jersey move of its own accord, of making color *dance*, that was Stephen Burrows. And, unsurprisingly, Burrows himself is often rendered photographically while dancing, on and off the runway. Thus, in this chapter, I seek to honor his creative vision while attempting to capture the putative rhythm of the time.

PARTYING AND PRANCING WITH THE "FASHION FAMILY" AT FIRE ISLAND

Any blueprint of Burrows's career would have to feature prominently the beachy queer haven of Fire Island; this site acted as a stomping ground for his cohort to comingle and hash out ideas while peacocking in his designs—from fringed patchwork leather pants to popsicle-hued jersey dresses. By the late 1960s, Burrows frequently spent the weekend "out east," nearly always with a set of friends in tow. The sleepy and remote hot spot served a diversity of roles for this bohemian crew. A narrow barrier island between Long Island and the Atlantic Ocean, approximately forty-five miles east of New York City, Fire Island was only accessible by private boat or ferry. Much of the action centered on Cherry Grove, the oldest continually inhabited town on the island, which in the decades after World War II became an ostensible second home for young gay men involved in advertising, publicity, design, and especially theater.[16] Elaborate theme parties were the norm, and it was not uncommon for men who designed department store window displays to recycle discarded bric-a-brac from their day jobs as festive party decorations, yet another example of the inventive practice of bricolage.

Burrows first visited Fire Island in 1965 at the invitation of his FIT classmate Roz Rubenstein, who shared a group house there. "It was a magical place. It was like the Garden of Eden. No cars were there. I'd never been to a place like that before," he mused.[17] Pat Cleveland first traveled there in 1970 at the invitation of Burrows, shortly after they first met; she remembers it in similarly fond terms, explaining in her memoirs that the island's small size meant that everyone became friends with one another immediately: "Fire Island was a sort of utopia built on having fun and being creative, and all doors were unlocked. It seemed like everyone there was connected with the business of art, as a designer, an interior decorator, a painter, a chef, a writer."[18]

By the mid-1960s, anthropologist Esther Newton states, Cherry Grove "had become a kind of informally organized gay theme park with an expanded resident population," who were entertained by "the gorgeous beach, of course, along with more lavish theme parties than ever before and round-the-clock communal sexual opportunities for men."[19] Soon after 1973, when Burrows and Calvin Klein (Lopez's high school classmate) both won their first of several Coty Awards, they became the indisputable "fashion stars of the island," according to fashion editor André Leon Talley.[20] In Burrows's words, "All the artists gravitated there every weekend, and dressed up and went to parties and danced at the Sandpiper, the Botel, and the Monster in Cherry Grove."[21] In one of Talley's photographs from 1976, Burrows is seen cutting his friend's hair in leopard-print drawstring pants of his design while Angelo Colon, one of Lopez's models and a body double of Grace Jones, is seen off to the side, sketching on a picnic table.[22]

Burrows took advantage of the idyllic setting as a source of personal rejuvenation and a golden opportunity to expand his professional network. Burrows, like Grace Jones and other artists in our story, experimented with psychedelic drugs and integrated these moments of expanded consciousness into his creative practice. He fondly recalls his first acid trips there, listening to Janis Joplin during the halcyon summers of the late 1960s. Thinking later about the generative friction between those psychic encounters and his design work, he remarked in an interview, "I think everything that happens to you contributes to what you expel when you're designing.... I was a product of the generation. I did everything."[23] Fashion historian Robin Givhan perfectly compares the kaleidoscopic play of color one experiences during an acid trip and Burrows's oft-noted use of saturated color combinations in his later collections. In addition, Burrows made use of his proximity to others of his ilk—urbane artistically inclined figures—taking advantage of the relaxed atmosphere as a reprieve from the grind of New York City. For instance, he befriended model Naomi Sims there; she won a scholarship to FIT and moved to New York City in 1966. Sims, as discussed in the previous chapter, was widely recognized as the first Black supermodel in the early 1970s. Before she broke out, she modeled Burrows's designs for a *Vogue* shoot on Fire Island. He also met fellow fashion designers like Halston and young upstart Willi Smith, who was model Toukie Smith's geeky brother. Burrows says, "I first met Willi at a party in the Pines on Fire Island in 1968. Most of the designers hung out there every weekend. I had heard about him through mutual model friends, and Willi and I became fast friends from then on."[24]

In the 1970s, the press repeatedly used the term *commune* to describe his friends. While rural hippie communes captured most media attention in the 1960s, such as the one Grace Jones briefly belonged to outside Philadelphia, the staggering variety of intentional communities in the era befuddled easy taxonomy. Peaking in number between the autumn of 1967 and the early 1970s, as cultural historian Timothy Miller stresses, these countercultural experiments in living included "Asian religious ashrams, group marriage experiments, communal rock bands, centers of radical politics, and back-to-the-land experiments in agricultural self-sufficiency."[25] They tended to be overwhelmingly white, with members often hailing from middle-class households. This is a reminder that the voluntary disavowal of material goods is a little more straightforward if your needs are already taken of.

Burrows's peer group, in contrast, was far more ethnically diverse. It included Italian jewelry designer and model Elsa Peretti (a close friend of Halston, who also provided financial backing to Burrows throughout his career), Puerto Rican photographer Charles Tracy (who later shot a *Vogue* editorial on Burrows in Central Park and was a contributor to Lopez's Puerto Rico issue of *Interview*), leather designer Bobby Breslau (who later became Burrows's assistant), and FIT friend and eventual business adviser Rubenstein. "It truly was like being in a Fellini film," recalls Rubenstein's husband, Randy Johnson. "[There were] just all kinds of people. Black people, gay people, straight people, Caucasian, Puerto Rican. It was absolutely delicious."[26] Playwright and FIT classmate Vy Higginsen concurs, alluding to the prevalent racial discord of the late 1960s: "There's turmoil everywhere. And here's this little group that looks like they're all getting along just fine," she says. "We would go out dancing in wild colors and walking down the boardwalk in Fire Island in these fabulous clothes. We became like a family, a sort of fashion family."[27] Intriguingly, as the quotation reminds us, this group envisioned itself as an alternative to the mainstream and all its social ills. But just as intriguing, they chose to manifest that alternative by partying and dressing up.

In a 1969 photograph, we see Burrows and his commune on a roof deck in Fire Island. Burrows—in red sunglasses, a red fringe top, and leather pants—is seated in a chair, surrounded by eight friends, all of whom appear to be wearing clothes he designed—color-blocked tops (some with matching pants) or fringed leather pants. In a second 1969 snapshot taken on the beach, Burrows and five of his friends pose, all at a choreographed distance from one another. All dressed in complementary outfits yet retaining their personas, they look like a fledgling rock band. In this sense, Burrows's commune was not unlike the peer groups of Jones or Lopez, harnessing an affinity for chromatic and sartorial difference as a shared badge of identity. Again, the politics of style transpires, as this self-identified group wields "styles of saying" that visually express a simultaneous camaraderie with one another and divergence from the status quo.[28]

Charles Tracy, Puerto Rico, circa 1971. Courtesy of Charles Tracy Archive.

I borrow this phrase from philosopher Nelson Goodman, who deploys it in a chapter on style in his 1978 text *Ways of Worldmaking*. Specifically, he uses it when discussing how different forms of cultural expression (he names painting, composing, and performing as examples) can be compared, even if they do not share a common subject or lack one altogether. Here, I am less interested in Goodman's philosophical explanation of how to distinguish style and subject than in his helpful suggestion that style is something that *speaks*. Style communicates, albeit not in a literal sense, he suggests. Across different genres, understanding forms of style "cannot be a matter of how they say something, for they do not literally say anything; they do other things; they mean in other ways."[29] Burrows and his peers were manipulating their clothing in this manner. They were not simply wearing his leather and jersey garments as a form of personal embellishment but rather to strategically project a group sense of difference and convey that rebellious message to the public.

The feedback loop between Fire Island and New York City was advantageous for many fashion designers who spent weekends there; for Burrows, it was instrumental. "Fire Island was the place fashion designers went for

Fire Island Pines, New York, 1969. *From left:* Roz Rubenstein, Gail Boggs, Bonnie Brownfield. Courtesy of Charles Tracy Archive.

inspiration," Pat Cleveland points out. Multiple costume changes were expected, whether for meals or parading at the beach. Still, they had an ultimate purpose, she noted: "Everyone would copy each other's style, mirroring similar colors, then take all their weekend energy, come back Monday, and bring it back into the clothes."[30] Burrows and Rubenstein first hatched the idea for opening a boutique together while out east at Fire Island; Rubenstein would run the business, and Burrows would design the clothes. Burrows also met

Fire Island Pines, New York, September 1969. *From left*: Don Fendley, Roz Rubenstein, Bobby Breslau, Hector Torres, Jim Valkus (*standing*), Stephen Burrows, Tony DiPace, and Harrison Rivera. *In front, seated*: Peter Capello. Courtesy of Charles Tracy Archive.

Fire Island Pines, 1970. *From left*: Daryl Meade, Hector Torres, Stephen Burrows, Bobby Breslau, Roz Rubenstein, Bobby Roveda. Courtesy of Charles Tracy Archive.

Jimmy Burkus, who—until he saw Burrows's clothing—had been determined to open a "bazaar" focused on fine art in New York City. Specifically, Burkus's idea was to showcase "anything he thought fit the category of art", Burrows clarified to me.[31] He "saw my things as art," Burrows explains, and thus envisioned combining "art and clothing as art together" in one space.[32] When Burrows and Rubenstein secured financial backing from an investor, they could begin to design and sell the clothes there, finally bringing their idea to fruition.

O BOUTIQUE'S COMMUNE OF CREATIVITY

O Boutique opened in 1968 on Park Avenue South and East Nineteenth Street, just below Gramercy Park. The store's name—pronounced like the English letter O—was chosen to evoke the Zen Buddhist symbol for infinity, which is visually represented as an imperfect circle. Burrows explained, in 2016, that the boutique "held a collection of paintings, sculpture and my clothes, all of which were made in the basement of the store."[33] O Boutique was another unusual hybrid—an art gallery and a clothing store—joining the list of nontraditional art spaces, along with the hair salon Cinandre and the department store Fiorucci, where aesthetic creation was forged. Moreover, its location near well-to-do Gramercy Park—the private, gated park (only accessible by a key) from which the neighborhood takes its name—was a helpful metaphor: It was neither uptown nor downtown, but rather in the murky space in between. (By 1973, Burrows was living near the area. His friend and model, Bethann Hardison, lived close by on Twentieth Street and Second Avenue.[34]) While Rubenstein worked on the financial side, the hive of artistic activity was in the basement workshop. There, the division of labor was split between Burrows and three others: William Hill, a friend from FIT, who was the patternmaker; Hector Torres, who worked on fabric design; and Bobby Breslau, a former package designer who met Burrows on Fire Island and evolved from a fan to serve as the group's leatherware designer. The four men worked together in the store's subterraneous space and lived in a tenement apartment near Second Avenue and East Seventh Street they rented for $150 a month.

By 1969, the boutique's buzz led to repeat profiles in the local press. For instance, the *Times* vividly rendered the store's electric atmosphere: "O, 236 Park Avenue South, is a groovy haven for the beautiful people. Stephen Burrows,

25, knows how to whip up sophisticated nothings as well as strikingly original clothes and accessories. O's sleek environment is punctuated with pop art, rock music and a flashing photo screen of Burrows's designs for men and women."[35] This evocative description gives a taste of the boutique's curated environment, where multiple senses were engaged and the store's decor was inseparable from its products. It is unclear whether mostly contemporary art was displayed for sale or if it was an intentional mixture of high and low. Still, the prominence of Pop Art in the store's environs mirrored a "significant rapprochement between the worlds of fashion and fine art" in the 1960s—be it Larry Aldrich's Op Art–inspired fabrics or Sonia Delaunay's textiles based on her abstract art.[36] New York City–based fashion designers associated Pop Art with a flash in the pan aesthetic, a quickness and ephemerality rather than durability, which they found particularly appealing. As a result, "pop fashion" emerged as a category. Future Hollywood director Joel Schumacher's clothing collection for the boutique Paraphernalia, which referenced the work of Pop artist Robert Indiana, is a primary example.[37] Juxtaposing Pop Art with Burrows's hippie-like fashions suggested continuity between the two, elevating his garments into an artistic enterprise. Burrows boldly defined himself elsewhere in such terms: "My artistic medium is fabric, and I like the way jersey moves and drapes—it's flexible."[38] The article situated O Boutique as a part of what the *Times* identified as a new direction within the more significant trend of New York City boutiques—"swingy shops owned and operated by Negroes or featuring black designers"—implying that Burrows's Blackness was as much an object of intrigue as his groovy, often-unisex clothes.[39]

Intriguingly, the following day, the *Times* published a second profile of O Boutique, highlighting Burrows's sportswear and imaginative color combinations.

> Sportive is the word for the fashions at the newly opened O Boutique at 236 Park Avenue South (at 19th Street). There are long dresses that look like overgrown football jerseys and matte jersey shirts that stand halfway between racing silks and an incarnation of Harlequin.
>
> Stephen Burrows, the young man who designs all of the shop's fashions, loves to juxtapose colors—the more the merrier. So the long-sleeved shirts, priced at $25, turn up with, say, an emerald green body, a bitter-green pointed collar (with a flap-front closing like a man's tee shirt), and pewter-gray sleeve with an inset of pale blue.[40]

O Boutique, 1969. *From left*: unidentified girlfriend of Bobby Breslau's brother, Roz Rubenstein, Bobby Breslau's brother, and Bobby Breslau. Courtesy of Charles Tracy Archive.

The writer suggests that Burrows's women's wear merged sartorial cues from a nearly schizophrenic gamut of sources, including the uniforms of horse jockeys and football players and the zany, tessellated patterns worn by the harlequin, the stock character of the Italian commedia dell'arte tradition. The lucid description of Burrows's wide-ranging colors, already emerging as one of the defining features of his clothes, mirrored the broader cultural shift in the late 1960s toward the "therapeutic and energizing nature of color," as fashion historian Phyllis Magidson underlines.[41] "The Age of Aquarius and psychedelia heralded the birth of an unprecedented color palette. Explosive oranges, Day-Glo greens, garish pinks and magentas" were worn with abandon.[42] And so was a fiery red, Burrows's favorite and oft-used color. (He even painted his entire living room red.[43]) The endgame was "to absorb their energy and radiate it back for all onlookers."[44]

Burrows's first editorial in *Vogue* was published in April 1969, within a few weeks of the *Times* profiles, a massive accomplishment in a short amount of time. Burrows had been embraced by the beacon of American women's fashion.

The feature was due to the persistence of fashion editor Carrie Donovan, who wanted to include Burrows in a section called "*Vogue*'s Own Boutique of Suggestions, Finds, and Observations." She asked his friend Charles Tracy to do the shoot, which became Tracy's debut as a fashion photographer. The magazine described the setting—staged in what looks like a recently designed playground, surrounded by anonymous brick buildings—as "a bare plot that's turned into one of those Manhattan oases.... One rainy afternoon everybody there was wearing something designed by Stephen Burrows for the new O' Boutique." One small black-and-white photograph showed an unnamed model, hands on her hips, wearing a hooded wool jersey tunic with snakeskin strips. Another, larger photograph showed a different model swinging on a rubber tire swing, wearing a "ravishing shirt of creamy, clingy jersey" and black "kid soft leather pants, fringed everywhere." The descriptions attest that *Vogue*'s first feature studiously avoided Burrows's sherbet-like colors, focusing instead on the tactility of his fabrics, such as "shiny brown snakeskin." It also suggests that uptown's embrace of downtown cool was still hesitant unless it conformed to established codes, especially regarding aspirational luxury.

While O Boutique operated as a showcase for Burrows's multicolored confections, what a publication like *Vogue* seemed to miss was how it also functioned, in fashion historian Robin Givhan's words, as a "commune of creativity" centered around Burrows's tight-knit friendships.[45] This collaborative spirit was intrinsic to the store's ethos, as model Bethann Hardison (who became his house model in the 1970s and, later, his PR person[46]) recalls. In her words, Burrows "started a company with a bunch of kids, and they did something called O Boutique, an actual store. And he and all those kids used to make all the clothes together—leathers and things."[47] Hardison's casual description seems appropriate for the laid-back environment Burrows created. The boutique was, of course, a business—though by all accounts, never particularly profitable—but just as important was that everyone involved was young, enthusiastic, and got to make things together. Collaborating was paramount to his process and integral to the store's philosophy, despite Burrows's sole name recognition in the press. Burrows, like Antonio Lopez and Grace Jones, created from within a close-knit community that prized fun and aesthetic innovation while acting as a support system and laboratory for new ideas.

O Boutique also benefited from its proximity to Max's Kansas City, the legendary restaurant and nightclub that became an epicenter of studied nonchalance and fabulous fashion. Model Berry Berenson, who was working for the back pages of *Vogue* at the time (and was briefly engaged to Richard Bernstein), said Burrows's store was "very hip, chic. Everyone used to go there and then go to Max's because it was across the street."[48] Max's Kansas City was the brainchild of creator and proprietor Mickey Ruskin, a lawyer manqué whose first "art bar" was the Ninth Circle in Greenwich Village, an establishment popular with poets and artists that opened in 1962. After leasing 213 Park Avenue South, a pharmacy turned restaurant, he renovated the space and opened Max's on January 15, 1966. It soon became the premier artists' hangout north of SoHo. It was partially encouraged by an unusual arrangement: Artists could donate works in exchange for a free tab (exclusive of liquor and tips). The artsy decor signaled its preferred clientele, including sculptures by Donald Judd and John Chamberlain; a fluorescent light sculpture by Dan Flavin; and an elaborate light beam installation by Forrest Myers, timed to illuminate each night from 8:00 p.m. to 4:00 a.m.[49]

The cliques congregated in distinct zones, Glenn O'Brien recalls: art world luminaries in the front by the bar, music business executives in the middle, and oddballs (like Warhol's contingent or the performance troupe the Cockettes) in the back room, illuminated by the red light of Flavin's sculpture. And then there was the glossy fashion world, from models and photographers to hairdressers and fashion designers. "Jackie Rogers, Tiger Morse, Betsey Johnson, Fernando Sanchez, Scott Barrie, and Stephen Burrows. They were all big personalities, even the quiet ones," O'Brien says.[50] Like Lopez and Jones, Burrows and his crew often worked and partied together; they would go to Max's on Saturday night, typically arriving around 1:00 a.m. and staying until the place closed at 7:00 a.m.[51]

We have seen again and again how central fashion was to the artistic and social life of New York City. According to Andy Warhol, nowhere was this more evident than at Max's—"the exact place where Pop art and pop life came together in New York in the sixties."[52] The assorted fashions of the 1960s, historian Peter Braunstein argues, "projected individual identity as a slide show of alternating roles, postures, and personalities—a sensibility that could be summed up as 'the many moods of me.'"[53] This sense of play was reflected in the clothing trends one could witness firsthand at Max's, which Warhol likened to a "fashion gallery" of sorts.[54]

Burrows's growing cult following undoubtedly led to his inclusion in a notorious showcase of Black fashion designers on May 20, 1969, a benefit fashion show titled "Basic Black."[55] It was held at Bergdorf Goodman, the luxury department store on Fifth Avenue in midtown Manhattan. For the event, the store hired Black makeup artists, hairstylists, and models (including Sims and women from Liaison, a networking group for professional Black women).[56] After the fashion show, an estimated seven to eight hundred guests were invited to a "soul food cocktail party."[57] There, they politely sipped champagne and ate fried chicken, chitlins, ribs, greens, and black-eyed peas—"pure radical chic" in 1969—while entertained by a jazz quintet dressed in daishikis.[58]

The event's true impetus, though, was the fractious racial climate of the time and the organizers' perhaps naive belief that fashion could act as a calming salve to those wounds. "People believed American fashion, in its choices and depictions of beauty, could help everyone get along," Givhan iterates.[59] Sims's inclusion was expected, given that she became the first Black model to be photographed for the cover of a major fashion magazine—in 1967, for the *New York Times' Fashion of the Times*. (Sims again made history when she became the first Black woman to appear on the cover of *Life* magazine, a few months after the Bergdorf event.) While well-intentioned, the stereotypical depiction of Black culture at the soiree was off-putting at best, perhaps even downright offensive and, as Givhan suggests, close to minstrelsy. In Rikki Byrd's words, "The event put blackness on display for the consumption of hundreds of guests, both black and white, but of course did little to impact race relations in the country."[60]

And for Burrows, while his participation signaled his inclusion in a small but growing lineage of successful Black fashion designers, it also implied yet again that his newfound fame was viewed through the prism of his race. In other words, Burrows was not interpreted as an American fashion designer tout court, even though it seemed this was how he viewed himself, given his reluctance in interviews to define his clothes through his racial identity. Again, this was likely due to the persistent notion that Burrows's clothes should be interpreted as a symbol of the so-called joy of Black life. This friction was emblematic of a shared skepticism surrounding the moniker *Black designer*. The fashion industry promulgated the term to group designers like Burrows into a catchall category. And that alignment may have been beneficial, and even desired, by at least some designers, who wanted to be perceived alongside their immediate and generational peers. Still, we can assume that other designers eschewed for multiple reasons what they interpreted as a fraught label to describe themselves. These could include the desire to reach a more extensive customer base beyond Black consumers and to resist the overtly political use of the term at the time. But perhaps another reason was the suspicion that the newfound attention Black designers were receiving was just another of fashion's famously fleeting trends, "in" one season and "out" the next. That tension would reappear in the early 1970s, even as Burrows's women's wear and color choices became more refined.

Despite the raves and Burrows's growing renown, O Boutique went out of business two years after it opened. Rubenstein could never figure out how to make Burrows's clothes profitable. "Despite all the press attention, O Boutique was a money pit. Burrows was not a businessman, nor were any of his friends," Givhan argues.[61] It is tempting to see O Boutique as an act of youthful folly. But that would be shortsighted. After all, Burrows's store attracted musicians and actresses of the day and exposed his clothes to a broader audience, which was remarkable given that he was in his mid-twenties and not an established designer. Jazz trumpeter Miles Davis, whose funk musician wife Betty posed in several of Antonio Lopez's Instamatics, wore suede pants by Burrows, for instance.[62] "People were pulling up in limousines for these clothes. They came from everywhere. This was like, *the* spot, *the* crowd, *the* group," Vy Higginsen recalls.[63] Burrows's ability to push the zeitgeist in new directions was also augmented by the attention he received from American *Vogue*. The magazine was "famous for aesthetic and rhetorical extravagances in the sixties" because of its editor in chief, Diana Vreeland, who recognized that it was time for American designers to be celebrated.[64] The ready-to-wear collection that Rubenstein and Burrows launched in 1969 for high-end department store Bonwit Teller (where many Pop artists first worked as window display designers) also evinced their growing recognition in the fashion industry.[65] In this sense, the store was a resounding success. O Boutique, likewise, caught the attention of another fashion broker who would become instrumental in the next stage of Burrows's career. While O Boutique shut down, the youthful energy of Burrows and his commune was only beginning.

THE HARD-CHIC AND TECHNICOLOR VIVACITY OF STEPHEN BURROWS WORLD

Shortly after O Boutique closed, Burrows took the Lexington Avenue subway line uptown for an appointment at Henri Bendel—known by many simply as Bendel's—arguably New York's most plush women's department store.

Founded in 1895, it was the first retailer in the United States to sell Coco Chanel's designs. Located at 10 West Fifty-Seventh Street, Henri Bendel was two blocks south of Central Park and one block west of Fifth Avenue, that famed thoroughfare lined on both sides with expensive retail stores, including Bergdorf's, which was one block away. He was meeting with store president Geraldine Stutz. The fortuitous meeting was brokered by Joel Schumacher, a Fire Island regular and champion of Burrows, who by day worked there assisting with window displays. In Burrows's words, "Joel worked for *Vogue* with Carrie Donovan. He came up to me on Fire Island and said, 'You have great style. We would like to shoot you for Vogue.' Joel also introduced me to Geraldine Stutz at [Henri] Bendel's. He suggested I go see her when O Boutique was closing."[66]

Bendel's was a twenty-five-thousand-square-foot store showcasing exclusive designers tailored to Stutz's vision—her ideal customer was a chic, moneyed, and very petite woman. Like Bonwit Teller, B. Altman, and Lord and Taylor, it catered to these economically elite consumers and their taste for European haute couture; prêt-à-porter copies of Dior and Chanel were some of its best sellers. However, the proximity to luxury stores belied "Bendel's role as a midtown outpost for downtown cool," as one writer recalled.[67] This description could easily describe the trendy sites of art-making we witnessed in the previous chapters, which also imported downtown artistic energy into midtown retail spaces. In the 1960s, Pop artist Andy Warhol earned a steady paycheck as the store's in-house illustrator. Meanwhile, the visionary Stutz created a "Street of Shops," where individual designers curated discrete spaces within the larger store, a precursor to the modern-day concept store. As Robin Givhan argues, "The Henri Bendel imprimatur was invaluable to a designer. It was where any newcomer wanted to be."[68] According to Burrows, he brought a few pieces of his own design with him to the appointment— pants, shirts, T-shirts, a couple of dresses—but it was a Melton wool coat he made that caught Stutz's eye. Reportedly, Stutz twirled around in the coat, intended as menswear, and declared that she loved it. The rest was history: "I met with her on a Thursday and I started the following Monday."[69] He was given space in the workroom of Bendel's Studio, the small manufacturing part of the store run by Pat Tennant (who became his mentor), along with a couple of sewing machines, assistants, and $250 a week.[70]

Like Antonio Lopez and Juan Ramos's move to Fiorucci shortly after its April 1976 opening, "Burrows's migration to 57th Street brought downtown funk to the more rarefied" midtown crowd.[71] His custom boutique, which opened on the third floor on August 1, 1970, was called Stephen Burrows World.[72] Schumacher designed the shop. Punctuated with metal studs, the black patent leather walls exuded a dark glamour. The distinctive interior was immediately impactful, as proven by a *Times* profile published that fall: "Stephen Burrows's world is a very special one. It includes the hard chic of black leather studded with nailheads and the youthful exuberance of bright colors that are mixed but never matched." The writer noted the similarities between the tactile surroundings and the clothes for sale: "Matching the black and chrome of his shop, a black leather jacket has jersey sleeves; the gaucho pants are also made of leather; the ornaments are silvery studs. The jacket, $100; the gauchos, $275." She informs the reader in a caption, "Everything is available on the third floor at Henri Bendel in a department called Stephen Burrows' World that is all gleaming black and chrome. That is Burrows himself at the far right, wearing one of his own hard-chic designs."[73] Fascinatingly, *hard-chic* is used twice here as an adjective: once to describe the black leather in his shop, and again to delineate his design aesthetic overall. This makes sense, given that one of the female models featured in the article is pictured wearing studded black leather pieces that perfectly mirror the black leather walls against which she is posing. But can this also be a metaphor for a sultry, sexually charged edginess that hovered between uptown and downtown sensibilities? Specifically, I am considering the contrast between Henri Bendel's elegant retail environment and the flirtation with black leather's multiple associations (masculinity, sexual kink, motorcycles) in Burrows's in-store boutique; hard-chic perfectly describes the confluence of uptown polish and downtown attitude captured in surfaces.

Stephen Burrows World is an addition to the other carefully designed environments we have seen, such as Cinandre or Paradise Garage, where artsy creatives devised new aesthetic and bodily styles.

In an unusual arrangement, Stutz hired Burrows and part of his downtown commune, bringing the loose collective vibe to Henri Bendel's posh environs. This was mainly due to Stutz's astute awareness of how instrumental the larger collective was to Burrows's success. She knew that there was a "particular chemistry of personalities fueling Burrows' creativity at O Boutique. Rather than risk disturbing that, she simply picked up the entire package and moved it uptown."[74] And yet, she didn't hire his whole collective,

Stephen Burrows World at Henri Bendel, 1970. *From left*: Roz Rubenstein, Hector Torres, Daryl Meade, Bobby Roveda, Stephen Burrows, Bobby Breslau. Courtesy of Charles Tracy Archive.

but only two members—Roz Rubenstein and Bobby Breslau. When I asked about their exact new roles, Burrows specified that Breslau was a salesman, while Rubenstein became the jewelry and accessories buyer for Bendel's.[75] Nonetheless, we can assume they were creatively valuable enough to Burrows that their presence was desired and needed. In contrast to the team of peers that made Burrows's clothes with him in the basement of O Boutique, sewers performed the bulk of the manual work in the workroom of Bendel's Studio. Hence, while his arrival at Bendel's was a career coup, one that also freed him from the day-to-day drudgery of running a boutique, it also meant a transition to a different (and classed) business model where the creativity and collective labor of friends was less prized than the cultivated persona of the individual designer.

Soon after opening his in-store boutique, Burrows was introduced to a young Pat Cleveland—Antonio Lopez's frequent model, as we know, and Grace Jones's friend—who had also developed connections within the

Stephen Burrows and Hector Torres at Bendel's Studio, 1970.
Courtesy of Charles Tracy Archive.

often-hermetic worlds of *Vogue* and Bendel's. *Vogue*'s Carrie Donovan first discovered the Harlem-raised Cleveland on the street. She was on her way home from school, wearing a garment that she and her mother, Lady Bird Cleveland, had designed. Soon after, in 1966, sixteen-year-old Cleveland began modeling for the Ebony Fashion Fair; the popular traveling fashion show brought high-end fashion, including Burrows's designs, to Black audiences throughout the United States.[76] Returning to New York City and hoping to become a fashion designer, Cleveland produced a clothing line with her

Carol LaBrie in Stephen Burrows headpiece, 1970. Courtesy of Charles Tracy Archive.

mother and aunt for designer Tiger Morse's boutique. In 1968, she was first featured in *Vogue*, photographed by Joel Schumacher in Central Park, in a lace shirt she and her mother designed.

After the shoot, Donovan informed Cleveland that she had sent her fashion sketches to Bendel's. The rest happened fast: "Bendel's liked my designs, and I set about making several skirts and blouses for the store. They bought them all, put my name on the label, and sold every last item."[77] Unfortunately, the deal evaporated just as quickly as her success had occurred. Cleveland explains that she and her mother mistakenly made everything in Cleveland's size. When the store asked for larger sizes, "it got complicated. I had to make darts in the blouses, which I'd never done before.... Because I didn't really know how to make the larger sizes, I lost the order."[78] Despite the understandable disappointment for her and her mother, *Vogue* hired Cleveland to be a fitting model, where she worked with the magazine's Brooklyn-born Filipino illustrator Maning Obregon. And yet, despite being one of a few Black models signed to the Ford Modeling Agency, her modeling career was at an impasse...until she met Burrows.

A mix-up by one of Donovan's scouts (who mistook Cleveland for another Black model, Norma Jean Darden) led to the impromptu meeting at Bendel's with Burrows, who needed a fitting model. After arriving at Bendel's from *Vogue*, Cleveland took the elevator to the eighth floor, where she met Bobby Breslau, who whisked her off to Burrows. In her memoirs, Cleveland describes what happened next:

> "Steve! It's just me. There's a young lady to see you." We waited for a few minutes, and Bobby rapped on the door again. It opened, and out poured a cloud of smoke and the sounds of Motown and R&B. The room was dark, with brightly colored drawings covering the walls. And there, amid a cluster of hanging flowering pants, he stood: Mr. Stephen Burrows, a beautiful African-American man of medium height whom I guessed to be around twenty-six, wearing fringed leather pants, an appliquéd T-shirt similar to Bobby's, and silver mirrored sunglasses, something I'd never seen. He had a mustache and was smoking a very tiny rolled cigarette.[79]

Burrows, Breslau, and Hector Torres were so enamored of how Cleveland looked in a signature Burrows look—a green wrap top and a skirt with yellow appliqués and bands of suede—that they used her in a *Vogue* shoot in Central Park that day. Published in the August 1970 issue, the editorial signaled Burrows's official arrival at Bendel's. Referencing the psychedelic colors of the animated Beatles film *Yellow Submarine*, the two-page Pepperland-inspired spread prominently featured the exuberant, color-blocked jersey clothes that made up Burrows's first collection for the department store. And, in typical fashion, Burrows's multiracial commune modeled the motley-colored ensembles. Subsequently, Burrows hired Cleveland as his fitting model, and she also walked in his first runway show at the store that August.

"Stephen Burrows in Pepperland," *Vogue*, August 1, 1970. Courtesy of Charles Tracy Archive.

Cleveland's encounter with Burrows was fortuitous; they developed an extensive working relationship and an abiding friendship. As a result, Cleveland began hanging out in Burrows's studio. She recalled, "The studio was such a lively, happy place, with a constant 'cookin' up something in the kitchen' quality that happens when creative people come together."[80] Cleveland attended chic industry parties with Burrows and began to travel with him and his crew to Fire Island, where she modeled in the impromptu photo shoots they would stage there. Almost immediately, she became part of his so-called 'fashion family.' "Becoming a member of Stephen's World was a turning point for me. It lifted my career—my whole life—from black and white to Technicolor," she remarked.[81] Seemingly the fleshly embodiment of Burrows's fashion sketches, Cleveland became a source of artistic inspiration. When asked about her in 1976, he said, "I never actually designed for Pat—I mean, I have little things. But I would think of Pat when I would design."[82]

Burrows's design process, such as his thinking about fabrics, evolved during his stint at Bendel's. In her 1978 book *The Fashion Makers*, fashion journalist Bernadine Morris succinctly summarized the shift: "He mixed up colors with an artist's eye, especially in his pieced or patchwork jerseys that established his first claim to fame. Later came fluttery chiffon dresses, delicate and charming."[83] Burrows's use of chiffon—"an elegant, sheer silk weave with a soft drape and shimmering translucence"—suggested a maturity and newfound sophistication that undoubtedly appealed to Henri Bendel's consumers.[84] Moreover, given Bendel's in-the-know clientele, the luxe material—long aligned with Parisian fashion houses—also signaled a degree of aspirational taste. Elspeth Brown argues that "knowledgeable American audiences associated the fabric with both French haute couture and with the glamour that France represented for 1960s audiences."[85]

Similarly, Burrows's use of color also morphed during his tenure at Bendel's, which was readily apparent in press coverage of his shows. A *Times* article by Morris from 1970, for his debut collection with Bendel's, noted his "absolute disregard for the established laws of color," stressing his affinity for a youthful mishmash of finger-paint–like colors: "Does a dress have a red top? He'll make the sleeves lime, the middle peach—and he'll add orange stockings for good measure. The strangest thing is, it works." Stutz, quoted in the article, concurs: "He stretches a rainbow over the body. It's never a hodgepodge."[86] Color was also the focus of an Irving Penn–shot feature in

Pat Cleveland and Stephen Burrows at the home of fashion photographer Sante Forlano, circa 1971. Courtesy of Charles Tracy Archive.

the September 1971 edition of *Vogue* called "Put Some Color in Your Life," which deemed Burrows the master of "sweater-fit clothes and color that moves." The latter phrase suggested that Burrows's vibrant colors were so vivid to the human eye that they seemingly refused to stay static, coming alive on the wearer's body. The adjective *Fauvist* was also to describe his manipulation of the chromatic spectrum, referencing an early twentieth-century avant-garde technique of painting in France that emphasized brilliant, nonnaturalistic colors. In interviews, Burrows said he inherited his mother's love of "strong color"; he recalled her teaching him how to draw as a child by using "a whole box of crayons to color one page," a telling description that sounds strikingly like how fashion journalists initially defined his early aesthetic.[87] Moreover, Burrows's characterization echoes others, like Cleveland and

Lopez, who absorbed early influences that later permeated their work; as art historian James Meyer argues, these similar shared "impressions" can shape a generation.[88]

Burrows's shift at Bendel's was not away from bright colors—he still used a panoply of shades in his work—but rather toward *fewer* colors, such as monochromatic dresses with a different-colored trim. (Recall the Burrows dress described by photographer Ming Smith in the previous chapter.) A review by Morris of his spring 1973 collection took notice of this palpable switch: "The mixing of different-color inserts in the same style is a Burrows signature that he has gone about refining. A green jacket has one yellow sleeve, one black sleeve, for instance. A couple of seasons back, it would have had a lot more colors."[89] Compared to earlier looks, his color-blocking seemed less haphazard and chaotic. Instead, the color juxtapositions appeared more intentional and elegant, often with a sizeable high-intensity color panel dominating the others, similar to Jones's Bauhaus-inspired maternity dress.

By 1973, one of Burrows's most widely known (and later copied) signatures was the "lettuce" edge on the hem of his dresses, initially the result of a workroom mishap. Cleveland recalls that during her first meeting with Burrows, she was at first perplexed when Bobby Breslau encouraged Burrows to put her "in the lettuce" until he "handed me a silk jersey dress with a hemline that looked like the round, feathery edges of several heads of lettuce."[90] For some dresses, Givhan discusses, Burrows used a very light Jasco-brand jersey (the same fabric favored by his peer Halston) usually used in lingerie; the difficulty of sewing such a buoyant fabric led to the accident: "Burrows pulled the stitching too tightly as he was hemming one of his jersey dresses, and the fabric curled. He liked the effect so much that he began using it not only along the hem but also along the cuff and at the neckline."[91] This effect of a wavy undulating hemline was only nicknamed "lettucing" after a meeting with *Vogue* editor in chief Diana Vreeland; she reportedly used the term *lettuce* to describe either an existing green dress of Burrows or one she envisioned him making for an upcoming shoot in Bali, according to different accounts. The October 1973 issue of *Vogue* featured actress Lauren Hutton in a black jersey dress with the signature finishing, shot by legendary photographer Richard Avedon.

Ever creative, Burrows also became known for other design innovations. His clothes often featured a blood-red zigzag topstitching, described by him as "the blood running through my anatomical clothes."[92] By 1973, this had become one of his most immediately recognizable elements: whether with a zigzag or lettucing, you always knew when you saw a Burrows. He also refused to use structural interiors or linings for his dresses, which made underwear superfluous and heightened the irresistible allure of his clothes. "The '70s was really about a newness that was coming around into fashion with everything being thin and light and not so serious. I liked to take the lining out of everything," he explained.[93] This sartorial feature also rendered these garments tailor-made for the body heat generated in discos, as we will shortly see.

In 1973, Burrows's success at Bendel's—selling close to half a million dollars' worth of his clothes a year—led to him becoming the first Black designer to win a Coty Award, the fashion equivalent of an Oscar.[94] Nominated in 1971 and 1972 before his first win in 1973, Burrows eventually would become a "Hall of Fame" member, winning the award three times. (He won his second in 1974 and his third in 1977.) His 1973 win, the result of a nationwide poll of four hundred fashion reporters, was remarkable, given that he was only twenty-nine years old. Paired with the other winner, thirty-year-old Calvin Klein (his Fire Island peer), it suggested that youthful neophytes were pushing aside the old guard. However, it also indicated that Burrows was no longer viewed solely as a Black designer. Just a year earlier, for instance, Alvin Ailey dancer Judith Jamison modeled a beige chiffon toga dress designed by him in a *Times* profile of three under-thirty Black designers: him, Scott Barrie, and Willi Smith. The article's title, "Young, Black, and Sophisticated," was an obvious riff on Nina Simone's 1969 song "To Be Young, Gifted, and Black," an anthem of Black solidarity.[95] And yet, in a June 1973 profile, *Women's Wear Daily* described Burrows as making "pure American fashion for the avant-garde contemporary woman," a characterization that does not explicitly mention his race.[96] Instead, he was perceived as producing cutting-edge women's wear in an artistic style now recognized as quintessentially American—a designation that implied a sizeable, diverse audience of consumers. In short, the cultural tide had shifted, and Burrows got his way.

Meanwhile, his presentation was an electrifying display of the appeal of his clothes. Held at Lincoln Center's Alice Tully Hall on June 21, 1973, the fashion show for the awards program was organized by Audrey Smaltz, the fashion editor of *Ebony* magazine. She introduced Burrows in Ebony Fashion Fair speak—"SB stands for Soul Brother. And here is Soul Brother Stephen Burrows"—before his models filled the stage.[97] In one surviving photograph of the proceedings, a trio of effervescent Black models in multicolored flowing dresses (one of whom appears to be Cleveland) poses upstage, microphones

Stephen Burrows's presentation at the 1973 Coty Awards, Alice Tully Hall at Lincoln Center, New York. *From left (foreground)*: Ramona Saunders, Pat Cleveland, Norma Jean Darden. Bethann Hardison, dressed in pink, stands in the background on the steps. Courtesy of Charles Tracy Archive.

in hand as if performing in a concert, as a longer line of models walk on tiered steps behind them. This more dramatic approach to modeling was a signature of Burrows's shows, as we will soon see. He became increasingly seen as a fresh face of American fashion and was offered a chance to represent the national industry that had suddenly embraced him in Paris. Naturally, he rose to the challenge with some help from his friends.

THE CHOREOGRAPHY OF BLACK MODELS AT THE BATTLE OF VERSAILLES

Soon after Burrows's Coty win, Eleanor Lambert, a savvy fashion publicist who helped establish the Coty Awards in 1943, invited him to participate in an evening fashion show staged at the Palace of Versailles. A seventeenth-century former royal residence built on the outskirts of Paris, the Palace of Versailles was an opulently baroque estate of twenty-three hundred rooms, including the famous Hall of Mirrors and the Royal Opera, where the show was ultimately held. However, it was badly in need of repairs, so Lambert shrewdly proposed the idea of a fundraising gala for its restoration, which she used as an opportunity to stage a showdown between American designers and the French fashion establishment. The latter was represented by an intimidating roster: Pierre Cardin, Emmanuel Ungaro, Hubert de Givenchy, Yves Saint Laurent, and Marc Bohan for Christian Dior. Determined to put the American fashion industry on the map, Lambert chose their American counterparts. Burrows was the fifth and last American designer she invited—Bill Blass, Anne Klein, Halston, and Oscar de la Renta made up the rest of the American contingent. Some perceived Burrows as an odd choice for the event, considering that he was a relatively young up-and-comer whose swift ascent was atypical amid the fashion elite. Moreover, he was the only Black designer in either camp. Officially called Le Grand Divertissement (The great entertainment), the event became known as the Battle of Versailles.

Remarkably, given the rigid system for choosing the models, Black models formed a sizable percentage of the bloc. The original ballot required a model to receive at least three votes from the five American designers to be cast.[98] Of the thirty-six slots, Black models were voted into eleven, several of whom were college graduates or Ebony Fashion Fair alums or had walked in Burrows's previous runway presentations. Burrows's friend and runway favorite Cleveland was a shoo-in; by then, she was one of "Antonio's Girls" along with Grace Jones and a "Halstonette," part of the entourage of models favored by Halston. (Halston, whom she met through Burrows, recognized her from her Ebony Fashion Fair days. "I watched you move to the music," he said when they first met.)[99] In addition to Cleveland, three more of the chosen— Alva Chinn, Billie Blair, and Amina Warsuma—also worked with Antonio Lopez. Harlem-bred Warsuma initially worked as a fitting room assistant at Bendel's. Burrows spotted her and eventually booked her for a show. The last chosen was Brooklyn-born Bethann Hardison, Burrows's house model at the time and a favorite of Halston's. Hardison, with a shaved head and attitude to spare, had been discovered by Willi Smith, Burrows's Fire Island peer, in 1967. (In a photograph from the event, she posed with Victor Fernandez, who began working as an assistant to Burrows that year and may have been romantically linked to him.)[100] Together, this group rose to the challenge of representing America.

The grand event took place on November 28, 1973, and even among the impeccably dressed guests and florid surroundings, the combination of Burrows's colorful, flowing dresses and the histrionics of the models who walked for him stole the show. After the lavish (and by all accounts, stiff) two-and-a-half-hour presentation of the French designers—which featured Russian ballet star Rudolf Nureyev dancing a scene from *The Sleeping Beauty* and the American expatriate Josephine Baker—it was finally America's turn. Burrows followed the opening segment: recent Academy Award winner Liza Minnelli's spirited rendition of "Bonjour, Paris!" and Klein's African-themed sportswear presentation. He showed his "famous lettuce edge on brightly colored jersey, interspersed with waves of multi-colored bibs, pop-art bodices, and long skirts with sweeping trains."[101] Hardison, one of the last to walk, strode the runway in a canary-yellow silk woven dress with a very long train that Burrows made explicitly for the proceedings as an homage to Paris couture. Hardison made an impression by "walking like a gangster," according to photographer Charles Tracy, a member of the commune Burrows asked to attend and photograph the proceeding; as Tracy described it, she affixed a death stare at the audience when she reached the front of the stage, before turning in the other direction.[102] Next, Cleveland, in her own words, walked in "Stephen's finale dress—a hot pastel multicolored creation with a dragon-tail train," just as the "trumpets and funky R&B guitar of Al Green's 'Love and Happiness' enveloped the whole theater." She held the elongated train of her dress and picked up speed as she walked, matching the music's tempo, until she got to the "front of the stage. And then—bam!—I dropped it hard with attitude and made a sharp turn. I could feel the weight of the train dragging behind me almost the length of the entire stage."[103]

Cleveland and Hardison's dramatic runway antics demonstrated how models' movements enhanced the design of Burrows's dresses in synthetic Pop Art shades—a looser, soulful, and more performative form of modeling influenced by Burrows. (According to Barry Ratoff, Charles Tracy's partner at the time, Tracy and Burrows collaborated on the choreography.)[104] Historian Elspeth Brown states, "Burrows encouraged his models to have fun, cut loose, and respond to the music: he preferred soul, especially Al Green, for its sensuality and groove."[105] Glenn O'Brien concurs that Burrows was a "fan of Motown, the Memphis sound, and the Philly sound" and that his models often "twirled down the runway to the music like it was the most enchanting party of all time."[106] Both writers suggest that the charm of Burrows's models was their joyful improvisation to R & B music, while showing how his clothes—and colors—moved.

A more nuanced perspective reveals how his models combined their quirks with his instruction to produce a specific theatrical effect. For instance, Cleveland recalled receiving tutelage in properly walking in Burrows's clothes from him, Bobby Breslau, and Hector Torres at Bendel's, learning "a modern couture walk but with a twist" that he invented. "I had to jut my hip bones forward as far as possible, then lean back with one leg forward and my tailbone tucked in. The idea was to get a straight line from my neck to my knee," while also adding "a few dancelike flourishes" of her own.[107] Thus, we can perceive how Burrows and Cleveland created this walking method *together*.

Dance and drama critic Clive Barnes later dissected the distinctive movement approach of the Black models at Versailles and their subsequent effect on fashion shows. In a 1978 *Vogue* article, he remarked that a white model was trained to be "a nonexistent coat hanger for what she was wearing," but "Black women are different. They have a triumphant assurance, a sense of bravado, of panache" that made them particularly well suited to the "new theatrical style fashion show."[108] His assertion implied that the dramaturgical skills of Black models, first perceived by many in Versailles, changed the culture of the modeling industry. Instead of simply wearing the clothes—but never upstaging them—the Black models at Versailles enlivened them. Like Lopez, Burrows recognized that collaborating with models with distinctive personalities and gestures *enhanced* the artistic process and, in Burrows's case, the visceral experience of fashion shows. The ever-astute Warhol, who attended the show and sat in the American box, also noticed. In a 1977 article by Bernadine Morris discussing a shift in the typical locale of fashion shows—from designer showrooms to hotel ballrooms, discos, off-Broadway theaters, and restaurants—he remarked that they were "the new art form, more exciting than theater."[109]

Burrows's models pushed the envelope even further that evening in Versailles. After Cleveland, the final model, completed her walk, she remained at the front of the stage, and the rest of the models joined her. Later, Cleveland recalled, they spontaneously vogued as a group. Here, on the outskirts of Paris, we have an unlikely connection to Paradise Garage, the industrial

Battle of Versailles Burrows's rehearsal, Paris, 1973. *From left*: Norma Jean Darden, Jennifer Brice, Heidi Gold, Alva Chinn, Nancy North, Amina Warsuma, Carla Araque, Karen Bjornsen, Chris Royer. Courtesy of Charles Tracy Archive.

downtown disco from the last chapter, where the attitude of gay ballroom culture was integral to its atmosphere. Amid DJ Larry Levan's propulsive sets, members of ballroom houses practiced and refined their moves, starting with the Ganzas, as the Xtravaganzas were nicknamed.[110] And again, we come back to Burrows's ostensible grab-bag of sources: American soul music and queer theatrical sensibilities mixed with bubbly mostly Black models and his lustrously colored dresses, described by *Vogue* as resembling "tropical-Pop-ical butterflies." The joie de vivre expressed in his presentation was the product of these divergent influences brought together and compelled to intermesh into a greater whole, not unlike the syncopated rhythms Burrows favored.

Style, in other words, existed on multiple registers here. And it was not limited to the discrete objects—the individual items of clothing—that we typically conceive of as the locus where style resides. Burrows's American models skillfully deployed bodily "fronts," projected out to the predominantly

French audience, manipulating the physical body as an instrument through which style could be displayed and actively calibrated. The addition of voguing to this informational vortex added yet another layer, since part of their "expressive equipment" was an emulation of a dance form drawn from a subterraneous Black and Brown queer sociality.[111] This suggested a bottom-up traversal of voguing from an antinormative subculture to a subset of Black models in an exclusive industry often rife with racism and snobbery. Ironically, voguing was meant to emulate and mimic successful print and runway models, the same elite group redeploying the art form in an invitation-only, aristocratic setting across the Atlantic. Burrows's models bodily invoked the shadow presence of New York City ballroom culture. As a means of intentional communication and nonverbal expression, style surfaced in this scene of colliding referents, mesmerizing color combinations, and gesturing bodies.

Burrows's presentation at the Battle of Versailles also illustrated that his loosely draped dresses were what Robin Bernstein would call "scriptive things," activated in the fruitful encounter between the inanimate object and the embodied gestures of the model.[112] In other words, what if we understood the friction generated by the imbrication of object and subject as an *event* in and of itself? In this force field, Burrows's jersey and chiffon dresses in painterly colors were props that came to life when worn by the dramatis personae, the lithe models cast in his shows. Admittedly, this notion could apply to any designer. However, the characterization offered by *Vogue*—that Burrows was a master at creating "color that moves"—suggests the performativity inherent in his clothes. The genesis of Burrows's designs—the club rather than fashion history—is also telling. His inspiration, at least initially, was rooted in creating dresses inspired by a body in motion, specifically the young women he would mambo with at the Palladium during his adolescence. The incorporation of voguing and soul music in his runway show at Versailles made sense, for his clothes, even years later, were imbued by the energy conjured on the dance floor. In an interview from 1977, he explained, "I can see a girl dancing, and immediately a dress pops in my head. A look. An image. Dancing is always in my clothes—the movement; that you can do anything and feel free in the garment."[113] This sense of freedom and unbounded movement would become even more pronounced in the late 1970s, when Burrows's barely there dresses became the attire of choice for the glamorous habitués of the discotheque, and nowhere more so than Studio 54.

CHAIN MAIL, CHIFFON, AND DISCO AT STUDIO 54

Despite the triumph of Versailles, the event ushered in a multiyear slump in his career. In the summer of 1973, as he was preparing for the Battle of Versailles, Burrows parted ways with Bendel's because it did not give him a raise despite his brisk sales. Stutz, unfortunately, found out about his departure through the press. With encouragement from his friend Halston and help from entrepreneur Ben Shaw, he ventured out on his own. He founded his company, Stephen Burrows Inc., on Seventh Avenue in the Garment District. That November, just before he flew to France, he showed his first collection alongside Halston's Ultrasuede shirtdresses; it was praised by the *New York Times* and *Women's Wear Daily* as further proof of his sartorial brilliance.[114] While this led to $900,000 in orders, only a third had been shipped to stores by the end of 1973. Factories had to figure out how to reproduce his signature zigzag stitching and "lettuce" edging. This learning curve led to shipping delays and canceled orders. In 1975, he became the first Black designer to gain a fragrance deal, signing a contract with Max Factor for $50,000 plus royalties, and launched the eponymous scent Stephen B that year. And yet, despite Max Factor's paying Burrows an almost $6 million advance, the lack of the necessary advertising support led the company to deem the fragrance only a "moderate" success.[115]

However, Burrows's decline seemed less about sales and more about the change in the creative process, from a commune of friends and collaborators housed in his boutique at Bendel's to an anonymous factory where his clothes could be efficiently mass-produced and quickly sold. Thus, one can surmise that the clothes lost a crucial part of their signature—if elusive—appeal: the community of peers whose friendship and love underpinned the garments and sustained his business.

In Burrows's case, as he quickly realized, his classic runway style—eclectic pieces that suggested a wearer's fashion sense—did not square with the imperative of department stores, which emphasized matching looks. As the head of his new company, Burrows also had a role in watering down his designs to appeal to a broader customer base. As one friend noted, "I knew it was all over when I stopped in the office one day and saw that people had been hired to do his sketches and help him choose colors."[116] This anecdote is telling; Burrows, the pioneer of "color that moves," was not in complete charge of his color schemes or drawing the clothes that usually sprung from his imagination. Burrows is blunt about his side of this story: "I thought I wanted to dress everybody. Then I saw who everybody was and all they wanted was polyester and they didn't care about anything as long it washed. I knew it wasn't for me."[117] Thus, Burrows's meticulous attention to craft—such as his "lettuce" hems or unusual fabric choices—was a particular value mainstream consumers neither appreciated nor shared. Dressing the world, it seems, required sacrificing artistic control and whimsy for capital and convenience.

Consequently, in the spring of 1976, Burrows contacted Stutz, hoping to repair the professional relationship he had badly fractured three years earlier with his sudden departure. By December 1976, he was back in his old boutique at Bendel's, plotting a career comeback.

In 1977, the ever-innovative Burrows ingeniously manipulated an unexpected material for his fall collection: metal mesh, produced by American manufacturer Whiting and Davis. This mesh, which looked like densely woven chain mail, was typically used for dainty accessories. Yet, when Burrows remixed it into slinky chain mail tops, the heavy material had a beautiful drape that accentuated the body's curves and shimmered under the lights like a disco ball.

He left behind the factory and the desire to dress everyone, and instead returned to making his clothes in his former studio at Bendel's. The impact was almost immediate. By the end of 1977, Pat Cleveland and Jerry Hall wore variations of the chain mail top to Studio 54. Grace Jones is photographed wearing one, as is model Iman. In another photograph taken that year, Cleveland wears a bronze version of the chain mail top and a magenta chiffon skirt, undulating in an airborne swirl. She wears the same outfit in a photo that accompanied an article published in the *Times* on June 5, 1977. Captioned "Burrows Is Back—with a Little Help from His Friends," the piece featured him photographed with some of his peers—Cleveland, Breslau, Hardison, Schumacher, and Stutz—and his mother and grandmother, all celebrating his rebound.

The same idea of a larger collective that underpinned Burrows's triumphant return to form was made more literal in a Mary Poppins–inspired *Vogue* shoot, also in 1977. Titled "Stephen Burrows: At the Top of His Form," the spread featured an umbrella-wielding Burrows held aloft by eight models, all dressed in his clothes. Hall wore a brass chain mail top and chiffon dress, while Cleveland wore a two-piece gold chain mail dress with deep

Pat Cleveland wearing Burrows in front of 9 West Fifty-Seventh Street for *New York* magazine, 1977. Courtesy of Charles Tracy Archive.

slits on the side. (Farrah Fawcett wore the same ensemble to the 1978 Academy Awards.) Alva Chinn, Iman, and Hardison were also prominent in the piece—and rightly so—not just as models for Burrows's clothes but also as his friends. In Hardison's case, her roles were multiple: She worked as an assistant to Burrows while modeling for him, first as his showroom model and then as his fitting model, and eventually was entrusted to run his studio. This suggests Hardison's level of influence and knowledge as a young model in the 1970s. (Later, she started her highly successful namesake modeling agency in 1984.) It is another example of horizontal art-making, rejecting typical vertical hierarchies that reinforce power structures and categorical distinctions, and instead delighting in the freedom to work across different genres and varying forms of expertise. Thus, as we have repeatedly seen, friendship and art-making flowed together.

It seems fitting that Burrows ascended to the "top of his form" by returning to his roots: the nightclub. With the success of his chain mail dresses and tops, Burrows became part of an elite group of fashion superstars in the late 1970s who created the sexually suggestive silhouettes that helped make Studio 54 famous. During its brief but legendary reign, the dance club was thronged by celebrities and dancers, all carefully dressed to impress. This made the venue another "fashion gallery," Warhol's term for Max's Kansas City. (Coincidentally, Studio 54 also hosted several fashion shows.) Burrows's peers included Halston, Norma Kamali, Calvin Klein, and Giorgio di Sant' Angelo. In addition to Burrows's chain mail tops, Halston's silk chiffon dresses, Kamali's sleeping bag coat, Klein's blue jeans, and di Sant' Angelo's advancement of the swimsuit with wrap skirt as evening wear (alternate variations of which were also designed by Kamali and Lopez) were all popular looks at Studio 54. The ever-fashionable Potassa de la Fayette, who partied with Jones and Cleveland and appeared in Lopez's Instamatics, was captured in a Burrows off-the-shoulder dress on the dance floor in 1978, her head thrown back in sheer ecstasy. "For the non-famous, the key to entry was fashion," Sonnet Stanfill writes, and those who did not indulge in designer fashions often relied on sheer outrageousness in their attire to gain admittance.[118] Like the other key stops in this cartography of the 1970s, Studio 54 was a playground for sartorial bombast and adventurous self-display.

Burrows's dresses, though, seemed to have a particular resonance with the disco scene, as fashion journalists and his peers confirmed. Jerry Hall appeared in the July 1978 edition of *Harper's Bazaar*, for instance, wearing a strapless drawstring silk dress designed by Burrows, which the magazine declared "upbeat dressing" fit for a "disco night."[119] This sentiment was shared by *Women's Wear Daily* and the *New York Times* in separate articles on his 1978 "Springtime Playtime" resort collection. Bernadine Morris noted that his pieces, "freewheeling, often in outrageous colors," were "especially marvelous for night. That's when the Burrows fan spends a lot of time at discotheques, and she can be assured that no matter what the crowd is wearing she won't be overlooked."[120] He was also praised for his "bright looks for evening playtime," such as a "shocking pink" matte jersey dress modeled by Cleveland, a hue prominent in previous discussions of Antonio Lopez and Grace Jones. Likewise, in an article published in *Life* magazine that year titled "Three Black Designers" and shot by photographer Gordon Parks, a caption indicated that Burrows's bias-cut top, while designed to float over matching pants, could also be worn separately as a "disco dress."[121] Burrows seemed to think of the less-is-more aesthetic of the disco era when discussing his ideal customer in 1977: "You have to have an attitude about yourself that's, well, almost snobby. My customer has to know who she is. Or else she's going to put my things on and say, 'I can't wear this! Everything's showing!' My customer wants to show it. She knows she's groovy."[122]

Meanwhile, Italian fashion editor Daniela Morera, photographed with Burrows and Hardison in 1977 at a Studio 54 party for Valentino, made clear that his clothes were synonymous with disco's primal rhythms. "They were exactly like the music itself, that enveloping, cocooning sound: sexy, sensuous, visceral vibrations," she says. And to her, the confident women who chose to wear Burrows's dresses "emanated the same shared aura, joining them together into an implicit community—the 'commune,' the hedonistic assemblage."[123] Others echo her description of the "chromatic and moving qualities" of his clothes. Glenn O'Brien likens Burrows's dresses to inert flowers that "bloomed into motion" when worn in the discotheque, since a "Burrows dress wasn't made to lean up against a wall in or sit in—it was made to twirl, leap, and undulate in, made to move." He adds, "Burrows made the first disco dresses, bias-cut masterpieces that accentuated curves and amplified the drama of dance, and all in colors that looked like the future. When a girl put on one of those dresses, a party started around her."[124]

More accurately, the collective space of the disco preceded and prompted the dress. Borrowing curator Naomi Beckwith's parlance, Burrows's process seems to exemplify an "artform emerging from social life," in which aesthetic experience is influenced by, rather than cleaved off from, everyday living.[125] The dance floor is arguably the best place to ponder the legacy of Burrows, who was so often visually portrayed dancing, as if translating that momentary bliss into a sensuously cut, body-hugging dress that came to life.

After all, Stephen Burrows was not only an artist who understood how to skillfully marry flesh and fabric through his legendary garments but also a dancer who knew how to infuse those aesthetic objects with the vitality of the crowded disco. He continued to sharpen his artistic vision as his career progressed and the times changed, moving from the leather pants and patchwork suedes he modeled on Fire Island in the late 1960s to the chiffon dresses he designed for the moneyed clients of Henri Bendel in the early 1970s. His sheer talent enabled him to bypass the standard rules of the fashion industry, notorious for its gatekeeping and overt racism, and rise through the ranks while not compromising the critical components of his artistic style—from visible seams to lettuce hems, from featherweight fabrics to vertiginous, psychedelic-like color. But what we also witnessed were the virtues of working together, as many members of Burrows's collective, or "fashion family," helped propel him forward as they traveled from the beaches of Fire Island to the sidewalks of downtown New York City and later the patrician Upper East Side. In doing so, friendship looms throughout the cartography of this chapter as a crucial support for the proliferation of Burrows's aesthetic point of view. This idiosyncratic network of models, leather-makers, photographers, jewelry designers, and other artistically inclined individuals shared a preoccupation with style as an instrument for hypercolorful aesthetic expression.

Some say that style enters where facts stop and feeling starts.

Nelson Goodman, *Ways of Worldmaking*

Afterword

Style Is a Feeling

We have traced the aesthetic breakthroughs and spatial wanderings of Antonio Lopez, Grace Jones, and Stephen Burrows as they blazed fiery, distinct paths of artistic expression. Each crossed—gleefully, relentlessly—over the typical limits between high art and popular cultures, blending erudite artsy ideas with the erotic sensuality of the disco and the gritty tenacity of the street. And we have witnessed how their artistic styles developed through the tension between established schemas and the creation of "something unique and individualized."[1] Under their spells, a department store window featured whimsical performance art, a trendy hair salon hosted a photo shoot for a fledgling model, and a runway show morphed into a sidewalk disco. They exhibited quiet concentration as they sketched in vast artist studios, configured their bodies in held poses, or toiled in workrooms amid the hum of sewing machines. They traded one kind of intensity for another when they cut loose at storied nocturnal venues such as Enchanted Gardens, Paradise Garage, Max's Kansas City, or Studio 54. This feedback loop, from daytime to nighttime and downtown to uptown, fed and informed their voracious appetites for more and better pleasures, a broader palette of inspiration, and the intangibility of the *new*. Throughout all this, each envisioned aesthetic creation as a collective enterprise. Therefore, they enlisted unconventional cohorts of like-minded peers in experimental endeavors: bathtub photo shoots, a disco baby shower turned performance, and a black leather-clad clothing boutique. They repeatedly epitomized working together—and *being-with*, to use José Esteban Muñoz's language—as a shared artistic philosophy and an intoxicating way of life.[2]

I have drawn our attention to style in these pages to illustrate that, far from a formless and ahistorical concept, it is an aesthetic medium constantly performed into being. In 1970s New York City, on the one hand, style was embodied; it was a delicate choreography of poses, clothing, and attitude, as demonstrated by models Pat Cleveland and Bethann Hardison at the Battle of Versailles. On the other hand, it described a recognizable artistic signature—Burrows's color-blocked jersey dresses, Lopez's three-by-three Instamatic grid, or Jones's campy theatricality. Each was inhabiting style and making art. While seemingly amorphous, style was the preferred medium of artistic expression, refined and actualized through these artists' outsize imaginations and deliberate efforts, as well as those of their friends. Collectively, they manipulated style like a pliable block of clay that could be sculpted into fascinating shapes, endowed with fresh and often provocative meanings.

Philosopher Nelson Goodman argues that "the discernment of style is an integral aspect of the understanding of works of art and the worlds they present."[3] We should recognize that the dominant style of any era tends to reflect and reiterate the social and political norms of the time. Since style constantly evolves, whatever is new—what rejects "the deadening givens of accepted practice," as art historian Thomas Crow suggests—tends to challenge rather than embody those norms.[4] Our protagonists and their coconspirators intervened in those rigid cultural logics, retooling them to reflect their honed sensibilities.

As the long 1970s segued into the 1980s, Lopez and Ramos continued collaborating and keeping busy in their Union Square studio. In 1981, after a chance meeting with the Bronx-based Rock Steady Crew, Lopez took photographs and made drawings of their urban bravado. That work led to an influx of Black and Brown teenagers to the studio. Lopez took casual Polaroids, on which they scribbled their names and contact information. In exchange, he captured their youthful insouciance and, for several, their hip-hop-inflected fashions: sleek Adidas tracksuits, fluffy Kangol bucket hats, and oversized glasses. In addition, *Playboy, Vogue,* and GQ commissioned Lopez's drawings of models and celebrities, and his illustrations also appeared in advertising campaigns for Bloomingdale's and Missoni. His work was also prominently featured in *Vanity*, an avant-garde and almost entirely illustrated fashion magazine he helped to cofound with Anna Piaggi.

While fashion illustration paid the bills, he and Ramos used the studio to pivot to more personal projects. They published two books: *Antonio's Girls* (1982), which included portraits from 1973 to 1981 of models Grace Jones, Pat Cleveland, and Jerry Hall; and *Antonio's Tales from the Thousand and One Nights* (1985), a visually lush rendering of select Middle Eastern folktales from the Arabian Nights. Fiorucci hosted the book release party for the former, with the Rock Steady Crew breakdancing in the store windows. From 1982 to 1985, he focused on the intricacies of the human form in a series of black-and-white pencil drawings and four large-scale watercolors of dancers from the Louis Falco Dance Company. He also staged workshops on both coasts—at his alma mater, FIT, and the ArtCenter College of Design in Pasadena, California—and in the Dominican Republic. In 1987, Lopez was in Los Angeles for two weeks for a show of his drawings at the Robert Berman Gallery in Santa Monica. According to Susan Baraz, one of Lopez's models in his FIT days, he became ill and was hospitalized before the opening. He died shortly thereafter at the UCLA Medical Center; he was only forty-four. The cause of death given by an obituary in the *Los Angeles Times* was Kaposi sarcoma, a rare form of cancer that often affects people with immune deficiencies.[5] It was not publicly discussed, given the stigma at the time, but Lopez had AIDS. Ramos continued living in the loft adjoining the studio with his partner Paul Caranicas, where he wrote the book *Antonio 60 70 80* (1995) and curated the accompanying exhibition.[6] Later that same year, before the exhibition opened, he died of AIDS-related causes; he was fifty-three.

It is worth briefly pausing here to acknowledge the definitive sense of an *end* that marks Lopez's premature death and the questions it provokes. For instance, did Lopez feel he was sufficiently recognized as a bona fide artist? Despite his prodigious output in various genres, Lopez desired that title—undoubtedly, for the fine-art legitimacy it would bestow on him. (According to his obituary in the *Times*, a show of his drawings was taking place in Munich at the time of his death.)[7] Lopez accomplished a staggering amount, personally and professionally, in his abbreviated life. But this is an undeniable loss. Lopez was perhaps the most drawn to the sensory delights of the street out of our trio of protagonists, interpreting it as a reliable indicator of the zeitgeist. In short, the street was where one could savor the city's flavors and be enchanted by Black and Brown "styles of saying."[8] Yet Lopez did not witness, for instance, hip-hop's increased flirtation with the mainstream during the decade after his death and the various urban-inspired fashion trends—some bubbling up from the outer boroughs—that circulated because of it. Ultimately, we do not know how these innovations or others would have affected his ever-mutating artistic style. We also lose the opportunity to see how he would have continued to evolve alongside Jones and Burrows as the decades accumulated.

Jones, who lived in Union Square with her then-boyfriend and artistic collaborator Jean-Paul Goude, released several creative projects in the early 1980s. Her fourth studio album, *Warm Leatherette* (1980), was a sharp departure from her previous music, shifting from disco to a new wave–reggae sound; its cover image, conceived by Goude, debuted Jones's new androgynous look, complete with her signature high-top haircut.[9] The follow-up, *Nightclubbing* (1981), was Jones's commercial and critical breakthrough, producing her first pop hit, "Pull Up to the Bumper."[10] That album cover, also by Goude—a painted photograph of her shirtless in a wide-shouldered Armani men's suit jacket, her skin tinged a deep blue-violet hue—crystallized Jones's pop persona. Similarly, the long-form music video *One Man Show* (1982), a mash-up of concert footage and music videos, adeptly displayed Jones's chameleonic stage presence and Goude's minimalistic set design.[11] (It was nominated for the inaugural Grammy for Best Long Form Music Video in 1984.)

Even as Jones, like Lopez, moved into other arenas—principally, music and film—she never entirely left behind her beginnings. She was and remains both a model and a performer who relishes artistic idiosyncrasy. This is particularly true in her relationship with Keith Haring, who met Jones in 1984 via Andy Warhol and eventually used her body as a literal canvas for his hieroglyphic-like markings. This creative act was documented by photographers Robert Mapplethorpe and Tseng Kwong Chi. The latter captured it in process at Paradise Garage in 1985, the downtown dance club Jones and Haring adored. The following year, Haring repainted her for her role as a vampire in the horror-comedy film *Vamp* (1986). That same year, he was shown painting a sixty-foot skirt in the music video for her single "I'm Not Perfect (but I'm Perfect for You)." Jones writhed in the enormous skirt at the end of the video, surfacing as a "pop-primitive explosion."[12] Nile Rodgers of

Chic, Warhol, and Tina Chow, one of Lopez's models, also made cameos. Jones's commercial work in the 1980s, in other words, seemed to draw continually on the collaborative ethos of the 1970s.

Meanwhile, Stephen Burrows was still working at his boutique within Henri Bendel as the 1980s rolled around. After his comeback in 1977 and participation in "The Best Six" fashion event in Tokyo in 1978 (where he was the only American designer invited), he remained at Bendel's until 1982, when his boutique closed.[13] His commercial success and his interest in it seemed to wane simultaneously. "I suffered from fashion burnout for a while," he noted in a 1993 interview with Bernadine Morris of the *Times*.[14] By and large, he seemingly withdrew from the mainstream fashion world. In the meantime, Burrows supported himself by making clothes for private clients and the theater while designing sportswear sold at Barneys New York.[15] On a more personal level, his relationship with Fire Island, once the summer playground of his "fashion family," also morphed. Burrows, a regular from 1965 until 1984, described how losing so many of his friends to the AIDS epidemic took the joy out of going.[16] This personal loss, plus the industry's breakneck pace, seemed to merge into a creative ennui.

Eventually, inspiration returned; in 1993, Burrows reemerged. After seeing his sketches, the president of Bendel's invited him to make evening wear and provided him with a niche on the fourth floor to sell his garments to the public. Burrows's clothes were made in his factory on Adam Clayton Powell Boulevard in Harlem, the neighborhood he now called home. "I have my own zigzag machines to do the scalloped edges so the factory people can't tell me they can't get the equipment"—likely hard-earned wisdom from his late-seventies relaunch. Morris described the new offerings, priced from $850 to $1600; they included "bodysuits, a short velvet flyaway jacket with chiffon godets at the sleeves and a single patchwork jacket, a reference to his color-block design days." In addition to skirts and pants, a "bathrobe jacket" indexed "the casual ease of fashion today."[17]

In perhaps further proof that all fashions are cyclical, a few decades later, during the 2010s, Lopez, Jones, and Burrows were each celebrated with retrospectives of their work alongside several publications and documentaries. Lopez's life and body of work were showcased in an art book (*Antonio: Fashion, Art, Sex, and Disco*, 2012), an exhibition ("Antonio Lopez: Future Funk Fashion," El Museo del Barrio, 2016), and a documentary (*Antonio Lopez 1970: Sex, Fashion, and Disco*, 2017). Similarly, Jones published a memoir (*I'll Never Write My Memoirs*, 2015), released a documentary (*Bloodlight and Bami*, 2017), and served as the underpinning of a group show ("The Grace Jones Project," Museum of the African Diaspora, 2016). Finally, an exhibition and accompanying book of the same title examined Burrows's trajectory ("Stephen Burrows: When Fashion Danced," Museum of the City of New York, 2013), while another exhibition, curated by André Leon Talley, coincided with Burrows's winning a lifetime achievement award named after him ("An American Master of Inventive Design," Savannah College of Art and Design, 2014). Museum and gallery exhibitions focused on each of our protagonists, or prominently featuring them, have continued into the 2020s, a testament to the enduring appeal of their work.[18]

Meanwhile, some of their equally noteworthy collaborators have also gained newfound visibility. Models Pat Cleveland and Bethann Hardison's experiences in the fashion industry are explored via the former's memoirs and the latter's documentary (which in turn featured Burrows and Cleveland as talking heads). The late Willi Smith, Burrows's Fire Island compatriot who passed away from AIDS in 1987, was the subject of a retrospective ("Willi Smith: Street Couture") at the Cooper Hewitt, Smithsonian Design Museum in New York City in 2020—the first exhibition and book in the institution's history dedicated to a Black designer. Ming Smith and Anthony Barboza's photography was part of a traveling show devoted to the Kamoinge Workshop, the overlooked working group of Black photographers of which both were members ("Working Together: Louis Draper and the Kamoinge Workshop," Virginia Museum of Fine Art, 2020). Finally, the recent rediscovery of Smith's poetic photography practice has led to a resurgence of interest in her body of work; this resulted in an eponymous book and, in a full-circle moment, a Museum of Modern Art exhibition ("Projects: Ming Smith," 2023).

Yet this is only part of the story; a more robust narrative accounts for the more extensive and ambiguous way their artistic contributions are embedded in the cultural landscape and how they affect what subsequent generations can do in their art. The most obvious example of this is Grace Jones. Her aggressive visual image, unusual for a Black female artist then, was a paradigm shifter that has seemingly permitted other musical artists of color to create bold, "loud," and highly aestheticized personas. Another instance is Stephen Burrows. His graceful Black models shimmied down the runway rather than simply strutting, responding to R & B music in his colorful garments.

That more soulful emphasis in fashion, one openly drawing on Black cultural traditions, is evident in numerous places, such as the label Pyer Moss, whose various collections have explored the legacies of Sister Rosetta Tharpe, Black cowboys, and FUBU, the streetwear label popularized by 1990s rappers.[19] Finally, Lopez's inclusive attention to those fashionable Black and Brown youth on the margins reminds me of the Telfar bag drop that took place at a Rainbow Shops fashion store on Fulton Street in Brooklyn in 2022. Consumers—primarily young, many queer, and virtually all of color—lined up to purchase what's been christened the "Bushwick Birkin," the covetable (and affordable) vegan leather bag designed by Telfar Clemens that is typically sold out online within minutes.[20]

Interestingly, even when these figures aren't explicitly referenced, we can see continuities between them and contemporary makers of color. For instance, the cultural pride Lopez, Jones, and Burrows possessed and filtered through their creative projects is mirrored by several prominent designers. Mexican American Willy Chavarria's zoot suit–inspired menswear, English designer Grace Wales Bonner's crochet-strip tracksuits mining Black diasporic imagery, and Dominican American Raul Lopez's tribute to his grandmother via his Ana handbag are some examples. Moreover, Christopher John Rogers's searingly bright hues and contrasting patterns in his women's wear are reminiscent of Burrows's saturated color palettes. Our three protagonists altered the cultural milieu in the 1970s, sometimes playfully and sometimes subtly rebuking the norms of the fashion establishment, especially its cultural insularity. But that work is never done.

These young designers of color also exude a mutual desire to fundamentally descramble the codes of the mainstream fashion industry, broadening its assumed artistic referents to include a rich sense of ethnic heritage while redefining what constitutes the high end of the fashion spectrum. For instance, Chavarria's spring 2022 collection was shown in a barbershop. It featured shirtless male models in super-high, cinched-in belted trousers with the exaggerated proportions of ball skirts, with satin boxers peeking over the waistbands.[21] Wales Bonner's sporty fall 2024 collection, called "Dream Study," was an homage to the collegiate style of students from Howard University, a historically Black college; to prepare, she conducted archival research at the institution, including sourcing 1990s yearbooks.[22] And Lopez, who says his collections for his label Luar (his first name spelled backward) have always been inspired by "bad bitches," titled his fall 2023 collection "Calle Pero Elegante"—which translates to "street but elegant"—as an homage to the "gangstresses" he grew up with in Williamsburg, Brooklyn.[23] Meanwhile, the legacy of spirited and outspoken models like Hardison, Cleveland, and Jones is mirrored by Paloma Elsesser and Precious Lee, curve and plus-sized supermodels who have been open about their precarity in a system defined by narrow ideals of racialized and physical beauty, especially in terms of body sizes.[24]

When filtered through the examples of Antonio Lopez, Grace Jones, and Stephen Burrows, we can see a continuum from then to today—a turf war over the aesthetic. Our trio shares with contemporary makers an explicit desire to widen the types of artistic influences recognized as legitimate and canonical sources of knowledge. These artists suggest that visual tropes from Black and Brown cultural lineages are too often treated as fads or, worse, gimmicks to garner publicity and sales.[25] However, this current generation of talented and highly motivated young creatives of color is emphatic about perceiving these as plush archives rather than mere trends. Across performance, fashion, and visual art, these artisans are leaping over categorical delineations and sparking cross-generational dialogues—for instance, Grace Wales Bonner used portraits by the artist Lubaina Himid, associated with the British Black Arts Movement in the 1980s, on her textiles.[26] In doing so, they refuse the tendency to water down diversity and inclusion to mere buzzwords, "in" one season and "out" the next. And, like Lopez, Jones, and Burrows, they know that aesthetic inspiration can come from unlikely and culturally specific sources, be it the abundant fabric of the zoot suit, the bling of nineties hip-hop culture, or the swag of the goddess from around the way—all fertile artistic styles that speak through vibrant vocabularies of their own making.

Our other central protagonist, New York City, continues to be a veritable magnet for aspiring artists seeking to generate new forms of aesthetic expression while radically invigorating existing ones. It is the capital of the art world, home to a thriving ecosystem of creatively inclined individuals and the more extensive global apparatus of galleries, museums, and art fairs that sustain them. But the artists themselves are the center of gravity, imbuing the city with their experimental flair and sense of drive. Writer M. H. Miller puts it nicely: "No part of this system would function—or have any meaning at all—without the artists themselves. They're the real reason New York and the art world are synonymous. Even now, when real estate prices have reached new heights that would shock those postwar pioneers, artists still live here and, more important, they still work here."[27]

Granted, it is easy to lament that rents are no longer cheap and that SoHo's enormous lofts, once occupied by artists in the 1970s, are now sought-after, multimillion-dollar apartments. This is the familiar story of New York City's rapid gentrification, which has made living and working in Manhattan untenable for many artists, pushing them out to neighborhoods in the outer boroughs. But, as Miller details, the communal vibe of artist-dominated buildings, while rarer, remains. Instead of the expansive Union Square studio Lopez and Ramos worked in, a small group of artists of color may share equipment and a studio paid for by one member—this is what the six photographers, who go by Mycelial Artists Collective, do in a space in Williamsburg. A studio may be a desk in a coworking space or a dimly lit closet; an exhibition space may be in a former Dunkin' Donuts; and a gallery may be the living room of a rented brownstone apartment in Crown Heights—I am referencing Medium Tings, the nomadic gallery founded and run by Stephanie Baptist.[28] Staging a fashion show can be prohibitively expensive for an emerging designer.[29] But there, too, innovation abounds—Pyer Moss, for example, staged a runway show at the Weeksville Heritage Center in Brooklyn, dedicated to one of the first free Black communities in the United States. Imagination continues to abound in nascent artistic styles and the spatial sites that nourish and enable them.

Like Lopez in the 1970s, a modern-day flaneur can easily observe that people are still making things, collaborating with friends, and living their lives beautifully and loudly. And the streets—from dense sidewalks to open-air subway platforms—continue to be thrilling displays of the sartorial braggadocio and carefully cultivated points of view that make people-watching a sport.

Perhaps the most notable difference from a half century ago is that there are no longer two primary gravitational centers—uptown and downtown. Instead, we have a polyglot collection of far-flung centers of creativity. And that creativity is often brilliantly on display not only in Manhattan but also in the outer boroughs. Hence, one can speculate that the contemporary equivalents of Lopez, Jones, and Burrows may be more likely situated in a Brooklyn neighborhood than Union Square. Like Jones, they may also bypass the gallery system, preferring more relaxed and industrial venues. They may also create fun concept stores like Fiorucci or Burrows's O Boutique, where clothes, visual art, and design share space. No matter the manner chosen, we can witness the steady proliferation of aesthetic vocabularies of style daily, be it the canvas on the easel or the body itself.

Throughout and beneath the story of inhabiting style and making art in 1970s New York City has been another narrative: my argument that we must broaden art history. We must expand the subjects of art history (i.e., people who have been ignored or understudied) and its theoretical approaches (i.e., style, the surface, and attention to the nonoptical, like sensations of feeling or the impact of the aural). This critique has emerged, in part, through the process of conceptualizing and writing this book: The protagonists I delineate in these pages are absent in the more traditional archives I consulted when starting my research. Hence, while I could *hear* the beginnings of a story in the musical rhythms of the time, I could not initially locate it in the places I had been trained to look for evidence. Grace Jones was the first member of this trio to emerge in my thinking; her absence from prototypical repositories, however, made it difficult to assess her working relationships with other artists (besides Jean-Paul Goude, the relationship academic scholarship tends to focus on). It was not until I first saw Antonio Lopez's work that I felt a palpable sensation—a feeling that his presence was foundational to this project, even if I knew nothing about him or his friendship with Jones. Similarly, though I had seen Stephen Burrows's dresses firsthand, it wasn't until I later read about him in Pat Cleveland's memoir that it became clear that he was the final member of this ensemble. And yet he, too, frustrated traditional methods, as there wasn't an easily identifiable source to turn to or a model for writing about a fashion designer through an interdisciplinary approach. Such is the difficulty and the delight of researching the underresearched; the details are fragmented, assembled slowly from numerous places, guided by instinctual meandering rather than a clear path. As a result, building this archive has been guided by an open-ended approach that, while attentive to historical facts, has been more guided by the almost-mythic stories of friendship and art-making that circulate throughout. By necessity, the archive I have constructed here supersedes any singular institution and is looser in its construction, encompassing a wider variety of what constitutes forms of knowledge and feeling.

Meanwhile, as the central figures of *Mavericks of Style* slowly clicked into place, my exhaustive research also turned outward to the demimonde of other visionary individuals and like-minded partygoers populating this illusory but not entirely faded history of 1970s New York City. The lore surrounding certain now-closed hotspots sparked my desire to trace and illuminate their spatial and affective outlines, hoping to capture their physical layout and, more importantly, the visceral sensations and sense of belonging they once ignited. My repeated turn to photographs throughout has been driven by a similar impetus: to see them as queer archival objects that hint at elusive feelings and zones of relation. Like extant vinyl records of Levan's legendary DJ sets, they offer momentary glimpses of a not fully knowable past.

Despite the "institutional illusiveness" of many of the objects and ephemera in this study, to use Krista Thompson's language, I have no desire for the opposite. The goal of "inclusion and recognition in more conventional art-historical paradigms" is beside the point.[30] Instead, as she and others suggest, we need a different model of art history, one taking place in the streets and the clubs rather than—or as well as—the museum. An art history that, rather than slotting artists of color into existing narratives, builds unconventional canons and conceptual frameworks. An art history that, to borrow from Muñoz, is concerned less with finite meanings and more with the affective force generated by aesthetic objects. An art history attuned to artists and performers, in Jennifer Doyle's words, who are "indifferent to galleries and their culture and to mainstream taste and values"—and, she adds, reject tacit understandings of art, identity, and politics as neatly aligned.[31] I offer one such model here, a more panoramic view of aesthetic creation that equally considers fine art alongside popular and commercial sources, looks to the residue left in the wake of performative acts, and thinks with the disarray and clutter that is the "stuff" of queer life, historical memory, and the archive, as Martin Manalansan suggests.[32]

Horizontal art-making, moreover, is a practice I emphasize to highlight how our notions of art and community shift when we don't assume vertical (and hierarchical) notions of value. As I have shown, a more equilateral relationship between different aesthetic forms allows us to chart a roving artistic sensibility, one that alters its form with each new medium it meets. Valuing the horizontal is crucial for distilling a milieu where one could, and was encouraged to, try out a different discipline and slip between understood boundaries, where the appellation 'artist' could encompass that limitless multiplicity. It also indicates the collectivism I have revealed above, where the group's ingenuity buttresses what, at first glance, may appear to be the genius of the singular artist. It is a bottom-up approach focusing on the friendship and love that sustains and encourages these pivots. And it foils metrics that emphasize categorizable works or genres, such as painting, that have traditionally been seen as more artistic than, say, fashion design or those whose origins reside in queer nightlife. Moreover, we should be suspicious of verticality itself, as Kemi Adeyemi urges, since it is not simply a neutral line; instead, it is a hegemonic norm that, in its emphasis on who or what rises to the top, reproduces unequal distributions of power.[33] Horizontal art-making, by contrast, is more interested in the movement *across*—the peregrination across streets, the traversal across forms, and the effort to build alliances across different identities.

Undoubtedly, even if not always conscious to me, my affective attachment to this archive has also been structured by desire and loss, particularly in the aftermath of the ongoing AIDS epidemic. In doing so, my research process—characterized by my admittedly obsessive historical documentation of the recent past—has been driven by an urge to come closer to a time that, while near, is not fully knowable. One of the reasons this recent past is so alluring and yet already a mystery is that death shadowed the joys of this moment. So many of the creators—both those who were larger than life and those who were quieter but equally memorable—had their lives cut short. Tina Chow, Keith Haring, Victor Fernandez, Bobby Breslau, and Richard Bernstein were all casualties of the AIDS crisis. DJ Larry Levan's heroin addiction was likely a contributing factor to his premature death from heart failure at the age of thirty-eight. Fashion journalist Berry Berenson—a former paramour of Bernstein's who chronicled Burrows's rise—was killed in one of the two New York–bound flights that left Boston on September 11, 2001. *Vogue* editor André Leon Talley recently died; one of the auctions of his belongings included a signed, dated, and inscribed poster from Lopez. (It sold for $1,600.) And Paradise Garage remains, for many of us, a landmark in the queer imagination, a brief bastion of sexual freedom and minoritarian collectivity that flourished before a tidal wave of devastation. For those like me, informed by a queer past we did not experience firsthand, research becomes a conduit for, in Ricardo Montez's words, "respond[ing] to an emotional call from archival matter" and understanding the "sensorial affective experience" of our longing.[34]

Style may be inherently superficial, but it is an access point to history and memory. The style that animates this narrative—delightful textures, synthetic surfaces, and bright colors—are portals to a queer past. Academia is still reticent to embrace style as a viable object of analysis because it fails to "mean" in proper ways. But as I finish writing this book, I am more convinced than ever that this reticence reflects a problem not with style but with how we define meaning. We need to expand how we assess meaning. We need, I believe, to explore a method of feeling style. Paying more attention to what we *feel*, rather than what we *know*, may prompt us toward a better understanding of the world. Feeling our way toward meaning enables us to appreciate that style is a tool for rehearsing other versions of the self. I argue for an attunement toward the multidimensionality of style in these pages—as a discourse and an artistic practice, as a badge of group belonging and a form of "doing," and as a way of life. I want us to see style as an elastic tool harnessed by creative folks with a tenacious drive to conjure other worlds. Therefore, the medium of style was also a means to open a fissure in the present social fabric, a vital means of summoning a new state of being. Blackness and Brownness were not simply descriptors of identity but emblems of the rainbowlike permutations of the possible.

Acknowledgments

Encouragement, advice, and moments to breathe and be present came in various manifestations from Bimbola Akinbola, Jamil Andrews, Stephanie Baptist, Tiffany Barber, Stephanie Batiste, Hershini Bhana, David Brody, Daphne Brooks, Walter Bryant, Connie Butler, Lucia Cantero, andré carrington, Sarah Cervenak, Joshua Chambers-Letson, Brittney Cooper, Erin Cristovale, Fred D'Aguiar, Field Trip Health, Henry Fields, Aisha Finch, Nicole Fleetwood, Tanisha Ford, Megan Francis, Lyndon Gill, Faye Gleisser, Macarena Gómez-Barris, Yogita Goyal, Joshua Guzmán, Jack Halberstam, Sarah Haley, Robeson Haley-Redmond, Jillian Hernandez, Stephan Herrera, Anthony Abraham Jack, Karen Jaime, Thomas Lax, Summer Kim Lee, Simone Leigh, Treva Lindsey, David Lobenstine, Chris Loperena, Marissa Lopez, Cassandra Lord, Saree Makdisi, Elizabeth Marchant, Tanya McKinnon, Sean Metzger, Robin Mitchell, Marie Moore, Joan Morgan, Bianca Murillo, Amber Musser, Tavia Nyong'o, Roy Pérez, Rafael Pérez-Torres, Elliott Powell, William Pruitt, Shana L. Redmond, Roger Reeves, Leah Wright Rigueur, Jonathan Rosa, Sandra Ruiz, Carlos Sandoval De

Leon, Kyera Singleton, Jonathan Square, Ronnie Thomas, Justin Torres, Dennis Tyler, Shane Vogel, Cally Waite, and Olivia K. Young.

Thank you to Bethann Hardison, Paul and Devon Caranicas, Anton Perich, Ming Smith, Barry Ratoff, and Rory Trifon for granting permissions and illuminating insights about the recent past.

Working with Courtney Berger as my editor for this project has been a true pleasure. I am immensely grateful for their steadfast commitment to this project and for shepherding the book through various stages. I also thank Laura Jaramillo, Lisa Lawley, Nicholas Taylor, and the staff at Duke University Press for their collective assistance in preparing the manuscript and images for the production process.

Engagements with enthusiastic audiences at various institutions, including Brown University, Bryn Mawr College, Cambridge University, Duke University, Edinburgh University, Emory University, Harvard University, Indiana University, Northwestern University, San Diego State University, Scripps College, University of California–Berkeley, University of Illinois–Urbana–Champaign, University of Maryland–College Park, University of Tennessee–Knoxville, University of Texas–Austin, University of Toronto, University of Wisconsin–Madison, and Yale University played a crucial role in nurturing this work. Your support and eagerness were invaluable. At UCLA, this project has been supported by a Research Excellence Award for Associate Professors from the Center for the Study of Women, the Division of Humanities, and the Institute of American Cultures and a Faculty Research Grant from the UC Consortium of Black Studies. I was in residence at the Radcliffe Institute for Advanced Study at Harvard University for the 2021–22 school year, which gave me crucial library access during the COVID-19 pandemic and much-needed time to focus on writing. I also thank Zoë Hopkins for serving as my nimble research assistant during my fellowship year. In 2023, I was awarded an Andy Warhol Foundation for the Visual Arts Writers Grant during the final stretch of completing the manuscript, affirming the institution's commitment to top-notch research and experimental writing on the visual arts. I am grateful for the support and recognition.

Speaking of the arts, my commissioned writing on contemporary artists of color sustained me during the painstaking research and slow accretion of words on the page this project required. I thank these various art institutions, artists, curators, and collaborators: Aperture, Brooklyn Museum, California African American Museum, Peggy Cooper Cafritz, Eddie Chambers, Renee

Cox, Adrienne Edwards, David Frantz, Genevieve Gaignard, Frye Art Museum, Maren Hassinger, Rujeko Hockley, Institute of Contemporary Art / Boston, Naima Keith, Senga Nengudi, ONE Archives, and Christina Quarles.

The graduate students in various iterations of my "Minoritarian Aesthetics" class were critical-thinking partners in interrogating interdisciplinary approaches to affective and performance-based archives.

I am grateful to the universe for its abundance and the ancestors' guidance and protection.

This book is dedicated to the next generation of creatives of color: aspiring dancers, writers, performers, models, visual artists, photographers, DJs, stylists, makers, and designers.

In Joe Roach's words, *pass it on.*

Notes

Introduction. Insurgent Aesthetics

1. As Hillary Miller discusses in the introduction to her book about theater and performance during the city's financial crisis in the 1970s, New York City's $13.5 billion budget was the largest municipal budget in the United States at the time, and the city was also the nation's most populous with its 7.5 million residents. After President Gerald Ford infamously denied federal assistance to the city—only to reverse himself later—a state-backed corporation, the Municipal Assistance Corporation (MAC), was formed by city and state officials to shore up the city's finances. However, Miller reminds us, the austerity measures that were put in place were unevenly distributed and thus affected neighborhoods and industries differently. For more on how these municipal infrastructures affected performance practices, particularly small independent and community-based theaters in the outer boroughs, see Miller, *Drop Dead*.
2. Keith Haring lovingly describes Paradise Garage repeatedly in such terms, emphasizing it as a space that had a significant effect on his life and the lives of others who frequented it. "Dancing [at the Paradise Garage] was really dancing in a way to reach another state of mind, to transcend being

here and getting communally to another place." See Keith Haring and Robert Farris Thompson's filmed interview for the BBC, November 1988, quoted in Haring, *Keith Haring's Journals*, xliii.
3. Als, "Spinning Tales," 26.
4. Miller, *Drop Dead*, 17.
5. Finch, *Style in Art History*; Ackerman, "Theory of Style." For similar works on style in art history, see Rothschild, *Style in Art*; and Ernest Hans Gombrich, "The Concept of Style in the History of Art," lecture notes [for] Fine Arts 190, Spring term, 1959.
6. Fischer, *Gay Seventies*; Hebdige, *Subculture*.
7. This echoes scholar Carol Tulloch's understanding of expressive style as an agentive process in the African diaspora. In her words, "I use the term 'style' as agency—in the construction of self through the assemblage of garments and accessories, hairstyles and beauty regimes that may, or may not, be 'in fashion' at the time of use. I see the styling practices of a layperson's articulation of everyday life though their styled body as exercising that agency." Tulloch, *Birth of Cool*, 276.
8. While the 1970s were recognized as the time when white gay men came to be regarded as tastemakers due to their heavy influence on disco culture, I chose not to use that term to describe these creators of color because of the Eurocentrism and colonial trappings associated with taste. Taste, in other words, is a highly cultivated sensibility that is deemed the proper provenance of an elite few. And it is a category that, historically, has been wielded against folks of color who are often deemed lacking. For more on white gay men as tastemakers, see Lawrence, *Loves Saves the Day*. For more discussion of taste, see Pham, *Asians Wear Clothes*; and Hernandez, *Aesthetics of Excess*.
9. Art historian David Getsy offers a useful description of street cruising's intricate mechanics: "Cruising is a strategic inhabitation of streets and other public and semipublic spaces, and it comprises coded signs, furtive but intentional looks, proxemic negotiations, gestural prompts, sartorial cues, and a heightened awareness of the city's geographic and social delineations." In the context of 1970s New York City, these "public performances of looking for and finding sex, sexual reciprocation, or mutual recognition of queer desiring were part of the experience of New York's streets, both day and night." Getsy, *Queer Behavior*, 27.
10. Barthes, "That Old Thing, Art...," 204.
11. Londoño, *Abstract Barrios*.
12. Pérez, "Glory That Was Wrong," 282.
13. Luckett, "Interview with Pat Cleveland," 41.
14. Jones, quoted in Padilha and Padilha, *Richard Bernstein*, 5.
15. Chuh, *Difference Aesthetics Makes*, 4.

16. Fashion designer Willi Smith's thoughts on creativity and commercialism, in 1978, ring true of how the other artists in this study, his peers, thought of the linkage between the two: "Today artists are afraid of becoming too commercial, but I don't believe my creativity is threatened by commercialism. Quite the opposite—I think that the more commercial I become, the more creative I can be, because I'm reaching more people." "Wear Willi Wear," *Fashion World*, August 28, 1978, quoted in Pastor, "WilliWear New Wave Graphics," 172.
17. As Chuh emphasizes, this "intense compartmentalization of knowledge" in the academy is salient "not only in disciplinarity, but also within disciplines." Chuh, *Difference Aesthetics Makes*, 13.
18. Heiser, *Double Lives in Art and Pop Music*.
19. Muñoz, *Disidentifications*, 33; Vazquez, *Listening in Detail*, 7. Jennifer Doyle neatly summarizes the field's collective focus: "The entire field of performance studies is structured by attention to the social space around performance" while "exploring the presence of the spectator or viewer to the work of art." Doyle, *Hold It Against Me*, 152n7.
20. Flatley and Grudin, "Introduction," 421. See also Stallings, *Funk the Erotic*; and Bradley, *Anteaesthetics*.
21. Muñoz, *Cruising Utopia*; Cheng, *Second Skin*; Cheng, *Ornamentalism*; Musser, *Sensual Excess*; Hernandez, *Aesthetics of Excess*.
22. Thompson, *Shine*, 5, 10. See also Brown and Phu, *Feeling Photography*; Campt, *Black Gaze*; Campt, *Listening to Images*; Mercer, *Welcome to the Jungle*; Smith, *American Archives*; Pinney and Peterson, *Photography's Other Histories*; Sharpe, *Ordinary Notes*.
23. I quote Jasmine Nicole Cobb and Derek Conrad Murray, respectively. See Brielmaier et al., "Institutionalizing Methods," 243, 248.
24. I borrow this phrasing from Kandice Chuh and her rumination on José Esteban Muñoz as a theorist of the aesthetic whose "theory of uncommon beauty" permeates his scholarship. See Chuh, "It's Not About Anything," 171.
25. Brielmaier et al., "Institutionalizing Methods," 253.
26. Ahmed, *Queer Phenomenology*. In terms of a deviant spatial orientation, I am also thinking of Saidiya Hartman's description of young Black women in early twentieth-century America and the "errant path they understood as freedom" as they sought to create beautiful lives for themselves in crowded cities. See Hartman, *Wayward Lives*, 288. I also concur with Mel Chen's suggestion to reconceive of queerness as not simply a sexual identity or as contact but rather as a form of "improper affiliation" across an array of subjectivities and spaces outside the heteronormative. See Chen, *Animacies*.
27. For more on everyday choreographies and maps of "what might be," see Hartman, *Wayward Lives*, 234.

28. Flatley and Grudin, "Introduction," 421.
29. Hernandez, *Aesthetics of Excess*, 7.
30. Cvetkovich, "Photographing Objects," 275.
31. Muñoz, *Cruising Utopia*. For more on the specific knowledges gained from the documentary traces of an event, see Jones, "'Presence' in Absentia."
32. Butt, introduction to *Between You and Me*.
33. Gopinath, *Unruly Visions*, 4. Moreover, in a more tangible manner, this book itself is indebted to models of queer curatorship, like the stewardship of Juan Ramos and Antonio Lopez's estate by Paul and Devon Caranicas and the attention Barry Ratoff has paid to Charles Tracy's photographic archive.
34. See Sewall-Ruskin, *High on Rebellion*.
35. Gopinath, *Unruly Visions*, 4.
36. Muñoz, *Disidentifications*, 34.
37. For discussions of both groups, see Shanks and Tepper, *Side by Side*. For more on Asco, see Chavoya and Gonzales, *Asco*; Chavoya and Frantz, *Axis Mundo*; Gleisser, *Risk Work*; and Guzmán, *Dissatisfactions*. For more on Studio Z, see Jones, *South of Pico*.
38. For more on the former, see Morris and Hockley, *We Wanted a Revolution*. For more on the latter, see Jaime, *Queer Nuyorican*.
39. For more on institutional critique, see Cahan, *Mounting Frustration*.
40. Its early participants were largely a mix of white suburban kids from the New York area, North Carolina, Pennsylvania, West Virginia, and the West Coast states, along with a smattering of artists from abroad, including Brazil, Italy, and Peru. See Magliozzi, "Art Is What You Make It," 14.
41. Gendron, *Between Montmartre and the Mudd*.
42. Cleveland, *Walking with the Muses*, 317.
43. Boch, *Mudd Club*, 101.
44. Lawrence, *Life and Death on the New York Dance Floor*, 77.
45. For more on these downtown party networks in New York City, see Lawrence, *Love Saves the Day*. For a design history of the nightclub that includes this period, see Kries et al., *Night Fever*. Finally, the Downtown Collection in the Fales Library at New York University is also a valuable resource of ephemera related to New York's City's various downtown scenes, especially Club 57, the Mudd Club, and Danceteria.
46. For instance, see Heiser, "Club Culture and Contemporary Art."
47. It has been characterized as a period of "compulsive artifice," where people adopted poses and identities that were contrived. The popularity of unisex styles, for instance, and idiosyncratic materials (such as leather and synthetics) encouraged this role-play. This idea of clothing and hair as both a form of disguise and a conduit to announce selfhood also per-

vaded Black consciousness—from blaxploitation films to "soul style." And *Vogue* in the seventies attempted to reframe the female body as a site of liberation rather than male pleasure, especially as more women entered the workforce and engaged in "power dressing." This focus on sartorial aesthetics and bodily embellishment showcases how seventies fashion was often employed as a form of "impression management" to influences viewers' interpretation of the sundry bodies they encountered in everyday life. See Françoise, "These Boots Were Made"; Powell, "Racial Imaginaries"; Ford, *Liberated Threads*; and Vogel, "State of Grace."

48. Miller, *Drop Dead*, 5.
49. Meyer, *Art of Return*, 42.
50. Hurston, "Characteristics of Negro Expression," 48.
51. Cleveland, *Walking with the Muses*, 30.
52. Writer Ocean Vuong's recent thoughts on photography, discussed alongside his poetry, resonates with my thinking on photography's power as a form. In his words, "I feel a very great kinship with photography in its ability to create a myth out of the real. You look at a photo, and anything you write about, it ends up being true, right? So the photograph because of how it's framed is very seductive and capacious and ends up being to me a very queer form because it sets up what is seemingly fixed. As we interpret [photography], or as we contextualize it, anything could happen. That's the closest I see to my own work in 'auto-fiction,' or auto-mythology, which is how I view my poems. Taking the lived experience and then mythologizing it towards other tropes...I think photography is really elusive in that way. It's seemingly so static, and so infinite. Every pixel, every frame is there, but the mystery is in the interpretation." Quoted in Stewart, "Ocean Vuong," 105.
53. Campt, *Listening to Images*, 9.
54. For a reflection on friendship and writing with art, see Doyle, "Just Friends."
55. Torres, "In Praise of Latin Night."
56. Vazquez, *Listening in Detail*, 20, 21.

Chapter 1. Mundane Made Spectacular: Antonio Lopez

Epigraph: Antonio Lopez, quoted in Laird Borrelli-Persson, "Before There Were Influencers, There Was Antonio, Illustrator Extraordinaire and Arbiter of Style," *Vogue*, September 5, 2018, https://www.vogue.com/article/antonio-lopez-1970s-sex-fashion-disco-documentary-by-james-crump.

1. *Nuyorican* and *Nuyorico*—which refer to the New York–born children of Puerto Rican parents who are familiar with the island's language and

culture—are, in Lawrence La Fountain-Stokes's words, "messy, irreverent neologisms that engage phonetic traits" or "insert non-English diacritics and capital letters in the middle of words," like *DiaspoRicans* (a synonym for Nuyorican). These negative slurs acquired new meaning in the late 1960s and early 1970s as Nuyorican cultural consciousness flourished: "As a practice of resistance, [they] entailed the proud affirmation of a new cultural identity, that of Puerto Ricans in the United States, and solidified through art making, site-specific artistic practices, community organizing and institution building." La Fountain-Stokes, *Queer Ricans*, 139, 138.

2. Banes, "Breaking," 14.
3. I borrow this wording from Juan Flores, who importantly emphasizes "the intensely overlapping and intermingling expressive repertories" of Black and Puerto Rican cultures in New York City that were foundational to hip-hop's formation. See Flores, *From Bomba to Hip-Hop*, 117.
4. This historically coincided with Operation Bootstrap, an economic shift and employment shortage in Puerto Rico, which led to the migration of a million people to the mainland between 1950 and 1965.
5. "Antonio Lopez at Art Center, 1983," short 1984 film directed by Leslie Ann Smith, posted April 7, 2016, by ArtCenter College of Design, https://youtu.be/XT6HU1_HxNU (hereafter Smith, "Antonio Lopez at Art Center, 1983").
6. Caranicas, *Antonio's People*, 126.
7. Malanga and Foye, "Grace to Be Born."
8. Malanga and Foye, "Grace to Be Born."
9. "Antonio Lopez (1986)—The Videofashion Vault," video interview with Lopez, last posted August 31, 2012, by Videofashion, https://youtu.be/uwq_zQQ2BgU.
10. O'Neill, "Antonio and Juan Stepping Out," 57.
11. Bourhis, "Antonio," 10.
12. James, "Juan Ramos."
13. Cleveland, *Walking with the Muses*, 197.
14. See Ruiz, *Ricanness*.
15. See Muñoz, *Sense of Brown*.
16. Smith, "Antonio Lopez at Art Center, 1983."
17. Amelia Malagamba-Ansótegui and Ramón Rivera-Servera, "Critical Desires: Race and Sexuality in the Work of Antonio," n.d., archived March 4, 2016, at https://web.archive.org/web/20160304045402/http://latino.si.edu/virtualgallery/antonio/bodyessay.htm.
18. Jones, *I'll Never Write My Memoirs*, 89.

19. Burt A. Folkart, "'Puerto Rican Henry Higgins': Fashion Illustrator Antonio Lopez Dies," *Los Angeles Times*, March 18, 1987. https://www.latimes.com/archives/la-xpm-1987o-03-18-mn-7649-story.html; Jennifer Krasinki, "Antonio Lopez Dazzles at El Museo del Barrio," *Village Voice*, August 10, 2016, archived at https://artwriting.sva.edu/journal/post/antonio-lopez-dazzles-at-el-museo-del-barrio.
20. For more on Potassa's modeling, see Carmack, "'I'm a Person Who Loves.'"
21. Frances Negrón-Muntaner identifies these dense cross-cultural relations as "Boricua pop." She pointedly notes, "Through a process of asymmetrical cultural exchange, artists producing for the mass media market have incorporated Puerto Rican and other subaltern practices while consistently erasing or displacing the source." Negrón-Muntaner, *Boricua Pop*, 31.
22. This elision is, moreover, not just limited to Lopez. Another critical example is fellow Nuyorican Juanito Xtravaganza (aka Juan Rivera). He helped his boyfriend Keith Haring stretch and paint his canvases while moving among elite and underground cultural spaces with him. Yet he has been subsequently marginalized, even sometimes erased from, the lore surrounding Haring's prolific aesthetic production in the late 1970s and early 1980s. See Cruz-Malavé, *Queer Latino Testimonio*.
23. See "How Kodak Will Exploit Its New Instamatic," *Business Week*, March 18, 1972, 46–48. As this article details, Kodak launched the newest addition to its "hot-selling Instamatic line" in 1972: the Pocket Instamatic. "Kodak's newest camera, roughly the size of a pack of cigarettes, will come in five models, selling for $30 dollars or less for the cheapest model to under $130 for the most sophisticated version." That same year, Eastman Kodak reported it planned a $30 million expansion of its Instamatic camera plant, which would be completed in late 1974. See "Kodak Plans to expand Instamatic Camera Plant," *Wall Street Journal*, October 13, 1972, 27.
24. McKenzie, "Interview."
25. Caranicas, *Antonio's People*, 9.
26. McKenzie, "Interview."
27. McKenzie, "Interview."
28. Caranicas, *Antonio's People*, 9.
29. Lopez's record collection was an eclectic mix of soul, disco, rock, and Afro-Cuban music, and his favorites included Donna Summer, the Doors, Toña La Negra, Vanilla Fudge, Marvin Gaye, James Brown, Barry White, and the Frenchies. Paul and Devon Caranicas, personal communication with the author, June 2020.

30. "And what I do with these girls is, it isn't just telling them what to do. You're supposed to set an example. You become what they want to be. Because when you dance with a girl, you can usually tell if they will listen to you or not. How well they will follow. And by dancing with these girls, I was able to lead them. And they trust me, and it was also a friendship." Smith, "Antonio Lopez at Art Center, 1983."
31. Quoted in Padilha and Padilha, *Antonio Lopez*, 274.
32. Caranicas and Ramos lived in the enormous, 3,500-square-foot loft with sixteen-foot ceilings, while Lopez lived at the nearby Chelsea Hotel. In Caranicas's words, "Built by a photographer, it had a dressing room and a dark room as well as professional equipment and props. This was the acme of the Instamatic photo period for Antonio. He was in the perfect environment to focus on what up until then had only been a brief experiment: sequences of photos exploring his fantasies." Caranicas, *Antonio's People*, 11. The third and last iteration of Warhol's Factory occupied the entire third floor of 860 Broadway, where he moved in August 1974. See Gopnik, *Warhol*, 787.
33. McKenzie, "Interview."
34. Garner, "Antonio and His Instamatic."
35. "Behind the scenes: in their lifetime Antonio and Juan created 9 books of instamatic grids chronicling their friends, travels, and experimental ideas in photography. In the archives we're restoring & scanning each book. Pictured here: book 2, page 1 viewed through velum; Rome c. 1974. #antoniolopez #instamatic #photography." See @the_antonio_archives, Instagram, February 7, 2019. https://www.instagram.com/p/BtmJKeZAFpF/. Lopez's photographic practice, especially his repeated use of the grid format, can be considered in relation to postminimalism. Despite the heterogeneity of practices included under this banner, such artists, as David Getsy emphasizes, "question the belief that geometric and serial forms can be used neutrally" while embracing "variation or error in the ad hoc systems they propose." Put succinctly, postminimalism "valued what Minimalism tried to expunge—the personal." Getsy, *Queer Behavior*, 21, 24.
36. O'Neill, "Antonio and Juan Stepping Out," 79. It is worth noting Puerto Rico's pride in Lopez's success. See Penny Maldonado, "A Puerto Rican Shines in Paris," *San Juan Star*, September 8, 1974, quoted in Padilha and Padilha, *Antonio Lopez*, 302.
37. See Meyer, "Jesse Helms Theory of Art."
38. Gester, "Flesh and Spirit," 249.
39. Getsy, *Queer Behavior*, 2.
40. Caranicas, *Antonio's People*, 17.
41. Langkjaer, "Urban Fitness, Gendered Practices," 197.

42. Caranicas, *Antonio's People*, 17; Langkjaer, "Urban Fitness, Gendered Practices," 197.
43. Caranicas, *Antonio's People*, 50; Padilha and Padilha, *Antonio Lopez*, 235.
44. *Newspaper*, published by Steve Lawrence, was an artists' magazine that ran for fourteen issues between 1968 and 1971 and featured the work of forty-eight artists. As Marcelo Gabriel Yáñez puts it, the periodical "functioned as an alternative exhibition space for photography that wasn't shown in galleries at the time" and a chronicle of a "queer-leaning downtown New York art scene of the late 1960s." In 1975, Lawrence briefly revived *Newspaper* as *Picture Newspaper* for three issues, running from June to August, and changed the printing to a mixture of black-and-white and color. Lopez's drawings and Instamatics were featured in all three of those issues and on the cover of the July 1975 issue. See Yáñez, "Steve Lawrence and *Newspaper*."
45. Langkjaer, "Urban Fitness, Gendered Practices," 195.
46. Padilha and Padilha, *Antonio Lopez*, 198.
47. McKenzie, "Interview."
48. Mercer, "Skin Head Sex Thing," 169–70.
49. Walker Evans, "Photography," quoted in Moore, "Starburst," 19.
50. See Kozloff, "Photography."
51. Moore, *Starburst*, 19.
52. Butet-Roch, "Perfectly Banal," 30.
53. McKenzie, "Interview."
54. Caranicas, *Antonio's People*, 17. Thorvaldson was featured in these ads from 1976 to 1986. For a reprint of the double grid, dated 1978, see Lopez, *Antonio's Girls*, 28–29. She also appears in a slightly related series, *Golden Mummy* (1978), in which she was covered in gold lamé. For an image of this double grid, see Lopez, *Antonio's Girls*, 50–51. For a reprint of one grid featuring Thorvaldson and another featuring Fernandez, both taken in New York City in 1977, see Lopez, *Instamatics*.
55. One of these, a set of Polaroids, is from circa 1976. The second, a set of Instamatics, is attributed to the year 1977 and was prominently featured in Lopez's exhibition at El Museo del Barrio in New York City, titled *Antonio Lopez: Future Funk Fashion*.
56. Paul and Devon Caranicas, personal communication with the author, June 2020. The ribbon motif would appear elsewhere in Lopez's work. Most explicitly, its influence surfaced in a Pop Art illustration Lopez produced for a department store in Tokyo in 1978 that showed four "ribbons" in hot pink, blue, and green, extending diagonally across a female face, one prominently featuring the words "Antonio's New York Story 78" in stylized typography. See Padilha and Padilha, *Antonio Lopez*, 282. A similar version, all in Japanese, has been archived on social media: "From

the archives: a flyer for Antonio's 1978 exhibition in Tokyo at Laforet. Swipe right to see the back. #antonio lopez #laforet," @the_antonio_archives, May 10, 2021, https://www.instagram.com/p/COsoUboA5gE/?img_index=1.

57. Meyer, "Mapplethorped," 241, 243. Ironically, his more homoerotic and s-m work was censored from that debut show by the eponymous gallery owner; it ran in a concurrent show at the Kitchen.
58. Warhol irreverently referred to this work as the *Cocks, Cunts, and Assholes* series. It is paired with another (and tamer) series, also begun in the fall of 1977, titled *Torsos*. Mapplethorpe experimented mainly with Polaroid photography from 1970 to 1975, developing the formal technique that would later bring him acclaim.
59. Hebdige, *Subculture*.
60. Muñoz, *Cruising Utopia*, 7.
61. Mercer, *Welcome to the Jungle*.
62. Cvetkovich, "Photographing Objects," 277.
63. Brown and Phu, *Feeling Photography*, 1.
64. Barthes, *Camera Lucida*.
65. My attention to my first encounters with the art object is inspired here by Muñoz, specifically his urge to follow a counterintuitive, art-historical approach to tracking our "associative belonging" to the artworks we study. See Muñoz, *Cruising Utopia*, 117.
66. St. Clair, *Secret Life of Colors*.
67. Muñoz, *Cruising Utopia*, 5; Taylor, *Archive and the Repertoire*.
68. Ramos remodeled the space into studio 10-A, where Lopez and Ramos worked, and studio 10-B, where Ramos and Caranicas lived. Lopez lived a few blocks away at 24 West Twenty-Third Street, near the Flatiron Building.
69. Vazquez, *Florida Room*, xiii.
70. Ramos's background contributed to his models' bodily vocabulary. Paul Caranicas emphasizes that Ramos trained with choreographer Alwyn Nikolai and "used his knowledge of body awareness and motion to advise models when they were starting out." Caranicas, *Antonio's People*, 72.
71. Brown, *Work!*, 212, 213.
72. Padilha and Padilha, *Antonio Lopez*, 162, 163.
73. Huck, "Mel Ramos, Albertina"; Gopnik, *Warhol*, 250.
74. For instance, in a 2010 interview, his matter-of-fact comments do little to dispel his reputation as a misogynist. "Yes, I've painted male portraits, but the main point is true, I'm interested in the female figure," he said. "Why is that? What can I say to that? I love women; I'm a healthy, male American. And women are objects of desire for me." Quoted in Greenberger, "Mel Ramos."

75. Caranicas, *Antonio's People*, 46.
76. Brown, *Work!*, 214.
77. Doyle, *Hold It Against Me*, xii.
78. Stallings, *Funk the Erotic*, xiii.
79. For more on the performance of objecthood by Black women artists, see McMillan, *Embodied Avatars*.
80. I borrow this idiom from art historian Robb Hernandez, who uses it, in a different context, to describe an "ideology by which to live (and die)" regarding fashionistas in the Melrose shopping district of Los Angeles in the early 1980s. For more on this "lifestyle based on the power of self-creation," see Hernandez, *Archiving an Epidemic*, 91.
81. Chambers-Letson, *After the Party*, 25.
82. See Jones, *I'll Never Write My Memoirs*, 104.
83. I discuss these themes in the context of Senga Nengudi and Maren Hassinger's collaborations and their membership in Studio Z in 1970s Los Angeles. See McMillan, "Sand, Nylon, and Dirt."
84. Lax, preface to *Side by Side*, ed. Shanks and Tepper.
85. Stephens, *Skin Acts*, 85.
86. Lawrence, *Love Saves the Day*, 261–64.
87. Schneider, *Vital Mummies*, 1.
88. Lopez designed black-and-white advertisements for the store—focused on blazers, belts, trousers, tuxedos, lingerie, and safari-inspired campaigns—published in the *Times*. He also created large black acrylic canvases that hung in the store windows and, in 1981, a line of custom-painted bags.
89. Marc Jacobs quoted in Owen, *Fiorucci*, 170.
90. Salibian and Socha, "Seminal Moment."
91. Bradbury, *Alternative Seventies*, 70.
92. Franco Marabelli quoted in Salibian and Socha, "Seminal Moment."
93. "Tobé Special Report Shops to See," July 26, 1977, quoted in Bradbury, *Alternative Seventies*, 68.
94. Taylor, "Tongue-in-Chic Boutique Revives the '60s."
95. Paul Caranicas, personal communication with the author, June 22, 2020.
96. Vazquez, *Florida Room*, x.
97. Caranicas, personal communication with the author, June 22, 2020.
98. Taylor, "Tongue-in-Chic Boutique Revives the '60s;" Hernandez, *Aesthetics of Excess*.
99. Cleveland, *Walking with the Muses*, 217.
100. Guarnaccia, *Elio Fiorucci*, 45. The photograph is reproduced on page 123.
101. Friend and artist Michael Thiele (who also built the stage for the *Candy Bar Wrapper Series*) fabricated the acrylic mannequins; Lopez's artis-

tic inspiration was the work of early twentieth-century Bauhaus artist Oskar Schlemmer, specifically the whimsical costumes of his *Triadisches Ballett* (Triadic ballet). This through line is evident in two preparatory mannequin studies Lopez drew in 1977. Lopez's tulle skirts debuted in 1976 and were displayed in Fiorucci's window in 1977.

102. Johnson, "Accidental Goddess," 182.
103. Magnuson, "Prime Time of Our Lives," 128. For a discussion of Club 57 within the context of the developing East Village pop performance scene in the early 1980s, see Parnes, "Pop Performance."
104. Magliozzi, "Art Is What You Make," 19. John Sex's performance (with Katy K) was titled "Valentine's Day Repose." Scharf's paintings were the focus of an exhibition titled "Fiorucci Celebrates the New Wave," which opened on May 8, 1979, and featured Nomi performing. Elio Fiorucci invited Haring and his protégé LA2 to paint murals in the Milan store in 1984.
105. Johnson, "Accidental Goddess," 182. Arias arrived in New York City in 1976.
106. Cavoulacos, "Downtown for Downtown," 31. Importantly, "Puerto Rican artists formed their own movement within the larger New York alternative art space movement." Emerging between 1969 and 1983, these multidisciplinary art spaces were situated in East Harlem/El Barrio, the Lower East Side/Loisada, and the South Bronx in addition to Lower Manhattan. Yasmin Ramirez has termed these collective endeavors the "Puerto Rican alternative art space movement." Dávila and Ramirez, *Nuyorican and Diasporican Visual Art*, 7, 8.
107. Magliozzi, "Art Is What You Make," 19.
108. Schneider, *Vital Mummies*, 37.
109. Stanfill, "Nightclub as Fashion Catwalk," 270, 271.
110. Johnson, "Accidental Goddess," 183.
111. Stanfill, "Nightclub as Fashion Catwalk," 262.
112. Lawrence, *Love Saves the Day*, 272.
113. Lopez was one of four artists solicited by Steve Rubell and Ian Schrager (who were past operators of the Lopez hangout Enchanted Gardens) to create brand-like logos for the club. He submitted a colored pencil drawing of Marilyn Monroe, recast as a disco diva. Lopez also designed dresses worn to the opening by Studio 54's publicist Carmen D'Alessio and Channel 5 reporter Judy Licht.
114. Langkjaer, "Urban Fitness, Gendered Practices," 204.
115. Langkjaer, "Urban Fitness, Gendered Practices," 207.
116. Goffman, *Presentation of Self*, 22.

Chapter 2. Neophyte to Muse: Grace Jones

1. *Anton Perich Presents: Grace Jones*, filmed concert at the Enchanted Garden, Queens, New York, 1976, posted February 15, 2022, by Anton Perich, https://youtu.be/SEgIKU2pf1s&t=20s.
2. Lopez, *Antonio's Girls*, 32.
3. For more on states of intoxication and ecstasy for the 1968 generation, see Waldmeier, "Life in Limbo." For more on LSD, see Pollan, *How to Change Your Mind*.
4. Lopez, *Antonio's Girls*, 32.
5. Lopez, *Antonio's Girls*, 32.
6. Lee, "Staying In," 30. My use of *wayward* here is purposeful, gesturing to Saidiya Hartman's extended treatment of the term as, for instance, cruising, strolling, seeking, drifting, wandering, and "a *beautiful experiment* in how-to-live." See *Wayward Lives*, 227–28.
7. Lopez, *Antonio's Girls*, 32.
8. Jones, *I'll Never Write My Memoirs*, 104. My use of Jones's memoir, at various points in the chapter, acknowledges that "self-fashioning and editorial control" is particularly important for Black women. In doing so, it can function as one of many "powerful new strategies by which Black women artists are disturbing the historical record in order to reclaim the pasts denied them by critics and institutions that have historically cared little for them." Brooks, *Liner Notes*, 313, 315.
9. Lopez, *Antonio's Girls*, 33.
10. Jones, *I'll Never Write My Memoirs*, 270–71.
11. The term *underground*, to describe the contemporary American underground, can be traced back to 1955 and the formation of the *Village Voice*, "the world's first underground newspaper." According to poet Jeff Nutall, the term didn't begin to circulate in New York City until approximately 1964. It was associated with the hippie and psychedelic movement, political rebellions of the 1960s, and the proliferation of antiestablishment newspapers, poems, and plays. Lawrence, *Love Saves the Day*, 50.
12. Mancuso held the first of these annual parties on Valentine's Day 1970 in his loft on 647 Broadway, just north of Houston Street, which became known as the Loft. He coined the term *third ear* to denote the spiritual and sensorial force unleashed by the alternative temporality of these parties. See Lawrence, *Love Saves the Day*, 9–10, 12. For more on out-of-body experiences in the 1960s and 1970s, see Nyong'o, "I Feel Love."
13. Hong, "Delusions of Whiteness."
14. Talley and Warhol, "New Again."

15. Hall, "What Is This 'Black'?"
16. Gwendolyn Brooks, *Maud Martha: A Novel* (New York: Harper and Row, 1953; repr. Chicago: Third World Press, 1993), 22, quoted in Hartman, *Wayward Lives*, 235.
17. Brody, *Punctuation*, 36.
18. Post, *Deadpan*, 12.
19. Schiche, "Iconic Photographer Ming Smith."
20. Ming Smith, personal communication with the author, July 28, 2023.
21. Reed, "Light and Shadow," 57.
22. Quoted from "Louis Draper's History of the Kamoinge Workshop, 1972" in Eckhardt, *Working Together*, 2. Formed in 1963, both the collective and the *Black Photographer's Annual* (which ran from 1972 to 1980) were instrumental in nourishing and preserving the work of Black photographers, as Deborah Willis argues, especially "at a time when most were being overlooked by publishers, journalists, curators, museums, and galleries." Willis, in preface to Eckhardt, *Working Together*, viii.
23. Barboza and Harris, "'Photograph Finds You,'" 35.
24. Jones, *I'll Never Write My Memoirs*, 70.
25. Barboza began to work for *Essence* magazine shortly after its launch in May 1970. The magazine aspired, according to its masthead at the time, to be "from a Black perspective" and to "delight and celebrate the beauty, pride, strength, and uniqueness of all Black women."
26. Barboza and Harris, "'Photograph Finds You,'" 35.
27. Smith and Talbert, "Portrait of the Artist," 12.
28. I am paraphrasing this insight about the Kamoinge Workshop, as a type of college, from Anthony Barboza. See Anthony Barboza oral history interview transcript, November 18–19, 2009, Smithsonian Archives of American Art, 7.
29. Smith and Obrist, "Flash of the Spirit," 229.
30. Taylor, "Salon That's Expanding."
31. Jones, *I'll Never Write My Memoirs*, 79.
32. Ming Smith, personal communication with the author, July 28, 2023; Jones, *I'll Never Write My Memoirs*, 107.
33. Ming Smith, personal communication with the author, July 28, 2023.
34. Galvão, "View from: Ming Smith," 30.
35. Ming Smith, personal communication with the author, July 28, 2023.
36. Ming Smith, personal communication with the author, July 28, 2023.
37. Ming Smith, personal communication with the author, July 28, 2023.
38. I am thinking of Johana Londoño's discussion of chromatic color versus color as "racially, ethnically, spatially, and politically significant." See *Abstract Barrios*, 71. See also Darby English's "artifactual color," a "sense of

color generated in the tension between color's racial connotations and its aesthetic meanings," in *1971*, 9.
39. Muñoz, *Sense of Brown*, 37.
40. Ming Smith, personal communication with the author, July 28, 2023.
41. Lobato, "Amazing Grace," 135, 136.
42. Kershaw, "Postcolonialism and Androgyny," 19, 20.
43. Guzmán and Ramos, "Mediated Identifications," 26.
44. Murray, "Beauty Is in the Eye," 127.
45. Murray, "Beauty Is in the Eye," 128, 129.
46. Smith and Talbert, "Portrait of the Artist," 15.
47. Brown, *Work!*, 231.
48. Detroit-born Peggy Ann Freeman, known professionally as Donyale Luna, was a precursor to both. She became the first Black woman to appear on the cover of any edition of *Vogue*, gracing the British edition in March 1966, and enjoyed wide success in Europe. See Powell, *Cutting a Figure*; and Brown, *Work!*
49. Cleveland, *Walking with the Muses*, 152.
50. For more on waywardness as a form of Black feminist refusal, see Hartman, *Wayward Lives*.
51. See Bradley, "Introduction."
52. For more on "haptic visuality," see Marks, *Skin of the Film*.
53. Barthes, "At Le Palace Tonight...," 48.
54. Quoted in "Portfolio II: Can You Feel It? Creating Environments and Experiences: Light and Sound Technologies," in Kries, Eisenbrand, and Rossi, *Night Fever*, 166.
55. Gyarkye, "Ecstatic, Elusive Art."
56. *Anton Perich Presents: Grace Jones, Haircut*, filmed haircut with Andre Martheleur, Cinandre, New York, 1978, posted May 24, 2022, by Anton Perich, https://youtu.be/_ED-vLWemWU.
57. Jones, *I'll Never Write My Memoirs*, 83.
58. Stephens, *Skin Acts*, 85.
59. Lopez, *Antonio's Girls*, 32. According to an *Ebony* article, this "discovery" occurred in 1974. While dining with friends, Jones "got so carried away when she heard *Dirty Old Man* by the Three Degrees that she jumped on the restaurant table and sang to the record. Her captivated audience applauded.... One of the models with her was so impressed by the impromptu performance that she told her boyfriend, who just happened to be a record producer." Norment, "Outrageous Grace Jones," 94.
60. Jones possessed that easily perceived but seemingly indescribable quality, that ineffable "it," that accrues in certain individuals. See Roach, *It*.

61. Schneider, *Vital Mummies*, 171n46.
62. Jones, quoted in Padilha and Padilha, *Richard Bernstein*, 5.
63. Jones, *I'll Never Write My Memoirs*, 141.
64. This insight on shine's aesthetic properties is paraphrased from Cheng, *Second Skin*, 115.
65. Jones, *I'll Never Write My Memoirs*, 147.
66. Padilha and Padilha, *Richard Bernstein*, 142.
67. Jones, quoted in Padilha and Padilha, *Richard Bernstein*, 5.
68. See Fleetwood, *On Racial Icons*.
69. See Sontag, "Notes on Camp."
70. Royster, "'Feeling Like a Woman,'" 78.
71. Goude, *Jungle Fever*, 102.
72. Walters, "As Much as I Can," 88.
73. This echoes José Esteban Muñoz's suggestion that, while camp is typically discussed as a "mode of reception" or a "subcultural lens for viewing the dominant culture," it should also be understood as "a style, even a means toward the enactment of the self in an adverse cultural climate." See Muñoz, *Disidentifications*, 212n2.
74. Geter, "Black Phenomena."
75. Mercer, *Welcome to the Jungle*, 119.
76. Jones, *I'll Never Write My Memoirs*, 204.
77. Warhol officially relaunched the magazine as *Andy Warhol's Interview* in May 1972. Critic Blake Gopnik chalks up the shift in its focus to Warhol's "Business Art" period in the 1970s, when the offering mattered more than profit. Moreover, he discusses, Warhol borrowed Halston's fashion world glamour, using his sartorial designs in fashion shoots and his models/friends like Pat Cleveland and Elsa Peretti for subsequent *Interview* issues. See Gopnik, *Warhol*.
78. Ottenberg, "Pat Cleveland on Partying."
79. Ottenberg, "Pat Cleveland on Partying."
80. Ottenberg, "Pat Cleveland on Partying."
81. Quoted in Gopnik, *Warhol*, 698.
82. Quoted in Schneier, "Man Who Made 'Everyone.'"
83. Mercer, *Welcome to the Jungle*, 121.
84. Crow, "Modernism and Mass Culture," 20–21.
85. Jones, *I'll Never Write My Memoirs*, 143.
86. Jones, *I'll Never Write My Memoirs*, 142.
87. Crow, "Modernism and Mass Culture," 4.
88. Jones, *I'll Never Write My Memoirs*, 203–4.
89. I borrow this term from Nicole Fleetwood's discussion of artist Fatimah Tuggar. See *Troubling Vision*, 177–205.

90. Music critic Vince Aletti, in a review of the album dated July 1, 1978, explicitly referenced the cover: "Finally 'Fame' is a marvellous combination of chutzpah and charisma from which Grace emerges quite triumphant. An added attraction: Richard Bernstein's ultra-fashionable cover." See Aletti, *Disco Files*, 423.
91. See McMillan, "Introduction."
92. Musser, *Sensual Excess*. I am also thinking of Elspeth Brown's discussion of excess, specifically, as an affective, sartorial, and gestural performance that is at once emblematic of queer notions of femininity and the figure of the diva, a performance that acts as a form of queer world-making. See her *Work!*, 15.
93. Jones, *I'll Never Write My Memoirs*, 204.
94. Montez, *Keith Haring's Line*, 86.
95. Nyong'o, *Afro-Fabulations*, 17.
96. For a reproduction of this photograph, see Padilha and Padilha, *Richard Bernstein*, 131.
97. Haring has used the term *painting as performance*, which could be applicable here. See Haring, *Keith Haring's Journals*, 39. Art historian Robert Farris Thompson also attended the 1985 performance. Later, he described Jones as Haring's ideal canvas, or "the theory most made flesh." See Thompson, "Requiem for the Degas," 138.
98. Quoted in Cruz-Malavé, *Queer Latino Testimonio*, 36.
99. Rosen, "Remembering New York's Legendary 70s Club."
100. Cruz-Malavé, *Queer Latino Testimonio*, 3.
101. Rosen, "Remembering New York's Legendary 70s Club."
102. Shapiro, "Saturday Mass."
103. Lawrence, *Love Saves the Day*, 361.
104. Quoted in Lawrence, *Life and Death*, 318.
105. Lawrence, *Love Saves the Day*, 2.
106. Goude, *Jungle Fever*, 106.
107. Goude, *Jungle Fever*, 106.
108. Howarth, "Postmodern Design."
109. Norment, "Outrageous Grace Jones," 90. This intriguing use of punctuation in the design of Jones's maternity dress also reminds us of how, as Jennifer Brody emphasizes, "punctuation choreographs and orchestrates thought." See Brody, *Punctuation*, 13.
110. Goude, *Jungle Fever*, 106.
111. Goude, *Jungle Fever*, 106.
112. For a reading of this image via postmodern style, see Adamson and Pavitt, "Postmodernism," 52.
113. Jones, *Warm Leatherette*.

114. See Guzmán and Ramos, "Mediated Identifications," 26.
115. See Lobato, "Amazing Grace," 136.
116. For a photograph of Jones performing in the maternity dress, see Borelli-Persson, "Grace Jones 1979 Baby Shower"; Goodman, *Ways of Worldmaking*, 23.

Chapter 3. Color That Moves: Stephen Burrows

1. For more on *Soul Train* and the grammar of Black (queer) dance, see Borelli, "You Can't Outdo Black People"; and Bragin, "Techniques of Black Male Re/dress."
2. Givhan, *Battle of Versailles*, 52.
3. Vega, *When the Spirits Dance Mambo*, 98. According to Vega, mambo dance nights at the Palladium were Wednesdays, Fridays, and Saturdays, and dance matinees were on Sundays.
4. Frank, "Stephen Burrows."
5. Magidson, "Backlash to Rebirth," 31.
6. O'Brien, "Stephen Burrows's World by Night," 44.
7. Feitelberg, "Stephen Burrows Reminisces in Rhythm."
8. Persson, "Revel, Rebel," 18.
9. Burrows's maternal grandmother, Beatrice Pennington Banks Simmons, worked as a nurse as well as a sample hand for fashion designer Hattie Carnegie. A self-made Viennese transplant, Carnegie ran a successful fashion empire out of her East Forty-Ninth Street boutique. These details are paraphrased from Persson, "Revel, Rebel," 16. The term *visual creator*, as well as the details of songs Burrows's models danced to, are from O'Brien, "Stephen Burrows's World by Night," 46.
10. Butler, "Fashion."
11. Butler, "Fashion."
12. Quoted in Morris, *Fashion Makers*, 53.
13. Persson, "Revel, Rebel," 16.
14. "SA Springburst: Happy, Bright with Color," *Women's Wear Daily*, November 3, 1978.
15. Myers, "Color Story," 207.
16. Newton, *Cherry Grove, Fire Island*, 13.
17. Givhan, *Battle of Versailles*, 54.
18. Cleveland, *Walking with the Muses*, 163.
19. Newton, *Cherry Grove, Fire Island*, 110.
20. Feitelberg, "Freedom and Summer Fun."
21. Quoted in Feitelberg, "Freedom and Summer Fun."
22. Feitelberg, "Freedom and Summer Fun," 32. This photograph was taken by André Leon Talley and is reproduced in the article.

23. Givhan, *Battle of Versailles*, 54.
24. Burrows, "Remembering Willi Smith," 222.
25. Miller, "Sixties-Era Commune," 328–29.
26. Quoted in Persson, "Revel, Rebel," 18.
27. Quoted in Givhan, *Battle of Versailles*, 112, 54.
28. Goodman, *Ways of Worldmaking*, 25.
29. Goodman, *Ways of Worldmaking*, 23.
30. Cleveland, "Remembering Willi Smith," 223.
31. Stephen Burrows, personal communication with the author, March 4, 2025.
32. Quoted in "Stephen B. Heart to Heart with Berry Berenson Perkins," *Interview*, September 1976, 34–36 (hereafter "Stephen B. Heart to Heart").
33. Quoted in La Ferla, "New York Fashion Week."
34. Stephen Burrows, personal communication with the author, March 4, 2025.
35. Peterson, "New Beat."
36. Lobenthal, *Radical Rags*, 80.
37. Paraphernalia opened in September 1965 and was located on Madison Avenue between Sixty-Sixth and Sixty-Seventh Streets. "A laboratory and showcase for untried design talent, Paraphernalia heralded a new epoch in fashionable New York." Lobenthal, *Radical Rags*, 78.
38. Quoted in Daniela Morera, "Burrows on Burrows," *Stephen Burrows*, 136.
39. Peterson, "New Beat."
40. Warren, "Helping Out the Togolese."
41. Magidson, "Backlash to Rebirth," 29.
42. Magidson, "Backlash to Rebirth," 31.
43. I confirmed that this was the living room of his Gramercy Park apartment, where he moved in 1973. Stephen Burrows, personal communication with the author, March 4, 2025.
44. Magidson, "Backlash to Rebirth," 31.
45. Givhan, *Battle of Versailles*, 111.
46. Stephen Burrows, personal communication with the author, March 4, 2025.
47. Quoted from "The HistoryMakers Video Oral History with Bethann Hardison," interview with Julieanna L. Richardson in New York on July 15, 2013, part of the HistoryMakers Digital Archive, https://da.thehistorymakers.org/storiesForBio;ID=A2013.190.
48. Quoted in Sewall-Ruskin, *High on Rebellion*, 205.
49. See Watson, "Art of Max's."
50. O'Brien, "Stephen Burrows's World by Night," 44.
51. Givhan, *Battle of Versailles*, 112.
52. Warhol and Hackett, *POPism*, 186.

53. Braunstein, "Forever Young," 246.
54. Warhol and Hackett, *POPism*, 187.
55. The event was a fundraiser for the Northside Center, a Harlem nonprofit founded by the married psychologists Mamie Phipps Clark and Kenneth B. Clark, whose doll tests were instrumental in the landmark *Brown v. Board of Education* Supreme Court decision in 1954.
56. Byrd, "When Bergdorf Served Chitlins."
57. Sheppard, "Basic Black"; see also Byrd, "On the Black Designer."
58. Givhan, *Battle of Versailles*, 63.
59. Givhan, *Battle of Versailles*, 65–66.
60. Byrd, "When Bergdorf Served Chitlins."
61. Givhan, *Battle of Versailles*, 113.
62. Agovino, "Ensembles of Miles Davis."
63. Givhan, *Battle of Versailles*, 112.
64. Vogel, "State of Grace," 179.
65. Jones, "Fashion History." Artists who worked as window dressers at Bonwit Teller include Robert Rauschenberg, Jasper Johns, James Rosenquist, and Andy Warhol.
66. Quoted in Feitelberg, "Freedom and Summer Fun," 30.
67. Crosley, "On and Off the Avenue."
68. Givhan, *Battle of Versailles*, 115.
69. Stephen Burrows, personal communication with the author, March 4, 2025.
70. Butler, "Fashion." Burrows clarified to me that while the samples were made at Bendel's, the clothes were made on Seventh Avenue. According to him, his boutique was on the third floor, the showroom was on the seventh floor, and the workroom—Bendel's Studio—was on the eighth floor. Stephen Burrows, personal communication with the author, March 4, 2025.
71. Quoted in "Introduction," *Stephen Burrows*, 11.
72. Jones, "Fashion History."
73. Schiro, "For the Young and Daring."
74. Givhan, *Battle of Versailles*, 120.
75. Stephen Burrows, personal communication with the author, March 4, 2025.
76. For more on the Ebony Fashion Fair, see Bivins, "Inspiring Beauty." Burrows, whose clothing was featured in the traveling fashion extravaganza, and Cleveland are both highlighted in an article celebrating the show's twentieth anniversary. See Lewis, "Two Decades of Ebony."
77. Cleveland, *Walking with the Muses*, 122.
78. Cleveland, *Walking with the Muses*, 122.
79. Cleveland, *Walking with the Muses*, 153.

80. Cleveland, *Walking with the Muses*, 156.
81. Cleveland, *Walking with the Muses*, 157.
82. "Stephen B. Heart to Heart."
83. Morris, *Fashion Makers*, 51.
84. Brown, *Work!*, 248.
85. Brown, *Work!*, 248.
86. Morris, "Look of Fashions."
87. "Stephen B. Heart to Heart"; Butler, "Fashion."
88. Meyer, *Art of Return*, 41.
89. Morris, "Fashion Talk."
90. Cleveland, *Walking with the Muses*, 154.
91. Givhan, *Battle of Versailles*, 117.
92. Quoted in Persson, "Revel, Rebel," 16.
93. Quoted in Persson, "Revel, Rebel," 18.
94. Sales figures are noted in Butler, "Fashion."
95. Peterson, "Young, Black, and Sophisticated."
96. "Stephen Burrows: Real American Fashion," *Women's Wear Daily*, June 7, 1973.
97. All details of Burrows's fashion show at the Coty Awards paraphrased from Givhan, *Battle of Versailles*, 117–18.
98. Draper, "Versailles '73," 98.
99. Cleveland, *Walking with the Muses*, 183.
100. This photograph appears on Bethann Hardison's website, https://www.bethannhardison.com. Recall that Fernandez was described as "assistant designer to fashion genius Stephen Burrows" in the *Interview* special issue on Puerto Rico that Antonio Lopez and Juan Ramos guest-edited in 1975. See "El Interman, Victor Fernandez," *Andy Warhol's Interview*, 7, no. 8 (1975), 6. According to Barry Ratoff, a mutual friend of both (and Charles Tracy's romantic partner), Fernandez worked for Burrows from early 1973 until roughly 1975 or 1976, and then pursued a career as a fashion stylist, working with Barry McKinley for GQ. Burrows also confirmed that Fernandez was his assistant on Seventh Avenue between 1973 and 1975. Barry Ratoff, personal communication with the author, March 17, 2023; Stephen Burrows, personal communication with the author, March 4, 2025.

    Curiously, it is only through social media that we get any inkling of a possible romance between Burrows and Fernandez during this period. In an Instagram post, Ratoff describes in vivid detail a memory of Fernandez in the early 1970s: "Fall 1972. A Sunday evening at the Limelight on Seventh Avenue South, quite possibly on a quaalude standing in front of Michael Capello's DJ booth (I can still probably name every song I ever heard there) when suddenly my friend Billy nudged me to take a look at the boy coming through the crowd he had a crush on. I turned my head to the left and could only see a glow. It was like the sun rising through the crowd. He was breathtaking, dressed head to almost toe in the choicest of Stephen Burrows one of a kind ready-to-dance garments. I instantly knew there was more to NYC gay life than what I'd seen over the last year and I wanted in. Victor was Stephen Burrows' boyfriend and soon to be assistant, a better representative for his clothes Stephen could not have found. He was the epitome of youth. He was that very moment. Victor Fernandez, 18, Cuban born, transplanted to San Juan, Puerto Rico and living in New York for about a year. Its indescribable what I saw in him that night but grateful to whatever forces put us in that room at the same time." Posted by the AIDS Memorial (@theaidsmemorial) on Instagram, March 28, 2023, https://www.instagram.com/p/CqWyWhNoseI/.

Besides these examples, I was not able to locate any discussion of Burrows and Fernandez's working or romantic relationship in any of the secondary material on Burrows, a perplexing erasure. Still, I concur with Kemi Adeyemi's suggestion that, as researchers, we should be critical of the "expectation if not demand that our interlocuters be wholly known to us." Instead, she argues, we should respect Black historical actors who embrace opacity as a form of protection, particularly those who "have long been mistreated in and by institutional study." See Adeyemi, *Feels Right*, 109, 110.

101. Draper, "Versailles '73," 100.
102. Quoted in Givhan, *Battle of Versailles*, 210.
103. Cleveland, *Walking with the Muses*, 267.
104. Barry Ratoff, personal communication with the author, March 17, 2023.
105. Brown, *Work!*, 234.
106. O'Brien, "Stephen Burrows's World by Night," 46. Burrows confirmed to me his affinity for the Motown sound for his runway music, especially the music of the Supremes, the Emotions, and the Marvelettes. Stephen Burrows, personal communication with the author, March 4, 2025.
107. Cleveland, *Walking with the Muses*, 161.
108. Barnes, "Black Models," 274.
109. Morris, "Fashion Shows as Theater."
110. Lawrence, "'Listen, and You Will Hear,'" 6.
111. My use of "fronts" and "expressive equipment" is drawn from Goffman, *Presentation of Self*.
112. See Bernstein, "Dances with Things."
113. Butler, "Fashion."
114. The *Times* article also featured an illustration of Burrows's tiered chiffon dress, rendered by Maning Obregon. See Lee, "1973."

115. Hyde, "Leaving for Stephen Burrows's World."
116. Quoted in Butler, "Fashion."
117. Hyde, "Leaving for Stephen Burrows's World."
118. Stanfill, "Nightclub as Fashion Catwalk," 262.
119. A photograph of this is reproduced in "Dance," *Stephen Burrows*, 159.
120. Morris, "Klein and Burrows at the Top."
121. "Three Black Designers," *Life*, November 1, 1978, 81.
122. Butler, "Fashion."
123. Morera, "Ascending to Freedom," 37.
124. O'Brien, "Stephen Burrows's World by Night," 46.
125. Beckwith, "Only Poetry," 51.

Afterword. Style Is a Feeling

1. Ackerman, "Theory of Style," 232.
2. For a discussion of Muñoz's adaptation of this phrase from Jean-Luc Nancy, see Chuh et al., "Being with José."
3. Goodman, *Ways of Worldmaking*, 40.
4. Crow, "Modernism and Mass Culture," 4.
5. Folkart, "Puerto Rican Henry Higgins."
6. After Ramos's death, Caranicas continued living in the loft until 1997. More recently, the 31 Union Square West studio where Lopez and Ramos worked, and where Ramos and Caranicas lived and worked, has been included in New York City's LGBT Historic Sites Project. See https://www.nyclgbtsites.org/site/antonio-lopez-juan-ramos-studio-juan-ramos-paul-caranicas-residence-studio/.
7. Schiro, "Antonio Lopez Is Dead at 44."
8. Goodman, *Ways of Worldmaking*, 25.
9. Goude remarked extensively on the counterintuitive logic of Jones's haircut: "When Grace is dressed in a mini skirt, wearing female attire, she looks, as I've said, somewhat masculine. But if she wears *male* attire, the femininity of her features is immediately revealed, enhanced. The same goes for her haircut. The flat-top she wears now is a traditional Marine hairdo. For some reason, Grace's beauty is enhanced by that hairdo. The volumes of her face are so powerful they need to be brought out and exaggerated. This is why I cut her hair that way." Goude, *Jungle Fever*, 105–6.
10. For an assessment of that album and Jones's performance antics at the time, see Gibbs, "Grace Jones Has Great Cheekbones."
11. For a reading of *One Man Show* and its relationship to African diasporic artistic traditions, especially Jonkonnu, see Fulani, "Who Is Grace Jones?"
12. Importantly, as Ricardo Montez also notes, this is the only music video Jones directed herself. See Montez, *Keith Haring's Line*, 85.

13. For more details on this Japanese showcase of Western fashion, see "Six Designers to Show at New Event in Tokyo," *Women's Wear Daily*, October 12, 1978. Burrows's inclusion suggests the synchronicity of his designs with Japanese aesthetic concepts such as basara—a love of color and flamboyance—and the propensity of Japanese consumers for "visual newness" and "play" in fashion. See Fury, "Fashion's Ultimate Fantasist"; and Slade, *Japanese Fashion*, 52, 59.
14. Morris, "Return of an American Original."
15. Morris, "Return of an American Original."
16. Feitelberg, "Freedom and Summer Fun," 30.
17. Morris, "Return of an American Original."
18. For instance, Lopez's illustrations and Instamatics were the subject of two shows, "Let Me Hear Your Body Talk" (2020) and "Kind of a Drag" (2022), at the Daniel Cooney Gallery in New York City. Across the proverbial pond, Jones was the subject of an exhibition (*Grace Before Jones: Camera, Disco, Studio*, Nottingham Contemporary, 2020); for the first time, it brought together her editorial work with Tony Barboza alongside portraits by Antonio Lopez, Ming Smith, Richard Bernstein, and Jean-Paul Goude. Likewise, Burrows's work was featured in an homage to eight decades of American style, in which each item of clothing was featured as the embodiment of a crucial fashion concept (*In America: A Lexicon of Fashion*, Costume Institute at the Metropolitan Museum of Art, 2021). A wool jersey dress in multiple color panels, dated 1970–73, was grouped with other garments to represent the quality of "vibrancy."
19. Friedman, "Pyer Moss and the Power." "At the time of this writing, Pyer Moss's future as a clothing brand is unclear. Described on its still-functional website as a "wholly independent art project that operates in the mediums of art, fashion, film and sound," its last runway show was in 2021. As such, its inactivity indicates the persistent challenges implicit in running an independent brand in the current economic climate. For more discussion on the brand's potential and mishaps, see Tahirah Hairston, "The Promise of Pyer Moss," *The Cut*, January 30, 2023, https://www.thecut.com/article/pyer-moss-kerby-jean-raymond-designer.html.
20. Paoletto, "Inside Telfar's Rainbow Bag Drop." In November 2024, Clemens opened his first brick-and-mortar shop in SoHo at 408 Broadway to much fanfare. See Falb, "Telfar Takes SoHo!"
21. This garment was also included in the Met's "Lexicon of Fashion" exhibition. For runway photographs, see Farra, "Willy Chavarria Spring 2022."
22. Macellus, "Howard University Alumni."
23. Ukiomogbe, "Raul Lopez."
24. "Top Models Paloma Elsesser and Precious Lee Crowned 'The New Supers' by British *Vogue*," *The Grio*, March 21, 2023, https://thegrio

.com/2023/03/21/top-models-paloma-elsesser-and-precious-lee-are-crowned-the-new-supers-by-british-vogue/. See also Paton, "Why Did Ultrathin Models Make a Comeback at Fashion Week?"; and Testa, "What Does It Take to Be a *Vogue* Model?"

25. For an art-historical discussion of Black tropes, see Dickerman et al., "Afrotropes."
26. See "Grace Wales Bonner and Lubaina Himid in Conversation," *Dazed*, February 14, 2022, https://www.dazeddigital.com/art-photography/article/55456/1/grace-wales-bonner-and-lubaina-himid-in-conversation-tate-modern.
27. Miller, "Artist Is Present," 82.
28. See the Medium Tings website at https://www.mediumtingsbk.com/.
29. Recent estimates have put the cost in the low six figures. In an interview, Chavarria said his fall 2024 show cost $350,000 and was done with the help of sponsors, including tequila brand Don Julio and shoemaker Allen Edmonds. Designer Elena Velez has been equally frank about fashion's hidden costs; she disclosed that her company borrowed most of the $40,000 to finance a 2023 runway show she held at a Brooklyn warehouse from her mother's retirement fund. See Hine, "How Much Does It Actually Cost?"; Binkley, "High Employability of Willy Chavarria"; Testa, "Should Making It in Fashion Be This Hard?"
30. Thompson, *Shine*, 46.
31. Doyle, *Hold It Against Me*, 15, xi.
32. See Manalansan, "'Stuff' of Archives."
33. See Adeyemi, "Beyond 90 Degrees."
34. Montez, *Keith Haring's Line*, 18, 19.

Bibliography

Ackerman, James. "A Theory of Style." *Journal of Aesthetics and Art Criticism* 20, no. 3 (1962): 227–37.

Adamson, Glenn, and Jane Pavitt. "Postmodernism: Style and Subversion." In *Postmodernism: Style and Subversion, 1970–1990*, edited by Glenn Adamson and Jane Pavitt, 12–95. London: Victoria and Albert Museum, 2011.

Adeyemi, Kemi. "Beyond 90 Degrees: The Angularities of Black/Queer/Women/Lean." *Women and Performance: a journal of feminist theory* 29, no. 1 (2019): 9–24.

Adeyemi, Kemi. *Feels Right: Black Queer Women and the Politics of Partying in Chicago*. Durham, NC: Duke University Press, 2022.

Agovino, Michael J. "The Ensembles of Miles Davis Epitomized Cool." *New York Times*, March 11, 2016.

Ahmed, Sara. *Queer Phenomenology: Orientations, Objects, Others*. Durham, NC: Duke University Press, 2006.

Aletti, Vince. *The Disco Files, 1973–78: New York's Underground, Week by Week*. New York: Distributed Arts Publishers, 2018.

Als, Hilton. "Spinning Tales." 1996. Reprint, *New Yorker*, December 3, 2018, 26–29.

Banes, Sally. "Breaking." 1985. Reprinted in *That's the Joint! The Hip-Hop Studies Reader*, edited by Murray Forman and Mark Anthony Neal, 13–20. New York: Routledge, 2004.

Barboza, Anthony, and Mazie M. Harris. "'The Photograph Finds You': A Conversation with the Artist." In *Eye Dreaming: Photographs by Anthony Barboza*, edited by Anthony Barboza, Aaron Bryant, and Mazie M. Harris, 29–46. Los Angeles: J. Paul Getty Museum, 2022.

Barnes, Clive. "Black Models: A New Fashion Energy." *Vogue*, December 1978, 274.

Barthes, Roland. "At Le Palace Tonight…" 1978. Reprinted in *Incidents*, translated by Richard Howard, 43–48. Berkeley: University of California Press, 1992.

Barthes, Roland. *Camera Lucida: Reflections on Photography*. Translated by Richard Howard. New York: Hill and Wang, 1981.

Barthes, Roland. "That Old Thing, Art…" 1980. Reprinted in *The Responsibility of Forms: Critical Essays on Music, Art, and Representation*, translated by Richard Howard, 198–206. New York: Hill and Wang, 1984.

Beckwith, Naomi. "Only Poetry." In *The Freedom Principle: Experiments in Art and Music, 1965 to Now*, edited by Naomi Beckwith and Dieter Roelstraete, 39–57. Chicago: Museum of Contemporary Art Chicago in association with the University of Chicago Press, 2015.

Bernstein, Robin. "Dances with Things: Material Culture and the Performance of Race." *Social Text* 27, no. 4 (2009): 67–94.

Binkley, Christina. "The High Employability of Willy Chavarria." *Vogue Business*, February 11, 2024. https://www.voguebusiness.com/story/fashion/the-high-employability-of-willy-chavarria.

Bivins, Joy L. "Inspiring Beauty: 50 Years of Ebony Fashion Fair." NKA: *Journal of Contemporary African Art*, no. 37 (2015): 80–89.

Boch, Richard. *The Mudd Club*. New York: Feral House, 2017.

Borelli, Melissa Blanco. "You Can't Outdo Black People: *Soul Train*, Queer Witnessing, and Pleasurable Competition." In *The Oxford Handbook of Dance and Competition*, edited by Sherril Dodds, 515–30. New York: Oxford University Press, 2019.

Borrelli-Persson, Laird. "Grace Jones's 1979 Disco Baby Shower Was as Ridiculously Chic as They Come." *Vogue*, August 21, 2015. https://www.vogue.com/article/grace-jones-debbie-harry-childrenswear.

Bourhis, Katell le. "Antonio: An Artist's Dialogue with Fashion." In *Antonio 60 70 80: Three Decades in Style*, edited by Juan Eugene Ramos and Paul Caranicas, 8–13. Munich: Schirmer Art Books, 1995.

Bradbury, Oliver. *An Alternative Seventies: The Last Age of Radicalism*. London: Nantz Press, 2020.

Bradley, Rizvana. *Anteaesthetics: Black Aesthesis and the Critique of Form*. Stanford, CA: Stanford University Press, 2023.

Bradley, Rizvana. "Introduction: Other Sensualities." In "The Haptic: Textures of Performance," edited by Rizvana Bradley. Special issue, *Women and Performance: a journal of feminist theory* 24, nos. 2–3 (2014): 129–33.

Bragin, Naomi. "Techniques of Black Male Re/dress: Corporeal Drag and Kinesthetic Politics in the Rebirth of Waacking/Punkin.'" *Women and Performance: a journal of feminist theory* 24, no. 1 (2014): 61–78.

Braunstein, Peter. "Forever Young: Insurgent Youth and the Sixties Culture of Rejuvenation." In *Imagine Nation: The American Counterculture of the 1960s and '70s*, edited by Peter Braunstein and Michael William Doyle, 243–73. New York: Routledge, 2002.

Brielmaier, Isolde, Joshua Chambers-Letson, Jasmine Nicole Cobb, et al. "Institutionalizing Methods: Art History and Performance and Visual Studies." In *Saturation: Race, Art, and the Circulation of Value*, edited by C. Riley Snorton and Hentyle Yapp, 241–59. Cambridge, MA: MIT Press; New York: New Museum, 2020.

Brody, Jennifer DeVere. *Punctuation: Art, Politics, Play*. Durham, NC: Duke University Press, 2008.

Brooks, Daphne A. *Liner Notes for the Revolution: The Intellectual Life of Black Feminist Sound*. Cambridge, MA: Harvard University Press, 2021.

Brown, Elspeth H. *Work! A Queer History of Modeling*. Durham, NC: Duke University Press, 2019.

Brown, Elspeth H., and Thy Phu, eds. *Feeling Photography*. Durham, NC: Duke University Press, 2014.

Burrows, Stephen. "Remembering Willi Smith." In *Willi Smith Street Couture*, edited by Alexandra Cunningham Cameron, 222. New York: Rizzoli Electa, 2020.

Butet-Roch, Laurence. "Perfectly Banal." *British Journal of Photography* (May 2013): 24–33.

Butler, Jean. "Fashion." *New York Times*, June 5, 1977.

Butt, Gavin. Introduction to *Between You and Me: Queer Disclosures in the New York Art World, 1948–1963*, 1–21. Durham, NC: Duke University Press, 2005.

Byrd, Rikki. "On the Black Designer." *Fashion Studies Journal*. Accessed April 14, 2024. https://www.fashionstudiesjournal.org/essays/2016/9/11/on-the-black-designer.

Byrd, Rikki. "When Bergdorf Served Chitlins and Champagne: The Curious Case of Soul Food in Department Stores." *Racked*, November 8, 2017. https://www.racked.com/2017/11/8/16614056/soul-food-department-stores-neiman-marcus-bergdorf-goodman-woolworths.

Cahan, Susan E. *Mounting Frustration: The Art Museum in the Age of Black Power*. Durham, NC: Duke University Press, 2016.

Campt, Tina. *A Black Gaze: Artists Changing How We See*. Cambridge, MA: MIT Press, 2021.

Campt, Tina. *Listening to Images*. Durham, NC: Duke University Press, 2017.

Caranicas, Paul. *Antonio's People*. New York: Thames and Hudson, 2004.

Carmack, Kara. "'I'm a Person Who Loves Beautiful Things': Potassa de Lafayette as Model and Muse." *Journal of Visual Culture* 19, no. 2 (2020): 246–54.

Cavoulacos, Sophie. "Downtown for Downtown." In *Club 57: Film, Performance, and Art in the East Village, 1978–1983*, edited by Sarah Resnick, 24–41. New York: Museum of Modern Art, 2017.

Chambers-Letson, Joshua. *After the Party: A Manifesto for Queer Life*. New York: NYU Press, 2018.

Chavoya, C. Ondine, and David Evans Frantz, eds. *Axis Mundo: Queer Networks in Chicano L.A.* New York: Prestel, 2018.

Chavoya, C. Ondine, and Rita Gonzalez, eds. *Asco: Elite of the Obscure, a Retrospective, 1972–1987*. Los Angeles: Los Angeles County Museum of Art, 2011.

Chen, Mel. *Animacies: Biopolitics, Racial Mattering, and Queer Affect*. Durham, NC: Duke University Press, 2012.

Cheng, Anne. *Ornamentalism*. New York: Oxford University Press, 2019.

Cheng, Anne. *Second Skin: Josephine Baker and the Modern Surface*. New York: Oxford University Press, 2000.

Chuh, Kandice. *The Difference Aesthetics Makes: On the Humanities "After Man."* Durham, NC: Duke University Press, 2019.

Chuh, Kandice. "It's Not About Anything." In *Saturation: Race, Art, and the Circulation of Value*, edited by C. Riley Snorton and Hentyle Yapp, 171–81. Cambridge, MA: MIT Press; New York: New Museum, 2020.

Chuh, Kandice, Joshua Javier Guzmán, Ricardo Montez, Tavia Nyong'o, Alex Pittman, and Jeanne Vaccaro. "Being with José: An Introduction." *Social Text* 32, no. 4 (121) (2014): 1–7.

Cleveland, Pat. "Remembering Willi Smith." In *Willi Smith: Street Couture*, edited by Alexandra Cunningham Cameron, 223. New York: Rizzoli Electa, 2020.

Cleveland, Pat. *Walking with the Muses*. New York: Altria, 2016.

Crosley, Sloane. "On and Off the Avenue: Bye Bye, Bendel's." *New Yorker*, December 27, 2018. https://www.newyorker.com/culture/on-and-off-the-avenue/bye-bye-bendels.

Crow, Thomas. "Modernism and Mass Culture in the Arts." In *Modern Art in the Common Culture*, 3–37. New Haven, CT: Yale University Press, 1996.

Cruz-Malavé, Arnaldo. *Queer Latino Testimonio, Keith Haring, and Juanito Xtravaganza: Hard Tails*. New York: Palgrave Macmillan, 2007.

Cvetkovich, Ann. "Photographing Objects as Queer Archival Practice." In *Feeling Photography*, edited by Elspeth Brown and Thy Phu, 273–96. Durham, NC: Duke University Press, 2014.

Dávila, Arlene, and Yasmin Ramirez, eds. *Nuyorican and Diasporican Visual Art: A Critical Anthology*. Durham, NC: Duke University Press, 2025.

Dickerman, Leah, David Joselit, and Mignon Nixon. "Afrotropes: A Conversation with Huey Copeland and Krista Thompson." *October* 162 (Fall 2017): 3–18.

Doyle, Jennifer. *Hold It Against Me: Difficulty and Emotion in Contemporary Art*. Durham, NC: Duke University Press, 2013.

Doyle, Jennifer. "Just Friends." In *Otherwise: Imagining Queer Feminist Art Histories*, edited by Amelia Jones and Erin Silver, 51–71. Manchester: Manchester University Press, 2016.

Draper, Deborah Riley. "Versailles '73: American Runway Revolution." *Nka: Journal of Contemporary African Art* 37 (2015): 94–102.

Eckhardt, Sarah L., ed. *Working Together: Louis Draper and the Kamoinge Workshop*. Richmond: Virginia Museum of Fine Arts, 2020. Exhibition catalog.

English, Darby. *1971: A Year in the Life of Color*. Chicago: University of Chicago Press, 2016.

Falb, Sam. "Telfar Takes SoHo! Inside the Brand's Store Opening Bash with Lil' Kim, Ellie the Elephant, and More." *Vogue*, November 25, 2024. https://www.vogue.com/article/inside-the-telfar-soho-opening-2024.

Farra, Emily. "Willy Chavarria Spring 2022 Menswear Collection." *Vogue*, September 9, 2021. https://www.vogue.com/fashion-shows/spring-2022-menswear/willy-chavarria.

Feitelberg, Rosemary. "Freedom and Summer Fun in the Seventies." *Women's Wear Daily*, July 2, 2020.

Feitelberg, Rosemary. "Stephen Burrows Reminisces in Rhythm." *Women's Wear Daily*, March 20, 2013.

Finch, Margaret. *Style in Art History: An Introduction to Theories of Style and Sequence*. Metuchen, NJ: Scarecrow Press, 1974.

Fischer, Hal. *The Gay Seventies*. San Francisco: Gallery 16, 2019.

Flatley, Jonathan, and Anthony E. Grudin. "Introduction: Warhol's Aesthetics." In "Andy Warhol," edited by Jonathan Flatley and Anthony E. Grudin. Special issue, *Criticism* 56, no. 3 (2014): 419–23.

Fleetwood, Nicole. *On Racial Icons: Blackness and the Public Imagination*. New Brunswick, NJ: Rutgers University Press, 2015.

Fleetwood, Nicole. *Troubling Vision: Performance, Visuality, and Blackness*. Chicago: University of Chicago Press, 2011.

Flores, Juan. *From Bomba to Hip-Hop: Puerto Rican Culture and Latino Identity*. New York: Columbia University Press, 2000.

Folkart, Burt A. "Puerto Rican Henry Higgins: Fashion Illustrator Antonio Lopez Dies." *Los Angeles Times*, March 18, 1987.

Ford, Tanisha. *Liberated Threads: Black Women, Style, and the Global Politics of Soul*. Chapel Hill: University of North Carolina Press, 2015.

Françoise, Anne-Lise. "These Boots Were Made for Walkin': Fashion as Compulsive Artifice." In *The Seventies: The Age of Glitter in Popular Culture*, edited by Shelton Waldrep, 155–75. New York: Routledge, 2000.

Frank, Alex. "Stephen Burrows: The Dancing Designer." *The Fader*, April 25, 2013. https://www.thefader.com/2013/04/25/stephen-burrows-the-dancing-designer.

Friedman, Vanessa. "Pyer Moss and the Power of Black Truth." *New York Times*, September 9, 2019.

Fulani, Ifeona. "Who is Grace Jones?" In *Archipelagos of Sound: Transnational Caribbeanities, Women and Music*, edited by Ifeona Fulani, 234–57. Kingston, Jamaica: University of the West Indies Press, 2012.

Fury, Alexander. "Fashion's Ultimate Fantasist Makes a Comeback." *New York Times Style Magazine*, July 24, 2017. https://www.nytimes.com/2017/07/24/t-magazine/fashion/kansai-yamamoto-revival.html.

Galvão, Carolina Abbott. "The View from: Ming Smith." *Monocle*, no. 160 (2023): 30.

Garner, Phillipe. "Antonio and His Instamatic." In *Instamatics*, by Antonio Lopez, n.p. Santa Fe, NM: Twin Palms Publishers, 2011.

Gendron, Bernard. *Between Montmartre and the Mudd Club: Popular Music and the Avant-Garde*. Chicago: University of Chicago Press, 2002.

Gester, Phillip. "Flesh and Spirit: Robert Mapplethorpe, Sam Wagstaff, and the Gay Sensibility." In *Robert Mapplethorpe: The Photographs*, edited by Paul Martineu and Britt Salvesan, 245–55. Los Angeles: J. Paul Getty Museum, 2016.

Geter, Hafizah Augustus. "Black Phenomena: On Afropessimism and Camp." *Bomb*, September 23, 2021. https://bombmagazine.org/articles/2021/09/23/black-phenomena-on-afropessimism-camp/.

Getsy, David J. *Queer Behavior: Scott Burton and Performance Art*. Chicago: University of Chicago Press, 2022.

Gibbs, Vernon. "Grace Jones Has Great Cheekbones." *Village Voice*, August 5, 1981.

Givhan, Robin. *The Battle of Versailles: The Night American Fashion Stumbled into the Spotlight and Made History*. New York: Flatiron Books, 2015.

Gleisser, Faye Raquel. *Risk Work: Making Art and Guerilla Tactics in Punitive America, 1967–1987*. Chicago: University of Chicago Press, 2023.

Goffman, Erving. *The Presentation of Self in Everyday Life*. New York: Anchor, 1959.

Goodman, Nelson. *Ways of Worldmaking*. Sussex, UK: Harvester Press, 1978.

Gopinath, Gayatri. *Unruly Visions: The Aesthetic Practices of Queer Diaspora*. Durham, NC: Duke University Press, 2018.

Gopnik, Blake. *Warhol*. New York: HarperCollins, 2020.

Goude, Jean-Paul. *Jungle Fever*. New York: Xavier Moreau, 1981.

Greenberger, Alex. "Mel Ramos, Painter of Sexually Suggestive Pop Pictures, Dies at 83." *ARTnews*, October 16, 2018.

Guarnaccia, Matteo. *Elio Fiorucci: Fashion Unfolds*. Milan: Moleskin SpA, 2015.

Guzmán, Joshua Javier. *Dissatisfactions: Queer Latinidad and the Politics of Style*. New York: NYU Press, 2024.

Guzmán, Joshua Javier, and Iván A. Ramos. "Mediated Identifications: José Esteban Muñoz and Visual Studies." *Afterimage* 49, no. 1 (2022): 26–31.

Gyarkye, Lovia. "The Ecstatic, Elusive Art of Ming Smith." *New York Times Style Magazine*, February 3, 2023. https://www.nytimes.com/2023/02/03/t-magazine/ming-smith-moma.html.

Hall, Stuart. "What Is This 'Black' in Black Popular Culture?" In *Black Popular Cultures*, edited by Gina Dent, 21–33. Seattle: Bay Press, 1992.

Haring, Keith. *Keith Haring's Journals*. 1996. Reprint, New York: Penguin, 2010.

Hartman, Saidiya. *Wayward Lives, Beautiful Experiments: Intimate Histories of Social Upheaval*. New York: W. W. Norton, 2019.

Hebdige, Dick. *Subculture: The Meaning of Style*. New York: Methuen, 1979.

Heiser, Jörg. "Club Culture and Contemporary Art: A Relationship." In *Night Fever: Designing Club Culture, 1960–Today*, edited by Mateo Kries, Jochen Eisenbrand, and Catharine Rossi, 173–88. Weil am Rhein, Belgium: Vitra Design Museum, 2018.

Heiser, Jörg. *Double Lives in Art and Pop Music*. Cambridge, MA: MIT Press, 2020.

Hernandez, Jillian. *Aesthetics of Excess: The Art and Politics of Black and Latina Embodiment*. Durham, NC: Duke University Press, 2020.

Hernandez, Robb. *Archiving an Epidemic: Art, AIDS, and the Queer Chicanx Avant-Garde*. New York: NYU Press, 2019.

Hine, Samuel. "How Much Does It Actually Cost to Put on a Fashion Show?" *GQ*, September 15, 2023. https://www.gq.com/story/nyfw-ss24-runway-show-cost.

Hong, Cathy Park. "Delusions of Whiteness in the Avant-Garde." *Lana Turner: A Journal of Poetry and Opinion*, no. 7 (November 2014).

https://shc.stanford.edu/arcade/interventions/delusions-whiteness-avant-garde.

Howarth, Dan. "Postmodern Design: Grace Jones's Maternity Dress by Jean-Paul Goude." *Dezeen*, September 11, 2015. https://www.dezeen.com/2015/09/11/postmodernism-fashion-design-grace-jones-maternity-dress-jean-paul-goude/.

Hyde, Nina S. "Leaving for Stephen Burrows's World." *Washington Post*, November 30, 1976.

Huck, Brigitte. "Mel Ramos, Albertina." *Artforum* 50, no. 1 (2011). https://www.artforum.com/print/reviews/201107/mel-ramos-28904.

Hurston, Zora Neale. "Characteristics of Negro Expression." In *You Don't Know Us Negroes and Other Essays*, edited by Henry Louis Gates Jr. and Genevieve West, 47–65. New York: HarperCollins, 2022.

Jaime, Karen. *The Queer Nuyorican: Racialized Sexualities and Aesthetics in Loisaida*. New York: NYU Press, 2021.

James, Charles. "Juan Ramos: Engineer of the Impossible." In "The Puerto Rico Issue." Special issue, *Interview* 7, no. 8 (1975): n.p.

Johnson, Dominic. "The Accidental Goddess: An Interview with Joey Arias." In *The Art of Living: An Oral History of Performance Art*, 175–94. London: Palgrave, 2015.

Jones, Amelia. "'Presence' in Absentia: Experiencing Performance as Documentation." *Art Journal* 56, no. 4 (1997): 11–18.

Jones, Grace. Foreword to *Richard Bernstein: Starmaker, Andy Warhol's Cover Artist*, by Roger Padilha and Mauricio Padilha, 5. New York: Rizzoli, 2018.

Jones, Grace. *I'll Never Write My Memoirs*. New York: Gallery Books, 2015.

Jones, Grace. *Warm Leatherette*. Island ILPS 9592, 1990, 33⅓ rpm.

Jones, Kellie. *South of Pico: African American Artists in Los Angeles in the 1960s and 1970s*. Durham, NC: Duke University Press, 2017.

Jones, Veronica. "Fashion History: Stephen Burrows." *New York Beacon*, February 18, 2021.

Kershaw, Miriam. "Postcolonialism and Androgyny: The Performance Art of Grace Jones." *Art Journal* 56, no. 4 (1997): 19–25.

Kozloff, Max. "Photography: The Coming to Age of Color." *Artforum* 13, no. 5 (January 1975): 30–35.

Krasinki, Jennifer. "Antonio Lopez Dazzles at El Museo del Barrio." *Village Voice*, August 10, 2016. https://artwriting.sva.edu/journal/post/antonio-lopez-dazzles-at-el-museo-del-barrio.

Kries, Mateo, Jochen Eisenbrand, and Catharine Rossi, eds. *Night Fever: Designing Club Culture, 1960–Today*. Weil am Rhein, Belgium: Vitra Design Museum, 2018.

Kushner, Rachel. *The Flamethrowers*. New York: Scribner, 2013.

La Ferla, Ruth. "New York Fashion Week: An Oral History, the First Shows." *New York Times*, September 7, 2016.

La Fountain-Stokes, Lawrence. *Queer Ricans: Cultures and Sexualities in the Diaspora*. Minneapolis: University of Minnesota Press, 2009.

Langkjaer, Michael. "Urban Fitness, Gendered Practices, and Fine Art: The Significance of Antonio Lopez's Sporty Styling of Fashion." *Fashion Practice: The Journal of Design, Creative Practice, and the Fashion Industry* 8, no. 2 (2016): 189–211.

Lawrence, Tim. *Life and Death on the New York Dance Floor, 1980–1983*. Durham, NC: Duke University Press, 2016.

Lawrence, Tim. "'Listen, and You Will Hear All the Houses That Walked There Before': A History of Drag Balls, Houses, and the Culture of Voguing." In *Voguing and the House Ballroom Scene of New York City, 1989–92*, edited by Stuart Baker, 3–10. London: Soul Jazz Books, 2022.

Lawrence, Tim. *Love Saves the Day: A History of American Dance Music Culture, 1970–1979*. Durham, NC: Duke University Press, 2004.

Lax, Thomas J. Preface to *Side by Side: Collaborative Artistic Practices in the United States, 1960s–1980s*, edited by Gwyneth Shanks and Allie Tepper. Vol. 3 of the *Living Collections Catalogue*. Minneapolis: Walker Art Center, 2020. https://walkerart.org/collections/publications/side-by-side/side-by-side-collaborative-artistic-practices-in-the-u-s-1960s-1980s

Lee, Summer. "1973—Stephen Burrows, Evening Dress." *Fashion History Timeline*, July 6, 2020. https://fashionhistory.fitnyc.edu/1973-stephen-burrows-evening-dress/.

Lee, Summer Kim. "Staying In: Mitski, Ocean Voung, and Asian America Asociality." *Social Text* 37, no. 1 (138) (2019): 27–50.

Lewis, Shawn D. "Two Decades of Ebony Fashion Fair." *Ebony*, December 1977, 146–52.

Lobato, Ramon. "Amazing Grace: Decadence, Deviance, Disco." *Camera Obscura* 22, no. 2 (65) (2007): 134–38.

Lobenthal, Joel. *Radical Rags: Fashions of the Sixties*. New York: Abbeville Press, 1990.

Londoño, Johana. *Abstract Barrios: The Crises of Latinx Visibility in Cities*. Durham, NC: Duke University Press, 2020.

Lopez, Antonio. *Antonio's Girls*. New York: Congreve Publishing, 1982.

Lopez, Antonio. *Instamatics*. Santa Fe, NM: Twin Palms Publishers, 2011.

Luckett, Kilolo. "Interview with Pat Cleveland." In *Halston and Warhol: Silver and Suede*, edited by Abigail Franzen-Sheehan, 39–45. Pittsburgh, PA: Andy Warhol Museum, 2014.

Macellus, Kerane. "Howard University Alumni on Being the Inspiration Behind Wales Bonners's Fall/Winter 2024 Show." *Essence*, February 27,

2024. https://www.essence.com/fashion/howard-university-alumni-wales-bonner-show/.

Magidson, Phyllis. "Backlash to Rebirth: New York's 1960s Fashion Youthquake." In *Stephen Burrows: When Fashion Danced*, edited by Daniela Morera, 24–30. New York: Skira Rizzoli, in association with Museum of the City of New York, 2013.

Magliozzi, Ron. "Art Is What You Make It: Club 57 and the Downtown Scene." In *Club 57: Film, Performance, and Art in the East Village, 1978–1983*, edited by Sarah Resnick, 11–23. New York: Museum of Modern Art, 2017.

Magnuson, Ann. "The Prime Time of Our Lives." In *Keith Haring*, edited by Elizabeth Sussman, 124–32. New York: Whitney Museum of American Art, 1997.

Malanga, Gerard, and Raymond Foye. "Grace to Be Born, and Live as Variously as Possible." *Gagosian Quarterly*, Fall 2023. https://gagosian.com/quarterly/2023/11/02/interview-grace-to-be-born-and-live-as-variously-as-possible.

Manalansan, Martin F., IV. "The 'Stuff' of Archives: Mess, Migration, and Queer Lives." *Radical History Review*, no. 120 (2014): 94–107.

Marks, Laura. *The Skin of the Film: Intercultural Media, Embodiment, and the Senses*. Durham, NC: Duke University Press, 2000.

McKenzie, Michael. "Interview: Antonio Lopez with Michael McKensie." 1976. Reprinted in *Instamatics*, by Antonio Lopez, n.p. Santa Fe, NM: Twin Palms Publishers, 2011.

McMillan, Uri. *Embodied Avatars: Genealogies of Black Feminist Art and Performance*. New York: NYU Press, 2015.

McMillan, Uri. "Introduction: Skin, Surface, Sensorium." In "Surface Aesthetics: Race, Performance, Play," edited by Uri McMillan. Special issue, *Women and Performance: a journal of feminist theory* 28, no. 1 (2018): 1–15.

McMillan, Uri. "Sand, Nylon, and Dirt: Senga Nengudi and Maren Hassinger in Southern California." In *We Wanted a Revolution: Black Radical Women, 1965–1985: New Perspectives*, 97–118. Brooklyn: Brooklyn Museum; Durham, NC: Duke University Press, 2018.

Mercer, Kobena. "Skin Head Sex Thing." In *How Do I Look? Queer Film and Video*, edited by Bad Object Choices, 169–210. Seattle: Bay Press, 1991.

Mercer, Kobena. *Welcome to the Jungle: New Positions in Black Cultural Studies*. New York: Routledge, 1994.

Meyer, James. *The Art of Return: The Sixties and Contemporary Culture*. Chicago: University of Chicago Press, 2019.

Meyer, Richard. "The Jesse Helms Theory of Art." *October* 104 (2003): 131–48.

Meyer, Richard. "Mapplethorped: Art, Photography, and the Pornographic Imagination." In *Robert Mapplethorpe: The Photographs*, edited by Paul Martineu and Britt Salvesan, 231–43. Los Angeles: J. Paul Getty Museum, 2016.

Miller, Hillary. *Drop Dead: Performance in Crisis, 1970s New York*. Evanston, IL: Northwestern University Press, 2016.

Miller, M. H. "The Artist Is Present." *New York Times Style Magazine*, March 3, 2024, 82.

Miller, Timothy. "The Sixties-Era Commune." In *Imagine Nation: The American Counterculture of the 1960s and '70s*, edited by Peter Braunstein and Michael William Doyle, 327–51. New York: Routledge, 2002.

Montez, Ricardo. *Keith Haring's Line: Race and the Performance of Desire*. Durham, NC: Duke University Press, 2020.

Moore, Kevin. "Starburst: Color Photography in America, 1970–1980." In *Starburst: Color Photography in America 1970–1980*, edited by Kevin Moore, 8–36. Ostfildern, Germany: Hatje Cantz Verlag, 2010.

Morera, Daniela. "Ascending to Freedom." In *Stephen Burrows: When Fashion Danced*, edited by Daniela Morera, 34–41. New York: Skira Rizzoli, in association with Museum of the City of New York, 2013.

Morera, Daniela. "Burrows on Burrows." In *Stephen Burrows: When Fashion Danced*, edited by Daniela Morera, 130–37. New York: Skira Rizzoli, in association with Museum of the City of New York, 2013.

Morera, Daniela. "Dance." In *Stephen Burrows: When Fashion Danced*, edited by Daniela Morera, 152–71. New York: Skira Rizzoli, in association with Museum of the City of New York, 2013.

Morera, Daniela. "Introduction." In *Stephen Burrows: When Fashion Danced*, edited by Daniela Morera, 8–11. New York: Skira Rizzoli, in association with Museum of the City of New York, 2013.

Morris, Bernadine. *The Fashion Makers*. New York: Random House, 1978.

Morris, Bernadine. "Fashion Shows as Theater." *New York Times*, June 15, 1977.

Morris, Bernadine. "Fashion Talk." *New York Times*, November 20, 1972.

Morris, Bernadine. "Klein and Burrows at the Top of Their Form." *New York Times*, April 29, 1978.

Morris, Bernadine. "The Look of Fashions for the Seventies in Colors That Can Dazzle." *New York Times*, August 12, 1970.

Morris, Bernadine. "The Return of an American Original." *New York Times*, August 10, 1993.

Morris, Catherine, and Rujeko Hockley, eds. *We Wanted a Revolution: Black Radical Women, 1965–85: A Sourcebook*. Durham, NC: Duke University Press, 2017.

Muñoz, José Esteban. *Cruising Utopia: The Then and There of Queer Futurity*. New York: NYU Press, 2009.

Muñoz, José Esteban. *Disidentifications: Queers of Color and the Performance of Politics*. Minneapolis: University of Minnesota Press, 1996.

Muñoz, José Esteban. *The Sense of Brown*. Edited by Tavia Nyong'o and Joshua Chambers-Letson. Durham, NC: Duke University Press, 2020.

Murray, Yxta Maya. "Beauty Is in the Eye." In *Ming Smith: An Aperture Monograph*, edited by Brendan Embser, 126–30. New York: Aperture Foundation, 2020.

Musser, Amber Jamilla. *Sensual Excess: Queer Femininity and Brown Jouissance*. New York: NYU Press, 2018.

Myers, Tanya Danielle Wilson. "Color Story: Stephen Burrows's Impact on the World of Fashion." In *Black Designers in American Fashion*, edited by Elizabeth Way, 195–218. London: Bloomsbury Visual Arts, 2021.

Negrón-Muntaner, Frances. *Boricua Pop: Puerto Ricans and the Latinization of American Culture*. New York: NYU Press, 2004.

Newton, Esther. *Cherry Grove, Fire Island: Sixty Years in America's First Gay and Lesbian Town*. Durham, NC: Duke University Press, 2014.

Norment, Lynn. "The Outrageous Grace Jones." *Ebony*, July 1979, 84–94.

Nyong'o, Tavia. *Afro-Fabulations: The Queer Drama of Black Life*. New York: NYU Press, 2018.

Nyong'o, Tavia. "I Feel Love: Disco and Its Discontents." *Criticism* 50, no. 1 (2008): 101–12.

O'Brien, Glenn. "Stephen Burrows's World by Night." In *Stephen Burrows: When Fashion Danced*, edited by Daniela Morera, 42–46. New York: Skira Rizzoli, in association with Museum of the City of New York, 2013.

O'Neill, Alistair. "Antonio and Juan Stepping Out." In *Visionary Writing: Antonio Lopez, Juan Ramos*, edited by Devon Caranicas, Tema Demichel, Anne Morin, 53–87. Madrid: diChroma photography, 2019.

Ottenberg, Mel. "Pat Cleveland on Partying with Richard Bernstein and the Factory Crew." *Interview*, April 22, 2022. https://www.interviewmagazine.com/art/pat-cleveland-on-partying-with-richard-bernstein-and-the-factory-crew.

Owen, David, ed. *Fiorucci*. New York, Rizzoli, 2017.

Padilha, Roger, and Mauricio Padilha. *Antonio Lopez: Fashion, Art, Sex, and Disco*. New York: Rizzoli, 2012.

Padilha, Roger, and Mauricio Padilha. *Richard Bernstein Starmaker: Andy Warhol's Cover Artist*. New York: Rizzoli, 2018.

Paoletto, Isabella. "Inside Telfar's Rainbow Bag Drop." *New York Times*, September 12, 2022.

Parnes, Uzi. "Pop Performance in the East Village Clubs." *Drama Review* 29, no. 1 (1985): 5–16.

Pastor, Julie. "WilliWear New Wave Graphics." In *Willi Smith Street Couture*, edited by Alexandra Cunningham Cameron, 160–73. New York: Rizzoli Electa, 2020.

Paton, Elizabeth. "Why Did Ultrathin Models Make a Comeback at Fashion Week?" *New York Times*, March 11, 2023.

Pérez, Roy. "The Glory That Was Wrong: el 'Chino Malo' Approximates Nuyorico." *Women and Performance: a journal of feminist theory* 25, no. 3 (2015): 277–97.

Persson, Laird. "Revel, Rebel." In *Stephen Burrows: When Fashion Danced*, edited by Daniela Morera, 14–21. New York: Skira Rizzoli, in association with Museum of the City of New York, 2013.

Peterson, Patricia. "New Beat." *New York Times*, May 25, 1969.

Peterson, Patricia. "Young, Black, and Sophisticated." *New York Times*, November 5, 1972.

Pham, Minh-Ha. *Asians Wear Clothes on the Internet: Race, Gender, and the Work of Personal Style Blogging*. Durham, NC: Duke University Press, 2015.

Pinney, Christopher, and Nicolas Peterson, eds., *Photography's Other Histories*. Durham, NC: Duke University Press, 2003.

Pollan, Michael. *How to Change Your Mind: What the New Science of Psychedelics Teaches Us About Consciousness, Dying, Addiction, Depression, and Transcendence*. New York: Penguin, 2018.

Post, Tina. *Deadpan: The Aesthetics of Black Inexpression*. New York: NYU Press, 2022.

Powell, Richard. *Cutting a Figure: Fashioning Black Portraiture*. Chicago: University of Chicago Press, 2008.

Powell, Richard. "Racial Imaginaries from Charles White's Preacher to Jean-Paul Goude and Grace Jones' Nigger Arabesque." In *Back to Black: Art, Cinema, and the Racial Imaginary*, edited by Richard Powell, David Bailey, and Petrine Archer-Straw, 9–27. London: Whitechapel Art Gallery, 2005.

Reed, Ishmael. "Light and Shadow: The Artistry of Ming Smith." *Rhapsody in the Street: A Magazine Curated by Grace Wales Bonner*, no. 22 (2021): 48–59.

Roach, Joseph. *It*. Ann Arbor: University of Michigan Press, 2011.

Rosen, Miss. "Remembering New York's Legendary 70s Club Paradise Garage." *i-D*, December 16, 2021. https://i-d.co/article/paradise-garage-new-york/.

Rothschild, Lincoln. *Style in Art: The Dynamic of Art as Cultural Expression*. New York: Thomas Yoseloff, 1960.

Royster, Francesca. "'Feeling Like a Woman, Looking Like a Man, Sounding Like a No-No': Grace Jones and the Performance of 'Strangé' in the Post-Soul Moment." *Women and Performance: a journal of feminist theory* 19, no. 1 (2009): 77–94.

Ruiz, Sandra. *Ricanness: Enduring Time in Anticolonial Performance.* New York: NYU Press, 2019.

Salibian, Sandra and Miles Socha. "Seminal Moment: Why the Fiorucci Store Was the Mother of All Retail Concepts." *Women's Wear Daily*, December 14, 2020.

Schiche, Ericka. "Iconic Photographer Ming Smith Brings Invisible Subjects into the Light with Houston Museum Exhibition, National Tour." *PaperCity Magazine*, September 29, 2003. https://www.papercitymag.com/arts-houston/ming-smith-photographer-shines-light-houston-camh-museum/.

Schiro, Anne-Marie. "Antonio Lopez Is Dead at 44; Was Major Fashion Illustrator." *New York Times*, March 18, 1987.

Schiro, Anne-Marie. "For the Young and Daring." *New York Times*, September 20, 1970.

Schneider, Sara K. *Vital Mummies: Performance Design and the Store-Window Mannequin.* New Haven, CT: Yale University Press, 1995.

Schneier, Matthew. "The Man Who Made Everyone Look So Famous." *New York Times*, September 7, 2018.

Sewall-Ruskin, Yvonne. *High on Rebellion: Inside the Underground at Max's Kansas City.* New York: Thunder's Mouth Press, 1998.

Shanks, Gwyneth, and Allie Tepper, eds. *Side by Side: Collaborative Artistic Practices in the United States, 1960s–1980s.* Vol. 3 of the *Living Collections Catalogue*. Minneapolis: Walker Art Center, 2020. https://walkerart.org/collections/publications/side-by-side/contents

Shapiro, Peter. "Saturday Mass: Larry Levan and the Paradise Garage." *Red Bull Music Academy Daily*, April 22, 2014. https://daily.redbullmusicacademy.com/2014/04/larry-levan-feature.

Sharpe, Christina. *Ordinary Notes.* New York: Farrar, Straus and Giroux, 2023.

Sheppard, Eugenia. "Basic Black: Fashion Show Breakthrough for 5th Avenue." *Los Angeles Times*, May 26, 1969.

Slade, Toby. *Japanese Fashion: A Cultural History.* New York: Berg, 2009.

Smith, Ming, and Hans Ulrich Obrist. "Flash of the Spirit." In *Ming Smith: An Aperture Monograph*, edited by Brendan Embser, 227–33. New York: Aperture Foundation, 2020.

Smith, Ming, and Janet Hill Talbert. "A Portrait of the Artist." In *Ming Smith: An Aperture Monograph*, edited by Brendan Embser, 9–20. New York: Aperture Foundation, 2020.

Smith, Shawn Michelle. *American Archives: Gender, Race, and Class in Visual Culture.* Princeton, NJ: Princeton University Press, 1999.

Sontag, Susan. "Notes on Camp." 1964. Reprinted in *Against Interpretation and Other Essays*, 275–92. New York: Picador, 1966.

Stallings, L. H. *Funk the Erotic: Transaesthetics and Black Sexual Cultures*. Urbana: University of Illinois Press, 2015.

Stanfill, Sonnet. "The Nightclub as Fashion Catwalk." In *Night Fever: Designing Club Culture, 1960–Today*, edited by Mateo Kries, Jochen Eisenbrand, and Catharine Rossi, 258–70. Weil am Rhein, Belgium: Vitra Design Museum, 2018.

St. Clair, Kassia. *The Secret Life of Colors*. New York: Penguin, 2016.

Stephens, Michelle. *Skin Acts: Race, Psychoanalysis, and the Black Male Performer*. Durham, NC: Duke University Press, 2014.

Stewart, Chris. "Ocean Vuong." *Gayletter*, no. 16 (2022). https://gayletter.com/ocean-vuong/.

Talley, André Leon, and Andy Warhol. "New Again: Grace Jones." 1984. Reprint, *Interview*, July 16, 2014. https://www.interviewmagazine.com/music/new-again-grace-jones.

Taylor, Angela. "A Salon That's Expanding While Others Fold." *New York Times*, July 19, 1973.

Taylor, Angela. "A Tongue-in-Chic Boutique Revives the '60s." *New York Times*, November 9, 1976.

Taylor, Diana. *The Archive and the Repertoire: Performing Cultural Memory in the Americas*. Durham, NC: Duke University Press, 2003.

Testa, Jessica. "Should Making It in Fashion Be This Hard?" *New York Times*, May 25, 2023.

Testa, Jessica. "What Does It Take to Be a *Vogue* Model?" *New York Times*, September 28, 2023.

Thompson, Krista. *Shine: The Visual Economy of Light in African Diasporic Aesthetic Practice*. Durham, NC: Duke University Press, 2015.

Thompson, Robert Farris. "Requiem for the Degas of the B-Boys." *Artforum* 28, no. 9 (May 1990): 135–41.

Torres, Justin. "In Praise of Latin Night at the Queer Club." *Washington Post*, June 13, 2016.

Tulloch, Carol. *The Birth of Cool: Style Narratives of the African Diaspora*. London: Bloomsbury, 2016.

Ukiomogbe, Juliana. "Raul Lopez Is Doing It for the Culture." *Elle*, September 13, 2023, https://www.elle.com/fashion/a45049268/raul-lopez-laur-fashion-interview-2023/.

Vazquez, Alexandra T. *The Florida Room*. Durham, NC: Duke University Press, 2022.

Vazquez, Alexandra T. *Listening in Detail: Performances of Cuban Music*. Durham, NC: Duke University Press, 2013.

Vega, Marta Morena. *When the Spirits Dance Mambo: Growing Up Nuyorican in El Barrio*. New York: Three Rivers Press, 2004.

Vogel, Amber. "State of Grace: American *Vogue* in the Seventies." In *The Seventies: The Age of Glitter in Popular Culture*, edited by Shelton Waldrep, 177–92. New York: Routledge, 2000.

Waldmeier, Martin. "Life in Limbo: Intoxication and Drugs." In *Ecstasy: In Art, Music, and Dance*, edited by Ulrike Groos, 176–200. New York: Prestel, 2019.

Walters, Barry. "As Much As I Can, as Black As I Am: The Queer History of Grace Jones." *Pitchfork Review*, no. 7 (2015): 86–97.

Warhol, Andy, and Pat Hackett. popism: *The Warhol '60s*. New York: Harcourt Brace Jovanovich, 1980.

Warren, Virginia Lee. "Helping Out the Togolese." *New York Times*, May 26, 1969.

Watson, Steven. "The Art of Max's." In *Max's Kansas City: Art, Glamour, Rock and Roll*, edited by Steven Kasher, 8–16. New York: Abrams Image, 2010.

Yáñez, Marcelo Gabriel. "Steve Lawrence and *Newspaper*: A Timeline." In *Newspaper*, edited by Marcelo Gabriel Yáñez, n.p. New York: Primary Information, 2023.

Index

abstraction, 44, 46, 49, 126, 135
addiction, 176
Adeyemi, Kemi, 176, 203n100
adult magazines, 38, 51
advertisements, 40, 91, 193n88
aesthetics: aesthetic forms and, 13–14, 79, 119, 166, 175; of Burrows, 124; of excess, 63; Fiorucci, 61–62, 67; gay, 87; generational, 18, 186n47; of Lopez, A., 28, 30, 46–47, 63; Puerto Rican, 30; queer, 15–16, 46; surface and, 14, 99, 101, 110–12, 117, 119, 142; transformation of, 91, 114
affective labor, 113
agency, 114, 184n7
AIDS epidemic, 167, 169–70, 176
Ailey, Alvin, 4
airbrush, 97–109, 113
Aldrich, Larry, 135
Aletti, Vince, 199n90
Algarín, Miguel, 17

Alice Tully Hall, Lincoln Center, 151–52
Als, Hilton, 2–3
Alvin Ailey American Dance Theater, 68–70, 72
ambivalence, 39, 54, 59
American Bandstand (television program), 121
American fashion designers, 140, 153, 169
androgyny, 104, 119, 168
Andy Warhol's Factory, 6, 12, 34, 79, 103, 111, 190n32
Andy Warhol's Interview magazine, 105–9, *109*, 198n77
Angelo, Giorgio di Sant', 161
Antonio 60 70 80 (Ramos), 167
Antonio's Girls (Lopez, A.), 96, 167
Antonio's Tales from the Thousand and One Nights (Lopez, Ramos), 167
Anton Perich Presents Grace Jones, Haircut (video), 77, 94–96, *96*
Araque, Carla, *156*

Arias, Joey, 29–30, 64, 67
ArtCenter College of Design, 167
art history, 174–76
artistic medium, style as, 8, 24, 110, 163, 166
artistic practices, 12–15, 17, 80–81, 87–88, 188n1; artists of colors and, 3–4, 8–10, 30, 46, 59, 170, 173, 175, 180. *See also specific artists*
artist-muse relationships, 80, 100–102, 111–12, 114
artist studios, 12, 148, 165; of Lopez, A., and Ramos, J., 26–28, 166, 173
art-punk club scene, 17–18
Asco (Chicanx group), 17
avant-garde, 9, 17, 72, 78, 109–11
Avedon, Richard, 150

Baker, Josephine, 154
Baldwin, James, 81
ballroom culture, gay, 156–57
Bamberger's department store, 123
Baptist, Stephanie, 173
Barboza, Anthony, 81–82, 196n25, 196n28; Jones and, 94, 206n18; Kamoinge Workshop and, 170
Barnes, Clive, 155
Barrie, Scott, 151
Barthes, Roland, 9, 47, 92, 98–99
"Basic Black" (benefit fashion show), 138–40
Basquiat, Jean-Paul, 18
Battle of Versailles (event), 127, 152–57, 156, 166
Bauhaus, 117, 192n101
Beatles, 146
beauty, 17, 20, 54, 81, 88, 105; androgyny and, 119; Black, 86; male, 40; as performative act, 95
Beaux Arts Ball (1958), 19
Beckwith, Naomi, 162–63
belonging, 88, 175–77, 192n65
Berenson, Berry, 137–38, 176
Bergdorf Goodman, 138–39, 141
Berkowitz, David, 1
Berlin, Eileen, 97
Berlin, Sy, 97

Bernstein, Richard, 9, 80, 97–114, 99, 101–3, 106–9, 176
Bernstein, Robin, 157
Bjornsen, Karen, 156
black-and-white photography, 39–40, 87–88, 92, 100, 109
Black beauty, 86
Black Beauty agency, 86
Black culture, 139–40
Black designers, 170
Black diaspora, 17, 104, 119, 171
Black fashion designers, 95, 122–27, 138–40, 151–53, 158, 162
Black feminism, 54
Black models, 15–16, 50, 80–82, 138–39, 152–57, 170; Burrows's use of, 124, 127, 129; first wave of, 91; peer-to-peer relationships of, 114. *See also specific models*
Blackness, 79, 135, 139
blackout (1977), New York City, 1–2
Black photographers, 17, 81–94, 170
Black Photographer's Annual, 196n22
Black Power, 9
Black Soul (band), 97
Black supermodels, 91, 129
Black women, 80, 91, 124, 155, 185n26, 195n8, 196n25, 197n48
Blair, Billie, 7
Blass, Bill, 153
Bloomingdale's, 62, 84, 100
Blueboy magazine, 38
Blue Water Series, 33, 36, 78
Boggs, Gail, 132
Bonwit Teller, 140
Boricua pop, 189n21
Bourdin, Guy, 38–39
Bowie, David, 104
Bradley, Rizvana, 92
Braithwaite, Fred, 18
Braunstein, Peter, 138
Brazil, 12
breakdancing, 23–24, 70
breathing, 26, 28
Breslau, Bobby, 130, 133–34, 133, 136, 143, 143, 146, 155
Brice, Jennifer, 15, 156
bricolage, 46

British Black Arts Movement, 172
British *Vogue*, 30
Brody, Jennifer, 79, 199n109
Brooklyn, 173
Broom Closet Series, 36
Brown, Elspeth, 47, 50, 148, 154, 199n92
Brownfield, Bonnie, 132
Brownness, 28
Brown v. Board of Education, 202n55
Bryne, Sean, 7
Burkus, Jimmy, 132, 134
Burrows, Stephen, 4–5, 82, 120, 125, 133, 143–44, 147, 149, 176, 201n43, 202n70, 205n13, 206n13; Battle of Versailles and, 152–57, 156; Black models used by, 124, 127, 129; Cleveland, P., and, 122, 143–49, 152–56, 159; collaborative ethos of, 127, 134–35, 137, 142–43, 146, 158–60; Colon and, 24; color-blocked jersey dresses by, 126, 148, 166; dance and, 123–24, 157, 163; at Fashion Institute of Technology, 5–6, 123–24; Fernandez and, 203n100; Fire Island and, 125, 127–34, 132–33, 141, 148, 163, 169; Henri Bendel and, 127, 140–52, 158–59, 163, 169; "lettuce" edge hems by, 150–51, 158–59; Lopez, A., and, 12; models working with, 81, 124, 127, 129, 138–39, 146, 152–55, 159–63; on music, 154–55, 204n106; O Boutique and, 16, 127, 134–40, 143; Smith, M., and, 81–82; on *Soul Train*, 12, 121–22; Studio 54 and, 158–59, 161–63; use of color by, 9–10, 122, 126, 129, 135–36, 148–50, 157–59, 170–71; *Vogue* and, 129, 136–37, 140, 147–50, 159–60; zigzag stitching by, 150–51, 158
Byrd, Rikki, 139

Café Society Series, 33–34
camp, 104–5, 198n73 166
Campt, Tina, 20, 47
cancer, 167
candid photography, 55, 57, 59, 113
Candy Bar Wrapper Series (Lopez), 32, 48–60, 69

Capello, Peter, 133
capital, cultural, 79
Caranicas, Paul, 49, 167, 190n32, 205n6; on Lopez, A., 33–34, 62–63
Caribbean, 6
Carnegie, Hattie, 200n9
Carnegie Hall, 26
Carnegie Hall Studios, 26
Canival, Jean-Eudes, 33–34
censorship, 9, 32, 36, 192n57
chain mail, 159, 161
Chambers Brothers, 81
Chanel, Coco, 140–41
Chavarria, Willy, 171, 206n21, 207n29
Chelsea Hotel, 190n32
Chen, Mel, 185n26
Cherry Grove, Fire Island, 128–29
Chi, Tseng Kwong, 168
chiffon, 148, 150–61, 163
Chinn, Alva, 7, 50, 153, 156, 161
Chow, Tina, 29–30, 33
Chuh, Kandice, 185n17, 185n23
Cinandre, 83–89, 84–85, 87, 134, 142
citizenship, US, 28
Clark, Dick, 121
Cleveland, Lady Bird, 18–19, 144
Cleveland, Pat, 17–19, 29–30, 37, 65–66, 96–97, 109, 147, 149, 152, 160, 166–67, 170; Burrows and, 122, 143–49, 152–56, 159; on collaborative ethos, 107–9; at Enchanted Gardens, 76; at Fiorucci, 61, 63, 65–66, 73; Fire Island and, 128, 131–32, 148; on *Interview*, 107–9; Lopez, A., and, 28, 37, 61, 65, 73; models used by, 7, 12, 91, 146, 152–55, 159–61; on *Soul Train*, 122; *Vogue* magazine and, 91, 143–47
Club 57, 6, 17, 63–64, 186n40
Coddington, Grace, 30
Colacello, Bob, 108
collectivism: collaborative ethos and, 4–6, 8, 10, 13, 17–20, 165–69, 173–76; of Burrows, 127, 134–35, 137, 142–43, 146, 158–60; Cleveland on, 107–9; of Jones, 78–81, 97–98, 100–104, 112–14; of Lopez, A., and Ramos, J., 26–29, 32, 43–48, 79

INDEX 227

Colon, Angelo, 24, 73, 129
color, 11–13, 93; Bernstein use of, 98–100, 105–11; Burrows's use of, 9–10, 122, 126, 129, 135–36, 148–50, 157–59, 170–71; Lopez, A., use of, 9, 33, 47–48
color photography, 10, 39–40, 88
commedia dell'arte, 136
commercial art, 6, 78, 80
commercial fashion design, 62–63
commercialism: creativity and, 13, 70, 185n16
commercial photography, 32, 81, 94
communication, style as, 8, 109, 119, 131, 157, 168
Cooper, Wilhemina, 86
Cooper Hewitt, Smithsonian Design Museum, 170
Cordero, Bill "Blast," 23
Cornelius, Don, 121–22
Coty Awards, 128, 151–52, *152*
counterculture, 129–30
couture walk, model, *155*
Croland, David, 109
Cross Bronx Expressway, 2
cross-disciplinarity, 13, 70, 90
Crow, Thomas, 109–11, 166
cruising, 9, 184n9
Cruz-Malavé, Arnaldo, 115
cultural capital, 79
cultural pride, 14, 171
Cunningham, Bill, 29–30, 98
curation, 15–16
Cvetkovich, Ann, 15, 46

dance: dancing, 2, 4, 34, *154*; Burrows and, 123–24, 157, 163; by Cleveland, P., 61; in Fiorucci window displays, 61, 63–64, 67–68; Jones and, 75–77, 89–90; on *Soul Train*, 12, 121
Darden, Norma Jean, 152, *156*
Davis, Betty, 35–36, 140
Davis, Miles, 140
deaths, 167, 176, 205n6
Deep South Suite, The (Ailey), 70
Delaunay, Sonia, 135
department stores, 122–23, 165; Bergdorf Goodman, 138–39, 141; Bloomingdale's, 62, 84, 100; Bonwit Teller, 140; Fiorucci, 60–70, 132; Henri Bendel, 3, 127, 140–52, 158, 163, 169; window dressers for, 44, 128, 141, 165, 202n65
DePino, David, 116
diaspora, 10, 14; Black, 17, 104, 119, 171; Puerto Rican, 5–6, 24–25
DiPace, Tony, *133*
disco culture, 2, 20, 110, 165, 168, 184n8; Burrows and, 161–63; Cleveland, P., and, 60–61; Jones and, 4, 51, 75, 89, 97, 100, 104–13, 115–19
division of labor, 43, 134
DJ culture, 23–24, 62
"doing": style as, 8, 114, 177
Dominican Republic, 167
Donovan, Carrie, 137, 141, 146
"Do or Die" (song), 100, *107*
downtown (New York City), 2–4, 18, 29–30, 67–68, 80, 173, 191n44
Doyle, Jennifer, 54, 175, 185n19
drag ball scene: in Harlem, 116
Draper, Louis, 82
drugs, 3, 176; psychedelic, 2, 5, 9, 76, 78, 115, 129
Du Bois, W. E. B., 88
Dunham, Katherine, 90

Ebony Fashion Fair, 144, 153, 202n76
Ebony magazine, 91, 117, 151, 197n59
El Museo del Barrio, 24, 47
Elsesser, Paloma, 172
Enchanted Gardens, 12, 18, 30; Jones performing at, 75–77
ephemerality, 15, 86, 135, 175
erasure, 30, 36, 98, 189n22
eroticism, 32–34 38–39, 50, 75, 165
Essence magazine, 81, 94, 196n25
Evans, Walker, 39
excess, 19, 39–40, 63, 199n92; Jones and, 89, 99, 119
exoticism, 86, 91, 119
expressive equipment: style as, 73, 157

Fader, The, magazine, 123
Fairchild Publications, 25

Fame (Jones), 100, 199n90
fashion: fashion design and, 10, 170, 172; American, 140, 153, 169; Black, 95, 122–27, 138–40, 151–53, 158, 162; commercial, 62–63; on Fire Island, 128–34; hip-hop, 166–67; mainstream, 169, 171
Fashion Institute of Technology, 5–6, 23–26, 91, 123–24, 167
Fashion of the Times (New York Times), 139
Fauvism, 149
Fayette, Potassa de la, 30, 31, 76, 161
female muses, 54, 96–114
femininity, 17, 87, 199n92, 205n9
feminism, 54–55, 60
Fendley, Don, 133
Fernandez, Victor, 36, 37, 40, 42, 43–44, 203n100
fetishism, 39, 112
financial crisis, New York City (1970s), 1, 183n1
fine art, 6, 17, 94
Fiorucci, 64–66, 84, 134, 142, 167, 194n104; Lopez, A., and Ramos, J., consulting for, 32, 60–70, 64–65, 75–76
Fiorucci, Elio, 61, 194n104
Fire Island, New York, 12; Burrows and, 125, 127–34, 141, 148, 163, 169; Lopez, A., and, 36
flaneur, 73, 173
Flatley, Jonathan, 15
flat-top haircut, 168, 205n9
Flavin, Dan, 138
Fleetwood, Nicole, 104
Flores, Juan, 188n3
Ford, Gerald, 183n1
Ford Modeling Agency, 146
Forlano, Sante, 149
France, 97; Battle of Versailles event in, 127, 152–57, 156, 166; Paris, 28, 32–34, 78, 98, 126, 152–58
Fred Astaire Dance Academy, 123
free Black communities, US, 173
Freeman, Peggy Ann (Donyale Luna), 197n48

friendships, 59, 127–30, 137, 142–43, 148, 158–59, 161; of Jones, 76–80, 86–87, 93, 97–107
futurity, 10, 162

Gaidarova, Nina, 43, 50
Gallery, the (disco), 116
gangs, 25
Ganzas (ballroom house), 156
Garment District, 158
garment trade workers, 6, 123
Garner, Phillippe, 35
gatekeeping, 4, 124, 163
gay aesthetics, 97
gay ballroom culture, 156–57
gay men, 4, 9, 29, 104–5, 128, 184n8; cruising by, 9, 184n9; as photographers, 32–44
gaze, 14, 105; photographic, 39, 88; white male, 54
gender, 17, 112, 186n47
generational aesthetics, 18, 186n47
gentrification, 173
Gester, Phillip, 36
gestures, 14, 91–92, 156–57
Geter, Hafizah Augustus, 105
Getsy, David, 38, 184n9, 190n35
Givhan, Robin, 123, 129, 137, 139–41, 150
Gold, Heidi, 156
gold lamé, 10, 69, 104, 191n64
Goodman, Nelson, 119, 131, 165, 166
Gopinath, Gayatri, 16
Gopnik, Blake, 198n77
Goude, Jean-Paul, 12, 29, 78–79, 101–2, 112, 115–16, 118, 168, 205n9
GQ magazine, 34, 38, 69, 71, 203n100
Grace Jones, Studio 54 (Smith), 89
Grace Jones at Cinandre (Smith), 87
Grace Jones at Studio 54 (Smith), 92
graffiti, 2, 63, 70
Grandmaster Flash, 24, 73
Green, Al, 154–55
Greenwich Village, 138
grid format, photography and, 7, 31–32, 35–36, 42–43, 166, 190n35, 191n54
group identities, 8
Grudin, Anthony, 15

Guarnaccia, Matteo, 63
Guzmán, Joshua Javier, 89, 118

hair (and haircuts), 94–96, 168, 205n9
hair salons, 80, 83–84, 134, 165
hairstyles, 86
Hall, Jerry, 29–30, 38, 159, 161–62, 167
Hall, Stuart, 79
Halston (fashion designer), 3, 12, 35, 129, 158, 161, 198n77
hard-chic designs, 142
Hardison, Bethann, 7, 81, 83, 137, 152–53, 152, 161, 166, 170
Haring, Keith, 63, 113–14, 183n2, 189n22, 194n104; Jones and, 5, 78–79, 112, 115, 168–69, 199n97
Harlem, 6, 169; drag ball scene, 116; Kamoinge Workshop based out of, 17, 170, 196n22, 196n28; Spanish, 18, 24–26
Harper's Bazaar magazine, 161–62
Harry, Debbie, 115
Hartman, Saidiya, 185n26, 195n6
Hebdige, Dick, 46
Henri Bendel (department store), 3, 127, 140–52, 158–59, 163, 169
Hernandez, Jillian, 15
Hernandez, Robb, 193n80
heteronormativity, 38
hierarchies, 6, 13, 72, 113, 161
Higginsen, Vy, 130, 140
high art, 40, 78, 165
high culture, 13, 67
High School of Art and Design. *See* School of Industrial Art
high-top haircut, 168, 205n9
Hill, William, 134
Himid, Lubaina, 172
hip-hop, 14, 24, 70, 166–68, 188n3
Holbrook, Thomas, 102
Holmam, Michael, 18
homoerotic works, 33–34, 36, 45–46, 192n57
homophobia, 9
horizontal art-making, 30, 70, 72, 90, 107–8, 109, 113, 161, 175–76

Howard University, 81, 171
Hugo, Victor, 44
Hurston, Zora Neale, 18–19
Hutton, Lauren, 150

I'll Never Write My Memoirs (Jones), 74, 195n8
Iman (model), 159, 161
Indiana, Robert, 135
individualism, 18–20, 165
"I Need a Man" Grace Jones), 88, 97–99, 99, 104–5
Ing, Francis, 100
inhabiting, style, 6, 126, 166, 174
institutional critique, 17
Interview magazine, 35–36, 64, 98, 103, 106–8, 126, 203n100
intimacy, 127
Italian *Vogue*, 34

Jamaica, 6, 30, 76
James, Charles, 26, 29
Jamison, Judith, 151
Japan, 4
Jet magazine, 91
Johnson, Beverly, 35, 91
Jones, Grace, 53, 56–58, 74, 77, 87, 90, 93, 96, 99, 101–3, 106–8, 118, 170, 195n8, 197nn59–60; baby shower for, 115–19; Barboza and, 81; body double for, 24, 129; in *Candy Bar Wrapper Series*, 51, 53, 54–55, 56–57, 58; at Cinandre, 83–89, 87; collaborative ethos of, 78–81, 97–98, 100–104, 112–14; disco culture and, 4, 51, 75, 89, 97, 100, 104–13, 115–19; at Enchanted Gardens, 75–77; excess of, 89, 99, 119; friendships of, 76–80, 86–87, 93, 97–107; gold lamé worn by, 10; Goude and, 12, 168, 205n9; haircut for, 94–96; Haring and, 5, 78–79, 112, 115, 168–69, 199n97; Lopez, A., and, 12, 29–30, 32, 51, 53–58, 73, 77–79, 116–19, 174; maternity dress for, 116–18, 118, 199n109; modeling by, 4–5, 19, 77–78, 80–82, 86–89, 94, 115; as muse, 80, 104, 111–12;

objectification of, 54, 111–12, 114; as recording artist, 80, 88–89, 96–111; at Studio 54, 10, 89–90, 90, 92–94, 93, 114; theatricality of, 166; Warhol, and, 79, 115. *See also specific music*
Joplin, Janis, 129
Jordan, Donna, 29–30, 66, 106
Juanito Xtravaganza (Juan Rivera), 189n22

Kamali, Norma, 69, 161
Kamoinge Workshop, 17, 81–83, 87–88, 170, 196n22, 196n28
Kaposi sarcoma, 167
Kenzo (fashion label), 100
Kershaw, Miriam, 89
kinship networks, 16, 19 104, 115, 187n52
Klein, Anne, 153–54
Klein, Calvin, 25, 128, 161
Kodak Instamatics, 4, 7, 9, 31, 37, 41, 42, 45, 56–58, 189n23, 190n32, 190n35, 191n44, 206n18. *See also* Lopez, Antonio: Kodak Instamatics by
Kushner, Rachel, 1

labor, 26, 28, 55, 62–63, 88, 109, 123; division of, 43, 134; of models, 113, 115; of racial icons, 104
LaBrie, Carol, 145
La Fountain-Stokes, Lawrence, 187n1
Lambert, Deanna, 11
Lambert, Eleanor, 152–53
Lange, Jessica, 33
Langkjaer, Michael, 38, 69
"La Vie en Rose" (Jones), 100
Lawrence, Steve, 38, 191n44
Lawrence, Tim, 68, 116
Lee, Precious, 172
Lee, Summer Kim, 77
Le Palace (disco), 92
Les Mouches (venue), 104–5
lettuce-edge hems, 150–51, 158–59
Levan, Larry, 2–3, 115–16, 156, 176
Life magazine, 139, 162
Lincoln Center, 151–52
linearity, 47
Lobato, Ramon, 89, 119

Loft, the, 2, 78, 195n12
logo design, 194n113
Londoño, Johana, 196n38
Look magazine, 11
Lopez, Antonio, 27, 28, 171, 189n29, 190n30, 190n36, 193n101, 194n113; advertisements by, 167, 193n88; aesthetics of, 28, 30, 46–47, 63; Alvin Ailey American Dance Theater and, 68–70, 72; Caranicas on, 33–34, 62–63; censorship of, 38; Cleveland, P., and, 7, 28, 37, 61, 65, 73; collaborative ethos of, 26–29, 32, 43–48, 79; consulting at Fiorucci, 32, 60–70; context-switching by, 13; death of, 167–68; downtown scene and, 29–30, 62–63, 69–70; fashion illustrations by, 4–5, 23–26, 28–30, 62, 68, 71–72, 167, 206n18; heavy breathing by, 26, 28; in *Interview* magazine, 35–36, 64; Jones and, 12, 29–30, 32, 51, 53–58, 73, 77–79, 116–19, 167, 174, 206n18; models used by, 23, 29–60, 63–73, 106–7, 153; in Paris, 28, 32–34; Polaroids photography by, 40, 70, 78; representation and, 32, 39, 46, 54; ribbon motif of, 191n56; street culture and, 22, 29, 69–70, 165, 167–68, 173; at Studio 54, 113–14; Thorvaldson photographed by, 191n54; Union Square studio of, 26, 27, 28, 49, 166, 173; Warhol on, 34, 48. *See also* Ramos, Juan; *specific works*
Lopez, Antonio: Kodak Instamatics by, ii, 4, 9, 33–34, 38–39, 44–60, 166, 190n32, 190n35, 191n44, 206n18; grids of, 31–32, 35–37, 40–43
Lopez, Raul, 171–72
Los Angeles, California, 167
Los Angeles Times, 167
Louis Falco Dance Company, 167
love, 59, 80
"Love Saves the Day" party, 78
low culture, 13, 24, 51, 67
LSD, 2, 5, 76, 78, 115
Luar (fashion label), 171–72
Lui magazine, 51, 53

Lundgren, Dolph, 102
Lyons, Lisa, 44

MAC, NY. *See* Municipal Assistance Corporation (MAC), NY
Magidson, Phyllis, 136
mainstream culture, 110–11, 168
mainstream fashion, 169, 171
Malanga, Gerard, 25
male models, 32, 36–47
mambo, 123, 157, 200n3
Manalansan, Martin, 175
Mancuso, David, 2, 78, 195n12
Mandate magazine, 38
Manhattan Gaze magazine, 44
mannequins, 24–25, 61, 63–64, 193n101
Mapplethorpe, Robert, 30, 35, 44, 168, 192n58
Marabelli, Franco, 62
marginalization, 3–4, 14, 30 88, 189n22
Maripol (fashion designer), 63
Martheleur, Andre, 84–85, *85*, 94–96
masculinity, 105, 205n9
mass culture, 14, 51
mass media, 54
mass production, 46, 48
materiality, 14, 99
maternity dress, for Jones, 116–18, *118*, 199n109
Max Factor, 158
Max's Kansas City, 12, 16, 106, 137–38
McCannon, Dindga, 17
McKinley, Barry, 203n100
Meade, Daryl, *133*, 143
"Me" decade, 1970s as, 18
Medium Tings, 173
memory, 10, 177
Men in Showers series (Lopez), 68–69
Mercer, Kobena, 39, 46, 109
Met Gala, 100
Meyer, James, 18, 148–49
Miller, M. H., 172–73
Miller, Timothy, 129–30
Minnelli, Liza, 35, 154
minorities, 9, 29, 105
minstrelsy, 139
misogyny, 192n74

mixtapes, 23, 47
Miyake, Issey, 29–30, 79
models and modeling, 166, 172, 192n70; Battle of Versailles, 153–57, *156*; Black, 15–16, 50, 80–82, 91, 114, 124, 127, 129, 138–39, 152–57, 170; of Burrows, 81, 124, 127, 129, 138–39, 146, 152–55, 159–63; by Cleveland, P., 7, 12, *37*, 65, 91, 146, 152–55, 159–61; by Jones, 4–5, 19, 77–78, 80–82, 86–89, 94, 115; labor of, 113, 115; of Lopez, A., 23, 29–60, 63–73, 106–7, 153; male, 32, 36–47; transgender, 30
Montez, Ricardo, 112, 176–77
Moreno, Rita, 35
Morera, Daniela, 162
Morris, Bernadine, 148, 155, 162, 169
Motown, 204n106
Mudd Club, 17
Municipal Assistance Corporation (MAC), NY, 183n1
Muñoz, José Esteban, 13, 166, 175, 185n24, 192n65, 198n73; on belonging, 88; on queer utopian aesthetics, 46
Murray, Yxta Maya, 89
Muse (Jones), 100, *106*, 112, 116
muses, 24, 36; artist-muse relationships, 80, 100–102, 111–12, 114; female, 54, 96–114; Jones as, 80, 104, 111–12
Museum Mile, New York City, 3, 24
Museum of Modern Art, 94, 170
Mycelial Artists Collective, 173
Myers, Tanya Danielle Wilson, 126

Negrón-Muntaner, Frances, 189n21
Newark, New Jersey, 123
New Jersey, 123
Newspaper magazine, 38, 191n44
Newton, Esther, 128
Newton, Helmut, 38–39
new wave–reggae, 168
New York City, 5, 13, 107, 120, 172, 174–75; alternative art space movement, 78, 134, 194n106; art-punk club scene, 17–18; Beaux Arts Ball, 19; cruising in, 9, 184n9; downtown, 2–4, 18, 29–30, 67–68, 80, 173, 191n44;

Jones moving to, 77; 1970s financial crisis, 1, 183n1; spatial cartography of, 16, 126–27; uptown, 3, 67–68, 80, 173. *See also specific locations*
New York Times, The, 25, 85, 125–26, 139, 158, 162
Nichols, Francis (DJ Frankie Knuckles), 116
Nightclubbing (Jones), 168
Nikon, 32
Ninth Circle, 138
Nixon, Richard, 1
Nomi, Klaus, 29–30, 63–64, 194n104
nontraditional art spaces, 78, 134, 194n106
nonverbal communication, 8, 157
North, Nancy, 156
Northside Center (nonprofit), 202n55
nostalgia, 3, 82
nudity, 36, 50–60
Nureyev, Rudolf, 154
Nutall, Jeff, 195n11
Nuyoricans, 17, 187n1, 189n22
Nyong'o, Tavia, 112

objectification, 54, 105, 111–12, 114
O Boutique, 16, 127, 134–40, *136*, 142–43
Obregon, Maning, 146
O'Brien, Glenn, 124, 138
O'Neill, Alistair, 25, 36
One Man Show (music video), 168
Onondaga Community College, 5, 76
"On Your Knees" (Jones), 100, *108*
Operation Bootstrap, Puerto Rico, 188n4
origami, 116–18

Padilha, Mauricio, 38–39
Padilha, Roger, 38–39
Palace of Versailles, 152–53
Palladium, the, 123, 157, 200n3
Paradise Garage, 2, 80, 142, 155–56, 168, 176, 183n2; Jones at, 114–19
Paragon Sports, 49, 69
Paraphernalia boutique, 135, 201n37
Paris, France, 28, 32–34, 126, 152–58; Jones in, 78, 98
Parks, Gordon, 162
Pasadena, California, 167

Peretti, Elsa, 130, 198n77
Performances: performance art, 13–15, 49, 60, 91, 183n1, 199n97; haircut as, 94–96; photography and, 118
performance studies, 13–14, 20, 185n19
Perich, Anton, 77, 94–95, *96*
Philadelphia Museum College of Art, 5–6, 123
photographers, 115; Barboza as, 81, 94, 170; Black, 17, 81–94, 170; Lopez, A., as, 30–64, 98; Smith, M., as, 81–94, 114; Tracy as, 137
photographic gaze, 39, 88
photography, 20, 28–29, 119, 174–75, 187n52, 191n44, 196n22; black-and-white, 39–40, 87–88, 92, 100, 109; candid, 55, 57, 59, 113; censorship and, 36; color, 10, 39–40, 88; commercial, 32, 81, 94; grid format and, 7, 31–32, 35–36, 42–43, 166, 190n35, 191n54; surface and, 92. *See also Kodak Instamatics*
Photo magazine, 51, 52
Phu, Thy, 47
Piaggi, Anna, 167
Picture Newspaper magazine, 191n44
pinup culture, 51
"Plastic Bag" (X-Ray Spex), 48
Plastic Series (Lopez), 33
pluralism, 10
Polaroid photography, ii, 166, 192n58; by Lopez, A., 40, 70, 78
politics, style and, 109, 130
Pop Art, 3, 9–10, 28–30, 48, 51, 126, 135
pop fashion, 135
popular culture, 165
Portfolio (Jones), 97–98, 100–103, *101–3*
Post, Tina, 80
postminimalism, 190n35
poverty, 18–19, 25
Presley, Elvis, 104
psychedelic drugs, 9, 129; LSD as, 2, 5, 76, 78, 115
Puerto Ricans, Puerto Rico and, 12, 187n1, 188n4, 190n36, 203n100; aesthetics, 30; diaspora, 5–6, 24–25; *Interview* magazine on, 35–36; queer, 46–47; subjectivity, 28; Young Lords as, 81

"Pull Up to the Bumper," 168
punctuation, 117–18, 199n109
Pyer Moss, 171, 173, 206n19

queerness, queer people and, 14–16, 175–77, 185n26, 186n33, 191n44, 199n92; censorship and, 38; desire and, 9, 39; Fire Island and, 127–28; kinship and, 115; sensibilities, 104–5; sociality, 157

racial bias, 8–9
racial difference, 14, 88, 112
racial icons, 104
racial identity, 10, 139
racialization, 54, 86, 105, 112, 172
racism, 91, 104, 157, 163
Ramos, Iván A., 14, 89 118
Ramos, Juan, 27, 28, 57, 167, 190n32, 192n68, 192n70, 192n74; consulting at Fiorucci, 32, 60–70; death of, 205n6; Lopez, A., and, 5, 25–28, 32–33, 43–48, 55
Ramos, Mel, 51
Ratoff, Barry, 203n100
R&B music, 154–55, 170
Real People (television program), 64
recording artist, Jones as, 80, 88–89, 96–111
Red Coat Series (Lopez), 33
rehearsal, 59–60
Renta, Oscar de la, 153
representation, 8–9, 14, 29; Jones and, 94, 119; Lopez, A., and, 32, 39, 46, 54
retrospectives, 169–70
Ribbon Series, The (Lopez), 32, 36, 40, 41, 42, 43–44, 45, 46–48, 55, 92
Rivera, Harrison, 133
Rivera, Juan, 115
Robert Berman Gallery, 167
Rock Steady Crew, 23, 70, 166–67
Rodgers, Nile, 168–69
Rogers, Christopher John, 171
Rolleiflex camera, 81
Roveda, Bobby, 133, 143
Royer, Chris, 156
Royster, Francesca, 104

Rubell, Steve, 75, 194n113
Rubenstein, Roz, 128, 130, 132, 132–34, 136, 140, 143, 143
Ruiz, Sandra, 28
runway shows, 165, 170, 173
Ruskin, Mickey, 138

sadomasochism, 39
Santa Monica, California, 167
Saunders, Michele, 115
Saunders, Ramona, 152
Scharf, Kenny, 63
Schlemmer, Oskar, 193n101
Schneider, Sara K., 61
School of Industrial Art, 25
Schrager, Ian, 194n113
Schumacher, Joel, 135, 141, 145
second-wave feminists, 54, 60
self-expression, 19, 80, 86, 97, 105
self-objectification, 9, 54
self-possession, 29, 91
self-presentation, 6, 49, 79, 110
Senegal, 97
sensory quality, surface and, 43
sensuality, 29, 34, 40–41, 126–27
Sex, John, 63, 194n104
sexism, 51
Sex Parts (Warhol), 44
sexuality, 15, 38–39, 50, 54, 86
Shaddick MacGregor, Virginia, 51, 52
Shaw, Ben, 158
Shoe Series (Lopez), 36
Siano, Nicky, 116
Simmons, Beatrice Pennington Banks, 200n9
Simone, Nina, 151
Sims, Naomi, 11, 91, 139
647 Broadway, 2, 129, 195n12
skin, surface and, 44
Sleeping Beauty, The (ballet), 154
Smaltz, Audrey, 151
Smith, Ming, 80–91, 82–85, 87, 90, 93, 112, 114, 170
Smith, Toukie, 95
Smith, Willi, 70, 95, 129, 151, 153, 170, 185n16
social media, 203n100

Sottsass, Ettore, 61–62
"soul style," 18
Soul Train (television program), 12, 76, 121–22
Spanish Harlem (El Barrio), 18, 24–26
Spanish Town, Jamaica, 76
sportswear, 68–70, 135–36
Stallings, L. H., 54
Stanfill, Sonnet, 68
Stavros, John, 36, 40, 41, 43–44, 47
Stephen Burrows Inc., 158
Stephen Burrows World, 127, 142–52
Stephens, Michelle, 59–60, 95
stereotypes, 112, 139–40
St. Jacques, Sterling, 31, 76
street culture, 165, 167–68, 173
streetwear, 68, 95, 171
Studio 54, 18–19, 68, 88, 113, 159, 161; Jones at, 10, 89–90, 92–94, 114
Studio Z, 17
Stutz, Geraldine, 141–42, 148, 158–59
style: as artistic medium, 8, 24, 110, 163, 166; bricolage, 46; as communication, 8, 109, 119, 131, 157, 168; as "doing," 8, 114, 177; as expressive equipment, 73, 157; hair, 86; inhabiting, 6, 126, 166, 174; politics of, 109, 130; "soul style," 18
subcultures, 8, 38, 46, 70, 110–11, 157
superficiality, 110–11
supermodels, Black, 91, 129
Supreme Court, US, 28, 36
surface: as aesthetic quality, 14, 99, 101, 110–12, 117, 119, 142; energy, 34, 111, 114; photography, 92; sensory quality and, 43; skin and, 44; theoretical approach to, 174
Syracuse, New York, 76

Talley, André Leon, 79, 128–29, 170, 176
tastemakers: taste and, 8, 184n8
Telfar, 171
Tennant, Pat, 141
"That's the Trouble" (Jones), 75
theatricality, 75–76, 79, 104, 155–56, 166
Thiebaud, Wayne, 51
Thiele, Michael, 49, 193n101

Thompson, Krista, 175
Thompson, Robert Farris, 199n97
Thorvaldson, Jane, 40, 43, 50, 191n54
Tiger Morse's boutique, 144–45
Times, The (newspaper), 62, 134–35, 142, 151, 169
"To Be Young, Gifted, and Black" (Simone), 151
Tokyo, Japan, 169, 191n56
Torres, Hector, 133, 134, 143–44, 146, 155
Torres, Justin, 20
Tracy, Charles, 35–36, 130, 137, 154
transformation, aesthetic, 91, 114
transgender people, 30
Tulloch, Carol, 184n7

underground culture, 2–3, 78, 111, 195n11
Union Square, Lopez, A., and Ramos, J., studio in, 26, 27, 28, 49, 166, 173
United States, 28, 36, 76, 173
Upper East Side, 3
upstate New York, 5–6, 76
uptown, New York City, 3, 67–68, 80, 173

Valkus, Jim, 133
Vamp (film), 168
Vanity magazine, 167
Vargas, Alberto, 51
Vazquez, Alexandra, 13, 49–50, 62
Vega, Marta Morena, 200n3
Velez, Elena, 207n29
verticality, 30, 113, 175–76
visual creators, 124, 200n9
Vogue magazine, 3, 12, 22, 26, 62, 147, 155–57, 197n48; British, 30; Burrows in, 129, 136–37, 140, 147–50, 159–60; Cleveland, P., and, 91, 143, 147; Italian, 34; Sims and Johnson in, 91
voguing, 155–57
Vollbracht, Michael, 113–14
Vreeland, Diana, 150
Vuong, Ocean, 187n52

Wales Bonner, Grace, 171–72
Walters, Barry, 105
Wangenheim, Chris Von, 38–39

Warhol, Andy, 3, 5, 15, 168, 192n58, 198n77; Bernstein and, 105–8, 113–14; Factory, 6, 12, 34, 79, 103, 111, 190n32; at Henri Bendel, 141; *Interview* magazine and, 35–36, 64, 98, 103, 106–8, 126, 203n100; Jones and, 79, 115; on Lopez, A., 34, 48; male models used by, 44; on Max's Kansas City, 138

Warm Leatherette (Jones), 168

Warsuma, Amina, 153, *156*

Watergate scandal, 1

Ways of Worldmaking (Goodman), 131

Weber's Originals, 124

Weeksville Heritage Center, 173

West Village, 26, 81

"Where We At" Black Women Artists Inc., 17

White, Renauld, *11*

white gay men, 184n8

"White Lines" (Grandmaster Flash), 24, 73

white male gaze, 54

whiteness, 28, 78

Whiting and Davis, 159

Wilhelmina Models, 86, 91

Willis, Deborah, 196n22

WilliWear, 70. *See also* Smith, Willi

window dressers, 44, 128, 141, 165, 202n65

Wolfe, Tom, 18

women of color, 29, 88–89, 124

Women's Wear Daily (journal), 5, 25, 151, 158, 162

World Trade Center, Lower Manhattan, 1

World War II, 128

X-Ray Spex (band), 48, 60

Xtravaganzas (ballroom house), 156

Yamamoto, Kansai, 104

Yáñez, Marcelo Gabriel, 191n44

Yellow Submarine (film), 146

Young Lords, 81

youth cultures, 29, 50

Zen Buddhism, 134

zigzag stitching, 150–51, 158